Doing Psychology Critically

Doing Psychology Critically

Making a Difference in Diverse Settings

ISAAC PRILLELTENSKY

and

GEOFFREY NELSON

First published 2002 by
PALGRAVE MACMILLAN
Houndmills, Basingstoke, Hampshire RG21 6XS and
175 Fifth Avenue, New York, N.Y. 10010
Companies and representatives throughout the world

PALGRAVE MACMILLAN is the new global academic imprint of the Palgrave Macmillan division of St. Martin's Press LLC and of Palgrave Macmillan Ltd. Macmillan® is a registered trademark in the United States, United Kingdom and other countries. Palgrave is a registered trademark in the European Union and other countries.

ISBN 0–333–92283–2 hardback
ISBN 0–333–92284–0 paperback

This book is printed on paper suitable for recycling and made from fully managed and sustained forest sources.

A catalogue record for this book is available from the British Library.

Library of Congress Cataloging-in-Publication Data
Prilleltensky, Isaac, 1959–
Doing psychology critically : making a difference in diverse settings / Isaac Prilleltensky and Geoffrey Nelson.
   p. cm.
  Includes bibliographical references and index.
  ISBN 0–333–92283–2—ISBN 0–333–92284–0 (pbk.)
  1. Critical psychology. I. Nelson, Geoffrey B. (Geoffrey Brian) II. Title.

BF39.9 .P75 2002
150′.23—dc21   2002070640

10   9   8   7   6   5   4   3   2   1
11 10 09 08 07 06 05 04 03 02

Printed and bound in Great Britain by
Creative Print & Design (Ebbw Vale), Wales

We dedicate this book to our children and partners,
our loving critics and ardent supporters.
Matan and Ora Prilleltensky;
Nicole, Laura, Dan and Judy Nelson.

Contents

List of Figures and Tables

Figures

Tables

Acknowledgements

We wish to thank our editor, Frances Arnold, for her enthusiasm, guidance and support. Her sensitive input improved the quality of the book. We also appreciated the comments by David Fryer, Ian Parker and Tod Sloan, who read a draft of the entire manuscript and provided wise advice. Ora Prilleltensky read various sections of the book and helped to improve its clarity. Ora also provided invaluable and unquantifiable support for Isaac. Laura Kiely assisted with preparation of the manuscript and checked and re-checked all the references and tables. Paul Bleazby assisted with the compilation of the index. Janine Jarski at Victoria University, assisted Isaac with multiple administrative tasks, related and unrelated to the book, that allowed him to dedicate more time to writing. Dot Bruck, Head of the Department of Psychology at Victoria University, showed great understanding when Isaac needed time for writing. Geoff received a travel grant to Australia from the Research Office of Wilfrid Laurier University that enabled him to meet with Isaac and complete the final draft of the book.

Preface

This book is about the implementation of critical psychology concepts in action. We felt the need to write a book that would articulate the practical implications of critical psychology. Critical psychology is not a special field but rather an approach to the entire field of psychology. This approach attends to the pervasive influence of power in all we do as psychologists; in our roles as therapists, researchers, writers, community consultants, evaluators, teachers, reviewers, supervisors and course and programme developers. Power shapes not only how we treat each other, but also the very subject matter of our study; how we understand psychology, how we create the theories we do create, how we endorse existing practices and how we accept the status quo. Foucault said that 'truth isn't outside power' (1984: 72). To that, we add that psychology isn't outside power, and that professional practice isn't outside power either. Power serves particular interests. As psychologists, we serve interests; our interests, our clients' interests, and a series of other interests of which we are not even aware, including the desires of those intent upon keeping society the way it is, with all its inequalities. Unless we understand how power pervades all we do, and become conscious of the interests we serve, we risk terrible ignorance. But this is only the first step. The next step is to transform that awareness into practices that promote well-being and liberation and that help community members to resist oppression. Although critical psychology is a young approach, very useful material has been written on how power becomes part of our daily discourse, and how we may inadvertently perpetuate injustice. Not a lot has been written, though, on how to practise from a critical psychology perspective. Here lies our potential contribution.

We want to offer suggestions for training and working in diverse settings using a critical psychology approach. Part I introduces foundational concepts in critical psychology. Part II deals with training in teaching, research, and applied work. Part III is where we articulate the implications of critical psychology for practising in clinical, counselling, educational, health, community, and work settings. The last part of the book discusses ways of integrating critical psychology across settings and across different spheres of life.

A main thrust throughout the volume is that we need to cross settings and mind-sets to advance the goals of critical psychology. Challenges in life derive from interactions of processes occurring simultaneously in different places and at different levels of analysis. Thus, we adopt a systemic approach that encourages psychologists to consider ways of intervention in an array of settings and modalities. Finding ways of collaborating with people in other disciplines, as well as means of integrating diverse helping forms is paramount. Equally important is the ability to view problems from multiple perspectives that defy compression of people's struggles in to either intra-psychic or social factors. Ussher (1991) and

Sedgwick (1982), among others, have demonstrated the disastrous effects of reducing the plight of women and people with psychiatric problems to either labelling, biology, gender, inner conflicts, or material/cultural determinants. Single-factor explanations simplify the human experience and are often an insult to those who suffer from diverse and converging problems that may include labelling, biology, gender, inner conflicts, material and cultural determinants and others.

We have tried to convey our ideas in an accessible style. We use pedagogical frameworks that illustrate and summarize the main points of the discussion in the various chapters. We hope that you will find the book stimulating and engaging. Most of all, we hope you will gain some ideas on how to do psychology critically.

Part I
Foundations

The words power, oppression and liberation were part of my vocabulary long before I knew what critical psychology was, or, for that matter, long before I really understood what they meant. I grew up in Córdoba, Argentina, in the 1960s and 1970s and I belonged to a Socialist Zionist youth movement. My participation in a political organization did not derive from a precocious sense of social responsibility but rather from historical circumstances: the repression of Argentinian people, and a longer history yet of Jewish persecution. In the youth movement, we learned how to question (paradoxically, in quite a dogmatic way) prevailing discourses and dominant figures. One of the most popular books we read in the youth movement was *How to Read Donald Duck*, an early deconstruction of American imperialism. Abuses of power, oppression, and resistance were all around us.

I studied and practised psychology in Israel and Canada. I brought to psychology the questioning attitude I absorbed in South America. After all, they taught me how to doubt official stories and how to distrust authority. Psychology, to me, looked like a series of official stories about normality, development, personality, and, most of all, conformity. I reacted negatively not only to the orthodoxy of some forms of psychoanalysis, but also to some of its theories that reduced complex human phenomena to unprovable assumptions.

I moved to Canada in 1984, where I worked in Winnipeg at a child guidance clinic and completed a PhD with a thesis entitled *Psychology and the Status Quo*. The politics of writing a non-empirical and controversial dissertation in a very traditional department of psychology were both colourful and explosive. This experience, if anything, cemented my resolve to pursue something like critical psychology.

I never quite 'discovered' that psychology individualized social problems and therefore was handmaiden to the status quo. It was, as if I always knew it, part of what we had learned in the youth movement: Psychology and other official stories were part of the ideological apparatuses that reinforced the system of domination.

Psychology's deflections of social problems into individual maladjustments, together with an abuse of power by professionals, led me to explore critical psychology. I was determined to practise a psychology that would not blame victims, that would not be divorced from social issues, and that would listen to people's concerns, in all their complexities. I have been searching for theories and practices that show the intricate connections between psychology, power, oppression, and domination. I have tried to articulate a set of values that will help me, and others, pursue social justice, self-determination, and collaboration and democratic participation in the outcomes and in the very processes of doing psychology. I have used these principles in working with schools, community groups, children, youth and families. Although these values are never quite fully achievable, I feel it's important to use them as a guide for alternative praxis. For me, one of the main challenges in practising critical psychology is how to stay true to the values I believe in. Institutional traditions within the university conflict with values of collaborative research and with political action. Peer support within critical psychology is crucial for developing an approach that promotes social justice.

We all need support in our effort to swim against the tide. Not too long ago, I was invited to present a paper at a conference on quality of life. Briefly, I argued that dignity and quality of life cannot be promoted in the absence of collective well-being, and that it, in turn, cannot be obtained in the absence of social justice. I discussed political inequities and poverty as barriers to well-being. I also noted how different political philosophies are conducive to very different social policies and outcomes. At the end of my talk a distinguished academic in the field asked me, without prelude or hesitation, *how is this science?* Although I cannot have the 'right' interpretation for his question, nor do I want to be overly paranoid, the question embodied, for me, derision about the ideas I presented, doubt about the merit of my proposition, and exclusion from a gathering that was supposed to be about 'real' science. This experience reminded me of why I'm a critical psychologist.

The level of power one can muster in any setting will determine, to a large extent, how a student, professional or academic will cope with intellectual and personal experiences of diminution. Power, in turn, will be increased by solidarity among people concerned to promote dignity and justice and oppose inequality. The path towards solidarity is comprised of partnerships among different groups. The notion of partnerships is crucial to us because it represents the preferred way of enacting values such as respect for diversity and collaboration and democratic participation. It is through these values of *interpersonal well-being* that we can hope to promote *personal well-being*. The safe space created by partnerships enables people to work in solidarity for the promotion of *collective well-being*. Our challenge is to form partnerships where students, colleagues, and community members alike can feel safe to explore the tenets of critical psychology, the need to resist oppression, and the role of power in quality of life.

Isaac Prilleltensky

Introduction

Critical psychologists share an interest in how power permeates professional discourse and action. Moreover, they have in common a commitment to reduce and eliminate oppression in society. But the focus of their attention, as well as their methodologies, vary a great deal. Some are engaged in discourse analysis, some in therapy, others in community work. Some critical psychologists use exclusively qualitative methods of research, while others incorporate quantitative designs as well. We also differ in our traditions, with some being heavily influenced by Latin American liberation psychology and others by the work of Foucault and German critical psychologists like Holzkamp. In this part of the book, we try to reflect diverse tendencies, but we cannot, nor do we want to, escape our own interpretation and use of critical psychology. We bring to this book our insights as well as our limitations.

As will be clear throughout the book, our orientation is informed primarily by the work of critical and community psychologists in several countries. We are also influenced by our experiences working in diverse settings and living in several continents. We want to communicate with people across settings and cultures. The two of us share an appreciation for clarity. There is a great deal of confusion in the language that psychologists of various persuasions use. Countless denominations within modern and postmodern psychology have questioned and multiplied the meaning of words like knowledge, values, and practice. In Part I of the book, we explain our own position with respect to foundational concepts in critical psychology. This is not to imply that our position represents *the* foundations of critical psychology, but rather that these concepts express *our* foundations in critical psychology.

Chapter 1 deals with the main concepts of our approach. We offer a definition of power that situates the individual as potential victim and abuser of it. In addition, we discuss how power is an essential ingredient in the attainment of well-being, the enactment of oppression, and the struggle for liberation. Liberation refers to the positive culmination of a process of resistance. Although complete liberation is an idealized state, we believe that partial liberations are possible and worth striving for. In Chapter 2, we evaluate the repercussions of theory, research, and action for the promotion of well-being. We do so by using a framework consisting of values, assumptions and practices. We ask what values lead to well-being and to the reduction of oppression. This tripartite framework of values, assumptions and practices informs the critique of mainstream practices and the construction of alternatives throughout the book. As a whole, the two chapters provide a set of tools for analyzing existing and alternative practices in psychology.

1

Power, Well-being, Oppression, and Liberation: Points of Departure

This chapter describes our basic approach to critical psychology. We begin with power because it is pivotal in attaining well-being and in opposing injustice. Then, we explore the remaining three foundational concepts of our work: well-being, oppression, and liberation. We discuss how these basic notions inform critical psychology practice. We pay particular attention to the need to cross boundaries in levels of intervention and disciplinary orientations. We also address the issue of clear communication and sensitivity to contextual considerations. We conclude with a brief overview of the book.

Power

Psychologists associated with critical psychology share an important insight: power and interests affect our human experience, our understanding of it, our definition of it, and our attempts to change it (Parker, 1999; Sloan, 2000). Discussing power in an interview, Foucault (1997) made the point that,

> In human relationships, whether they involve verbal communication such as we are engaged in at this moment, or amorous, institutional, or economic relationships, power is always present: I mean a relationship in which one person tries to control the conduct of the other. So I am speaking of relations that exist at different levels, in different forms; these power relations are mobile, they can be modified, they are not fixed once and for all (Foucault, 1997: 291–2).

Unlike typical psychological research, in which power is regarded as a variable existing 'out there,' affecting the behaviour of the people we study or treat, critical psychologists contend that power suffuses our very own actions as psychologists. We use our power to study power. Furthermore, we use our power to define power in such a way that we are not affected by it! This is not just a game of words. We find many examples of psychologists' 'declaration of independence'

5

from power (Herman, 1995). They usually come in the form of claims to objectivity and value-neutrality, announcing that psychologists study people 'out there' in a manner that is not affected by their own interests and power. For a long time, many of us were not even aware that power would be so pervasive and invisible at the same time. Power impregnates the very ways we think about power, psychology, and problems (Henriques *et al.*, 1984). Power operates in subtle ways because it is hidden under a mantle of neutrality.

In critical psychology we try to understand how our own power and subjectivity influence what we do and feel and study (Walkerdine, 1997). Our objective in this exercise is not to develop a new cadre of removed experts on power, but rather to use these insights in the pursuit of health and well-being.

Once we accept that power and interests affect what we do, we don't accept the premise that research is neutral, that interventions are not affected by politics, and that we are just healers. We have a doubting attitude towards the goals of the psychological industry (Rose, 1985, 2000). We just can't take it for granted that psychology pursues human welfare in a manner that is just and fair. Psychologists have contributed, directly and indirectly, wittingly and unwittingly, to oppressive domestic and foreign policies. In her 1995 book, *The Romance of American Psychology*, Ellen Herman documents the involvement of psychologists in formulating shameful policies. Although malevolent intent cannot necessarily be ascribed, psychologists helped to shape racist and inequitable policies, in the USA and abroad. Herman documents psychologists' involvement in project Camelot. This was a project funded by the US Department of Defence in the 1960s. It was designed to use social science to fight national liberation movements around the world. While some psychologists were uncomfortable with the idea of producing knowledge for military purposes, the majority regarded the project as a research opportunity that legitimized their role in public affairs. Many, in fact, were at pains to pronounce their neutrality, even as they endeavoured to produce research for the repression of liberation movements.

The point of this story is not to inculpate the behavioural scientists who worked for Camelot, but rather to show that psychologists are capable of claiming neutrality even as they offer advice on how to dominate other countries. 'Camelot's antiseptic language often emphasized the allegedly apolitical character of behavioural science, referring, for example, to "insurgency prophylaxis" rather than counterrevolution. Even at the height of the Cold War, psychology offered a convenient way to avoid all mention of capitalism, communism, or socialism' (Herman, 1995: 170–1). If we learned anything from Camelot, it is to realise how much power we have as psychologists. One thing is for sure, what looks neutral to a US psychologist looks very political to the average citizen of developing countries.

Camelot cannot be discounted as an aberration, for subtle and overt abuses of power are quite prevalent in psychology and the mental health professions (Parker *et al.*, 1995; Pilgrim, 1992). To break the silence around power, critical psychologists try to understand how cultural norms and systems of social regulation shape human experience. We see this, for example, in Walkerdine's (1996, 1997) efforts to comprehend the survival and coping mechanisms of working-class people, in Montero's (1993) and Martín Baró's (1995) work on power and ideology in

Latin America, and in the writings of Burman (1996) and colleagues dealing with social regulation and resistance. In this book we are interested in translating into practice what we know about the psychological, cultural, social and political sources and effects of power.

Power is multifaceted and omnipresent. There is material and psychological power, there is the power of the psychologist and the power of the client, power of parents and power of children, power to define mental illness and power to resist labels. Power, in our view, refers to the capacity and opportunity to fulfil or obstruct personal, relational, or collective needs. We note three primary uses of power: (a) power to strive for well-being, (b) power to oppress, and (c) power to resist marginalization and strive for liberation. In each instance, the exercise of power can apply to self, others, and collectives; and can reflect varying degrees of awareness with respect to the impact of one's actions. Whereas people may be oppressed in one context, they may act as oppressors in others. Power affords people multiple identities as individuals seeking well-being, engaging in oppression, or resisting domination.

Within a particular context, such as the family or work, individuals may exercise power to facilitate the well-being of some people but not of others. Across contexts, people may engage in contradictory actions that promote personal or collective well-being in one place but that perpetuate oppression in others. Due to structural factors such as social class, gender, ability, and race, people may enjoy differential levels of power. Degrees of power are also affected by personal and social constructs such as beauty, intelligence, and assertiveness; constructs that enjoy variable status within different cultures. The exercise of power varies not only across contexts, but also across time. Within a particular setting or relationship, people may occupy different roles at different times, making the exercise of power a very dynamic process.

Our concept of power merges elements of agency with structure or external determinants. Agency refers to ability and volitional activity, whereas structure refers to opportunity. The exercise of power is based on the juxtaposition of wishing to change something, on one hand, and having the opportunity to do so, on the other. Opportunities are afforded by social and historical circumstances. Adverse conditions block new opportunities. Ultimately, the outcome of power is based on the constant interaction and reciprocal determinism of agency and contextual dynamics.

Power is not tantamount to coercion, for it can operate in very subtle and concealed ways, as Foucault demonstrated in detailed historical analyses of population control (1979). Eventually, people come to regulate themselves through the internalization of cultural prescriptions. Hence, what may seem on the surface as freedom may be a form of acquiescence whereby citizens restrict their life choices to fit socially sanctioned options. In his book *Powers of Freedom*, Rose (1999: 88) claimed that:

> Disciplinary techniques and moralizing injunctions as to health, hygiene and civility are no longer required; the project of responsible citizenship has been fused with individuals' projects for themselves. What began as a social norm here ends as a personal desire. Individuals act upon themselves and their families in terms of the languages, values and techniques made available to them by professions, disseminated through the apparatuses of the mass media or sought out by the troubled through the market.

Thus, in a very significant sense, it has become possible to govern without governing *society* – to govern through the 'responsibilized' and 'educated' anxieties and aspirations of individuals and their families.

Internalized social prescriptions have direct implications for the self-perception of people with problems. Although coercion has not disappeared from the treatment of the mentally ill, we have, today, treatment methods characterized by kindness and compassion. However humanitarian, this trend is not without side effects, for it turns responsibility for problems and solutions inward. In the absence of apparent coercion, and in the presence of overt caring, there is nobody but oneself to blame for difficulties.

> The humanization of treatments of the insane encouraged the internalization of the difficulties they exhibited. The mad then had to take responsibility for cure, and the kind treatment which replaced the rods and whips would work its way inwards. The conscience of the mentally ill would act as a self-discipline all the more efficient than the social discipline of the general hospital (Parker *et al.*, 1995: 7).

Power, then, emanates from the confluence of personal motives and cultural injunctions. But, as we have seen, personal motives are embedded in the very cultural injunctions with which they interact. Hence, it is not just a matter of persons acting on the environment, but of individuals coming into contact with external forces that they have already internalized. Thus, we cannot take at face value that individual actions evolve from innate desires. Desires are embedded in norms and regulations. This is not to adopt a socially deterministic position however. For even though a person's experience is greatly shaped by the prescriptions of the day, agency is not completely erased. We concur with Martin and Sugarman (2000: 401) who claimed that:

> While never ceasing to be constructed in sociocultural terms, psychological beings, as reflection-capable, intentional agents, are able to exercise sophisticated capabilities of memory and imagination, which in interaction with theories of self can create possibilities for present and future understanding and action that are not entirely constrained by past and present sociocultural circumstances.

Resistance and collusion with oppressive structures co-exist. Indeed, contradictions abound. Humanists, for instance, wished to promote individual well-being without recognizing their contribution to the status quo by individualizing sources of suffering (Prilleltensky, 1994). They wished to advance personal liberation without changing social oppression.

Well-being

Well-being is achieved by the simultaneous and balanced satisfaction of personal, relational, and collective needs. In Table 1.1 we show the main values comprising the three domains of well-being and their respective needs.

Table 1.1 Personal, relational, and collective domains of well-being

Domains	Well-being		
	Personal well-being	**Relational well-being**	**Collective well-being**
Values	Self-determination and personal growth / Health	Respect for human diversity / Collaboration and democratic participation	Support for community structures / Social justice
Definition	Promotion of ability of children and adults to pursue chosen goals in life / Protection of physical and emotional health	Promotion of respect and appreciation for diverse social identities and for people's ability to define themselves / Promotion of fair processes whereby children and adults can have meaningful input into decisions affecting their lives	Promotion of vital community structures that facilitate the pursuit of personal and communal goals / Promotion of fair and equitable allocation of bargaining powers, obligations, and resources in society
Needs addressed	Mastery, control, self-efficacy, voice, choice, skills, growth and autonomy / Emotional and physical well-being	Identity, dignity, self-respect, self-esteem, acceptance / Participation, involvement, and mutual responsibility	Sense of community, cohesion, formal support / Economic security, shelter, clothing, nutrition, access to vital health and social services

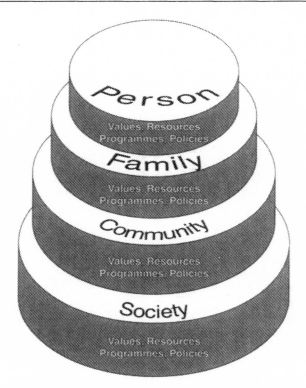

Figure 1.1 Ecological and hierarchical structure of well-being

Well-being is not only a multidimensional concept, but, as can be seen in Figure 1.1, a hierarchical one as well. The well-being of the individual is predicated on the well-being of the immediate family, which, in turn, is contingent upon community and societal conditions. As Cowen (1996:246) observed, 'optimal development of wellness . . . requires integrated sets of operations involving individuals, families, settings, community contexts, and macro-level societal structures and policies'. Despite what we know about the impact of various systems and levels on families, most interventions in psychology and mental health deal with individuals, dyads (for example, parent–child or marital relationships), or families (Cowen, 2000; Prilleltensky, 1997). Our actions lag behind our understanding of well-being. Much evidence points to the powerful impact of socioeconomic, cultural, and contextual factors in shaping the lives of children, adults, families and communities (Basic Behavioral Science Task Force of the National Advisory Mental Health Council, 1996; Cicchetti *et al.*, 2000; Garbarino, 1992; Keating and Hertzman, 1999a; McLoyd, 1998; Shonkoff and Phillips, 2000). Yet, in apparent disregard for this knowledge, many of us continue to focus on counselling, therapy, or person-centred prevention as the main avenues for well-being (Albee, 1996). We concentrate on individual interventions at our own peril, for the data suggest that we should be paying much more attention to socioeconomic determinants of health.

Differences in equity of income distribution is one of the principal determinants of differing health status among wealthy societies. Countries with highly unequal income distributions have poorer health status than those with more equitable income distributions. . . . This pattern suggests that health status (as a measure of human well-being) may be embedded in collective factors in society, not just in individual factors. . . . These findings led us to the conclusion that the underlying factors that determine health and well-being must be deeply embedded in social circumstances (Keating and Hertzman, 1999b:6–7).

Given this evidence, we cannot accept definitions of well-being that are based exclusively on intra-psychic factors. These definitions tend to be psycho-centric because they concentrate on the cognitive and emotional sources and consequences of suffering and well-being, to the exclusion of the social, material, and political roots and effects of lack of power. There is an ominous social reality 'out there' that impinges on how we feel and how we behave towards each other. While beliefs and perceptions are important, they cannot be treated in isolation from the cultural, political, and economic environment (Eckersley, 2000). We require 'well-enough' social and political conditions, free of economic exploitation and human rights abuses, to experience quality of life. All the same, we expect interpersonal exchanges based on respect and mutual support to add to our quality of life. Eckersley (2000) has shown that subjective experiences of well-being are heavily dictated by cultural trends such as individualism and consumerism; whereas Narayan and colleagues have claimed that the psychological experience of poverty is directly related to political structures of oppression (Narayan, Chambers et al., 2000; Narayan, Patel et al., 2000).

Much like our definition of power, Sen (1999a, b) describes poverty and well-being in terms of both capabilities and entitlements. Without the latter the former cannot thrive. Both in our definition of power and in Sen's conceptualization of poverty there is a dialectical relationship between personal capacities and environmental factors. But our approach to power and Sen's approach to poverty share another dimension. In both cases, capacities and resources are at once intrinsically meritorious and extrinsically beneficial. This means that a sense of mastery and control is both an end in itself as well as a means of achieving well-being. Access to preventive health care and educational opportunities are not only means to human development but also ends in their own right.

Well-being at the collective level is not only measured by the health and educational outcomes of a group of individuals, but also by the presence of enabling institutions and societal infrastructures. Hence, we define well-being in broad terms that encompass social progress and human development. As we explain in Chapter 8 dealing with health psychology, we cannot talk about psychological well-being in the absence of interpersonal and political well-being. The three kinds are mutually reinforcing and interdependent.

Sen (1999a, b) articulates the complementarity of diverse social structures in fostering what we call well-being and what he calls human development. Sen invokes the interaction of five types of freedoms in the pursuit of human development: (a) political freedoms, (b) economic facilities, (c) social opportunities, (d) transparency guarantee, and (e) protective security.

Each of these distinct types of rights and opportunities helps to advance the general capability of a person. They may also serve to complement each other. . . . Freedoms are not only the primary ends of development, they are also among its principal means. In addition to acknowledging, foundationally, the evaluative importance of freedom, we also have to understand the remarkable empirical connection that links freedoms of different kinds with one another. Political freedoms (in the form of free speeches and elections) help to promote economic security. Social opportunities (in the form of education and health facilities) facilitate economic participation. Economic facilities (in the form of opportunities for participation in trade and production) can help to generate personal abundance as well as public resources for social facilities. Freedoms of different kinds can strengthen one another (Sen, 1999b:10–11).

Our theory of well-being regards human development in terms of the mutually reinforcing properties of personal, relational, and societal qualities. Personal needs such as health, self-determination, and opportunities for growth, are tied to the satisfaction of collective needs such as adequate health care, access to safe drinking water, fair and equitable allocation of resources and economic equality.

The extent to which governments and states provide the population with these resources depends, in great measure, on the values they hold and the class interests they represent (Sen, 1999a, b). Well-being cannot be conceived out of context, a context in which 'nations suffer long term damage from "elite politics" that promote a government of corporations, by corporations, for corporations' (Pusey, in press: 10). These governments serve corporate interests that are often diametrically opposed to the needs of the poor. As Pusey claimed, 'most Anglophone nations have experienced a marked upward redistribution of incomes that generally reduces subjective well being, creates damaging social conflicts, endangers social cohesion and effective governance, and negatively impacts on the health of populations' (10). Developing countries fare no better. The wave of globalization that swept the world in the last twenty years decimated the minimal protections that citizens used to have in poor countries (Lustig, 2001).

The presence or absence of health-promoting factors at all levels can have positive or negative synergistic effects. When collective factors such as social justice and access to valued resources combine with a sense of community and personal empowerment, the chances are that psychological and political well-being will ensue. When, on the other hand, injustice and exploitation blend with a lack of resources, social fragmentation together with ill-health, suffering and oppression will emerge.

Oppression

Oppression can be regarded as a *state* or a *process* (Prilleltensky, in press; Prilleltensky and Gonick, 1994, 1996). Oppression is described as a state of domination where the oppressed suffer the consequences of deprivation, exclusion, discrimination, exploitation, control of culture, and sometimes even violence (for example, Bartky, 1990; Moane, 1999; Sidanius, 1993; Young, 1990). Mar'i

(1988:6) talks about oppression as a process: 'Oppression involves institutionalized collective and individual modes of behavior through which one group
attempts to dominate and control another in order to secure political, economic,
and/or social-psychological advantage'.

Much like well-being, oppression entails *political* and *psychological* dimensions.
We cannot speak of one without the other (Bulhan, 1985; Moane, 1999;
Walkerdine, 1997). Psychological and political oppression co-exist and are mutu-
ally determined. In Bartky's words,

> When we describe a people as oppressed, what we have in mind most often is an
> oppression that is economic and political in character. But recent liberation move-
> ments, the black liberation movement and the women's movement in particular, have
> brought to light forms of oppression that are not immediately economic or political.
> It is possible to be oppressed in ways that need involve neither deprivation, legal
> inequality, nor economic exploitation; one can be oppressed psychologically – the
> 'psychic alienation' of which Fanon speaks. To be psychologically oppressed is to
> be weighed down in your mind; it is to have a harsh dominion exercised over your
> self-esteem. The psychologically oppressed become their own oppressors; they come
> to exercise dominion over their own self-esteem. Differently put, psychological
> oppression can be regarded as the 'internalization of intimations of inferiority'
> (Bartky, 1990:22).

Oppression, then, entails a state of asymmetric power relations characterized by
domination, subordination, and resistance. Domination is exerted by restricting
access to material resources and imparting in people self-deprecating views about
themselves. It is only when people attain a certain degree of self-awareness that
resistance can begin (Bartky, 1990; Fanon, 1963; Freire, 1970; Memmi, 1968;
Prilleltensky, in press). Oppression applies to asymmetric power relations between
individuals, genders, classes, communities, and nations. These power relations
lead to conditions of misery, inequality, exploitation, marginalization, and social
injustice.

The dynamics of oppression are internal as well as external. External forces
deprive individuals or groups of the benefit of personal (for example, self-determination) collective (for example, distributive justice) and relational (for example,
democratic participation) well-being. These restrictions are often internalized and
operate at a psychological level as well, in which case the person acts as his or her
personal censor (Moane, 1999; Pheterson, 1986; Prilleltensky and Gonick, 1996).

Political oppression uses material, legal, military, economic, and/or other social
barriers to the fulfilment of self-determination, distributive justice, and democratic
participation. Such oppression results from the use of multiple forms of power.
Psychological oppression, in turn, is the internalized view of self as negative, and
as not deserving more resources or increased participation in societal affairs.
Political mechanisms of oppression and repression include actual or potential use
of force, restricted life opportunities, degradation of indigenous culture, economic sanctions, and inability to challenge authority. Psychological dynamics of
oppression entail surplus powerlessness, belief in a just world, learned helplessness,
conformity, obedience to authority, fear, verbal and emotional abuse (for reviews
see Moane, 1999; Prilleltensky, in press; and Prilleltensky and Gonick, 1996).

Poor people everywhere are subjected to experiences of injustice. Although absolute poverty is concentrated in the southern hemisphere, relative poverty and real deprivation are very much present in the North as well. 'In the UK, over a quarter of people live in low income households, with worse health, lower life-expectancy, lower levels of social participation, and worse life chances than those above the poverty line. Children are disproportionately disadvantaged' (Maxwell and Kenway, 2000:1). At the collective level, people in the South suffer from two sets of devastating experiences: (a) *insecurity, chaos, violence*, and (b) *economic exploitation*. Narayan and colleagues (Narayan, Chambers *et al.*, 2000; Narayan, Patel *et al.*, 2000) interviewed thousands of poor people who spoke of the fear of living with uncertainty and lack of protection. Lawlessness exacerbates the plight of the poor; it adds a dimension of terror to the material deprivation. Chaotic environments in politically unstable regimes are fertile grounds for crime and violence.

Economic exploitation is felt as a trap without escape. Children and adults working at slavery, or near slavery levels, have no choice but to relinquish their freedom and abide by rules of despotic employers.

> Officially, slavery no longer exists in Haiti. But through the lives of children in Haiti who live as *restaveks* we see the remnants of slavery. *Restaveks* are children, usually girls, sometimes as young as 3 and 4 years old, who live in the majority of Haitian families as unpaid domestic workers. They are the first to get up in the morning and the last to go to bed at night. They carry water, clean house, do errands and receive no salary . . . they eat what is left when the others are finished, and they are extremely vulnerable to verbal, physical and sexual abuse (Aristide, 2000:27).

Entire communities and countries experience economic exploitation. Poor communities working for starvation wages in fields feel trapped (Feuerstein, 1997). Poor countries feel equally trapped by international lending institutions that force governments to drop social services and lift tariffs on imports in the name of efficiency and economic growth. Korten (1995) reviews the cases of Costa Rica and Brazil. In both instances, structural adjustment programmes imposed by the International Monetary Fund (IMF) and the World Bank displaced millions of agricultural workers. Furthermore, many countries have 'become dependent on imports to meet basic food requirements' (Korten, 1995:49). Aristide (2000), in turn, reviews the case of rice production in Haiti. In a matter of ten years, from 1986 to 1996, Haiti increased its import of rice from 7,000 to 196,000 tons per year. During that period Haiti

> complied with lending agencies and lifted tariffs on rice imports. Cheaper rice immediately flooded in from the United States where the rice industry is subsidized . . . Haiti's peasant farmers could not possible compete . . . Haitian rice production became negligible. Once the dependence on foreign rice was complete, import prices began to rise, leaving Haiti's population, particularly the urban poor, completely at the whim of rising world grain prices (Aristide, 2000:11–12).

These stories are repeated throughout the entire South (Korten, 1995). The price of structural adjustment policies in countries like Haiti, Brazil and Costa Rica is unemployment and displacement for millions. Measures imposed at the collective level are felt very much at the personal level as well.

Economic policies that result in unemployment affect people in the South and in the North. Based on research in developed countries, Fryer (1998:78) asserts that 'unemployment is centrally involved in the social causation of mental health problems'. Furthermore, he claims that unemployment is psychologically debilitating because it 'disempowers by impoverishing, restricting, baffling and undermining the agency of the unemployed person' (Fryer, 1998:83). The impact of recessions can be felt in unemployment and on many other levels as well. Wages go down, health and working conditions deteriorate, and minorities are more visibly excluded from the job market (Fryer, 1998).

Policies and societal practices are very much felt at the individual and interpersonal levels. Just as well-being is brought about by the synergy of personal, relational, and collective needs, so is suffering caused by the synergy of unmet needs at all levels. 'Poor people report living with increased crime, corruption, violence, and insecurity amidst declining social cohesion. People feel helpless against forces of change' (Narayan, Patel *et al.*, 2000:222).

In the struggle for survival, social relations also suffer. Suffering at the relational level is marked by (a) *heightened fragmentation* and *exclusion* and by (b) *fractious social relations*. The personal dimension of suffering and victimization in the poor is characterized by (a) *powerlessness*, (b) *limitations and restricted opportunities in life*, (c) *physical weakness*, (d) *shame and feelings of inferiority*, and (e) *gender and age discrimination*. Impotence in the light of ominous societal forces like crime and economic displacement fuels the sense of powerlessness.

The oppressive experience of poverty is, at all levels, characterized by powerlessness. 'Poverty is like living in jail, living under bondage, waiting to be free' (A young woman in Jamaica, in Narayan, Chambers *et al.*, 2000:8). When rice farmers in Haiti work as hard as they can, abide by all the rules, and still cannot compete with American producers, there is a profound sense of oppression, powerlessness and lack of control. When little *restavek* girls work day and night and sustain multiple forms of abuse, hopelessness ensues. When poor women are subjected to humiliation, exclusion and violence, powerlessness is the most common outcome. Power differentials sit at the core of oppression for poor people of all ages. The power inequality expressed by poor people is not psychological or political but always both. Material and economic power are intertwined with feelings of shame and inferiority. In the light of so much adversity, it is against the odds that poor people still engage in acts of meaning, solidarity and liberation.

Liberation

Liberation refers to the *process* of resisting oppressive forces. As a *state*, liberation is a condition in which oppressive forces no longer dominate a person or a group. Liberation may be from psychological and/or political influences. There is rarely political without psychological liberation, and vice versa. Repressive cultural codes become internalized and operate as self-regulatory mechanisms, inhibiting defiance of oppressive rules (Moane, 1999).

Building on Fromm's dual conception of 'freedom from' and 'freedom to' (1965), liberation is the process of overcoming internal and external sources of subjugation (freedom from), and pursuing well-being (freedom to). Liberation from social oppression entails, for example, emancipation from class exploitation, gender domination, and ethnic discrimination. Freedom from internal and psychological sources includes overcoming fears, obsessions, or other psychological phenomena that interfere with the experience of well-being.

Liberation to pursue life satisfaction, in turn, refers to the process of meeting personal, relational, and collective needs. The process of liberation is analogous to Freire's concept of conscientization, according to which marginalized populations begin to gain awareness of oppressive forces in their lives and of their own ability to transform them (Freire, 1975). This awareness is likely to develop in stages (Watts, Griffith, and Abdul-Adil, 1999). People may begin to realize that they are subjected to unjust regulations. The first realization may happen as a result of therapy, participation in a social movement or readings. Next, they may connect with others experiencing similar circumstances and gain an appreciation for the external forces pressing down on them. Some individuals will go on to liberate themselves from oppressive relationships or psychological dynamics such as fears and phobias, whereas others will join social movements to fight for political justice.

The evolution of critical consciousness can be charted in terms of the relationship between the psychological and political dynamics of oppression. The level of critical awareness of a person or group will vary according to the extent that psychological mechanisms obscure or mask the external political sources of oppression. In other words, the more people internalize oppression through various psychological mechanisms, the less will they see their suffering as resulting from unjust political conditions. At times, the internalized psychological oppression will almost completely obscure the political roots and dynamics of oppression. Walkerdine (1996, 1997) documented how these processes of internalized oppression affected the lives of working-class women, whereas Allwood (1996) detailed the personal blame discourse of depressed women. In both cases, personal suffering and struggles are explained in terms of private ineptitudes divorced from systems of domination and exclusion.

Ideally, people go on to discern the political sources of their psychological experience of oppression and rebel against them. However, research on the process of empowerment indicates that individuals do not engage in emancipatory actions until they have gained considerable awareness of their own oppression (Kieffer, 1984; Lord and Hutchinson, 1993). Consequently, the task of overcoming oppression should start with a process of psychopolitical education that ends in greater awareness and action. This ideal outcome, however, should not be idealized too much because people may gain awareness of some facets of injustice and not of others. Liberation is not a fixated state at which people arrive and claim nirvana. New sources of oppression may emerge, or they may become oppressors themselves. The progression towards liberation is far from linear.

The relation between our own liberation as psychologists and the liberation of the people we work with is complicated. Some of us feel liberated or free from victimization, whereas others are subjected to discrimination in their lives because of disabilities or sexual orientation. Depending on our psychological experience we may project certain assumptions onto our clients, students, and community partners. The ethics of projecting onto others our own unresolved issues requires careful attention in case we define others' experiences based on our own inner conflicts.

We believe that the preferred way to contribute to the liberation of oppressed people is through partnerships and solidarity. We approach them in an attempt to work and learn from them. At the same time we try to contribute to their cause in whichever way we can (Nelson, Ochocka *et al.*, 1998; Nelson, Prilleltensky, and MacGillivary, 2001).

To promote liberation, critical psychology practice needs to engage with the political and the psychological at the same time. As Ussher (1991:293) pointed out, 'we need to operate on the level of the political and of the individual: at the level of discursive practices, and individual solutions for misery. The two must go hand in hand if we are to move forward'. Martín-Baró (1994), Moane (1999), and others, began to sketch the aims and methods of a liberation psychology. 'A liberation psychology aims to facilitate breaking out of oppression by identifying processes and practices which can transform the psychological patterns associated with oppression, and facilitate taking action to bring about change in social conditions' (Moane, 1999:180).

Table 1.2 shows how oppression, liberation and well-being are experienced at the levels of self, others, community, and society. At each of these levels, ideal values succumb under conditions of subjugation and re-emerge through a process of liberation. The ultimate outcome of this journey is to reach personal, relational and collective well-being. Although the table shows discrete paths for each one of the ecological levels, in actual fact all the levels are interconnected and interdependent. The path towards well-being requires solidarity; for nobody can reach liberation in isolation.

Doing psychology critically

The pressing question in this book is how to convert the insights about power, well-being, and liberation into practical interventions. We should not have to wait until clinics, schools, and community agencies embrace a critical psychology philosophy for us to promote critical practice. Power is ubiquitous and it pervades the way we think about and treat the people we work with. In all our interactions with service recipients we use our power with health-enhancing or deleterious effects. Which practices promote well-being and which assumptions perpetuate intimidation is not always clear. This is because even with the best intentions we can cause harm. A primary challenge, then, is to reflect on our own existing practices and scrutinize their effects. A subsequent challenge is to incorporate lessons about power, injustice, well-being and liberation into everyday practice.

We conceptualize practice broadly. We include psychological work in mental health clinics, in community settings, in schools, in workplaces, and in universities as well. The amount of work to be done to transform uncritical perspectives that blame victims and perpetuate asymmetric power relations is quite enormous.

Table 1.2 A journey of personal and political change

Ecological level	Values	Oppression (disempowerment)	Liberation and empowerment (processes to overcome oppression and achieve well-being)	Well-being (a state of personal, relational, and collective well-being)
Self	Personal (self-determination and health)	Internalized, psychological oppression	Conscientization situates personal struggles in the context of larger political and structural forces	Control, choice, self-esteem, competence, independence, political rights, and a positive identity
Others (relationships)	Relational (human diversity, collaboration and democratic participation)	'Power over', domination of, or by, others	'Power with', power sharing, egalitarian relationships, and peer mentoring support, individuals' and groups' quest for rights, identity, and dignity	Positive and supportive relationships, participation in social, community, and political life
Community and society	Collective (distributive justice, support for community structures)	Oppressive social practices manifested in policies and community settings	Empowering social practices manifested in policies and community settings provide larger structural context for wellness	Access to valued resources such as employment, income, education, and housing

From text deconstruction to therapy to community activism, critical psychologists have an important role to fulfil. To promote well-being and to resist oppression we believe that critical psychologists have to cross boundaries, develop clear communication with service recipients, and attend to contextual diversity.

Crossing boundaries

Awareness of power and politics did not necessarily come from within psychology. Rather, they came from disparate fields such as the sociology of knowledge, critical social theory, cultural studies, women's studies and radical politics. Without critiques from other disciplines, it would be hard for psychology to reflect on its own assumptions. We welcome such interrogations. These critiques forced psychology to look at its self-perception of healer and scientist (Rose, 2000).

Much like other disciplines threw light into psychology's role in society, allied fields helped to conceptualize human problems in broader terms. Hence, we know from sociology and biology and political economy that psychological symptoms are related to unemployment and organic malfunctions and class systems. The complexities of human beings extend far beyond the reach of psychology.

Crossing boundaries means not only looking at other sources of knowledge, but also at different levels of analyses. Traditionally we have looked into the 'mind' and its intra-psychic mechanisms for explanations of personal and interpersonal conflicts. We propose to broaden analyses of problems and sites of intervention to other ecological levels. In practical terms, this means more than a token recognition of family, community, and societal dynamics; it means a comprehensive view of how these parameters shape the life experience of the people we work with. But if holistic understanding is challenging, systemic intervention is harder yet. Connecting therapy with community interventions and social action may be difficult but not impossible.

Communication of meanings

Working across fields and with people who are often marginalized requires sensitivity to language. Language itself can be a source of oppression or a vehicle of solidarity. How can we expect to create bonds of solidarity when the people we work with do not even understand what we mean. Never mind our clients, even our colleagues and students sometimes don't understand what we're talking about. Obscuring language feeds into self-perceptions of stupidity in many people. We can't collaborate with community members when the terminology we use prevents access to knowledge. Critical psychologists are not immune to alienating people due to obfuscating language. The type of psychology we are promoting requires close collaboration with a range of people whose formal education may be different from ours. For us, promoting understanding is a matter of respect.

We don't believe that we'll lose something by communicating in simple language, but we do believe that we'll lose a lot by alienating partners. Language should build bonds of solidarity and not walls of alienation. But this is far from calling for a simplification of issues. The risk is not simplification of issues, but alienation from those we wish to work with. Freire (1975) showed how people with very little formal education could reach sophisticated levels of sociopolitical understanding. This was achieved through a process of popular education.

Practice in context

Critical psychology practice is always in context. But if contexts vary, as they invariably do, how can we apply a set of critical psychology principles across settings and cultures? We take it for granted that different contexts will have varied configurations of power and varied perceptions of well-being. We are not talking only about different cultures, but also about cultures within cultures, and subcultures within subcultures. Heterogeneity is often the norm and not the exception when dealing with seemingly discrete ethnic or minority groups. Each group subsumes subgroups with different prescriptive and proscriptive codes and beliefs. We cannot talk in general terms about all people with disabilities, or all people with psychiatric problems or all gays and lesbians.

Sensitivity to context means exploring our unique cultural heritage, taking the time to listen to the concerns and world views of others, and finding means of establishing a dialogue. James and Prilleltensky (in press) described a model of practice that attends to the interface among psychologists, their cultural values and assumptions, the ethnic identity of clients, and the unique position of the client within a subculture. The model alerts practitioners to potential projections of their own unchecked assumptions. This results in heightened sensitivity to the role of practitioners' and clients' cultures. Furthermore, it enables dialogue in dealing with diversity.

Book organization

This chapter has provided an overview of the central notions guiding our work in critical psychology. Chapter 2 introduces a framework for assessing the impact of theory, research, and action and provides a rationale for the values we believe in. Furthermore, we discern the basic parameters constructing the subject matter of psychology, including views about knowledge and ethics.

Part II of the book deals with training. We provide guidelines for preparing critical psychologists to work in applied settings, in research, and in teaching. The field of critical psychology needs models of training. Part III describes, in six chapters, the application of critical psychology tenets to practice in clinical and counselling, educational, health, community and work settings.

The last part of the book deals with the topics of integrations and transformations. We reflect on the need, and the struggle, to integrate critical psychology across settings and levels of intervention. The last three chapters of the book deal with change. They tackle, respectively, *agents, processes,* and *objects* of change.

2

Theory, Research, and Action: Oppressive and Emancipatory Effects

In this chapter we try to discern the oppressive and emancipatory effects of what psychologists do. What we do falls generally within the domains of theory construction, grounded investigations, and action. In all of our roles there are inherent beliefs driving our efforts.

Theory

Theories define, represent, and explain phenomena. As such, they are powerful tools. They can portray humans as active or passive, altruistic, or driven to violence. Whichever rendition of behaviour we prefer, the subjects of the theory are affected by the theory itself. We already know the effects of portraying women and Jews and blacks and migrants as inferior. A psychological theory of inferiority justifies policies of domination and engenders subjugation (Moane, 1999; Parker *et al.*, 1995).

Theories serve constraining or emancipatory purposes. Consideration of the potential oppressive effects of theories is an integral aspect of critical psychology. In our view, the confining effects of theorization ensue from three main sources: (a) the incomplete depiction of phenomena, (b) the affixing of people to immovable moulds, and (c) the obviation of power in theory construction itself. How do they work?

When we ignore crucial factors in explaining phenomena we run the risk of affirming relations of inequality and oppression. For example, when we ascribe women's unhappiness to unresolved 'inner' conflicts and we neglect 'outer' domestic violence, drudgery and unrelenting childminding, we formulate descriptions and prescriptions that focus on mentalistic accounts. These accounts render the objective conditions of inequality unaccounted and unaltered. As the subjects of such theorizing, women may surmise that they are not good at coping and that they need to change something within themselves. By leaving out objective conditions of suffering, the theory configures a phenomenon in psycho-terminology. As the recipient of such theorizing, the individual turns

21

inwards in search for solutions. This is an unjust outcome in that it internalizes problems and leads to self-deprecation. By failing to interrogate oppressive conditions within its domain, the theory normalizes the very circumstances which may have caused the suffering.

Because of its emphasis on the personal interpretation of events as causation of distress, rational emotive theory is particularly prone to incomplete descriptions of phenomena; although the same can be alleged of cognitive behavioural and certain psychoanalytic theories (Prilleltensky, 1994). Predominant theories of personality, clinical, and abnormal psychology have been historically susceptible to this type of reification. That is, the treatment of human behaviour as if it were an 'in-itself,' an entity abstracted from its social context (Hare-Mustin and Marecek, 1997; Sampson, 2001; Sloan, 1997). This charge is akin to psychological essentialism, whereby behaviour is explained in reductionistic terms of singular character traits (Martin and Sugarman, 2000). These traits and categories 'homogenize, essential-ize and naturalize as individual psychological qualities what are features of people's historical and current circumstances' (Burman *et al.*, 1996:73).

Affixing people, the objects of psychological theories, to set patterns and identities is another conduit of oppression. When we declare that somebody is psychologically disturbed we are not only describing but also prescribing and proscribing behaviour. Myriad stereotypes and labels are ascribed to groups and individuals, labels they cannot easily get rid of. These imputations constrain the horizons of the targets of stereotypes. Albeit in innocent ways, theories of development, personality and delinquency operate in a similar fashion. When our vocational preoccupation is with accurate diagnosis and prediction, it is not surprising that we spend endless time categorizing people (Sampson, 2001). However beneficial for communication purposes, diagnoses carry within them the risk of narrowing the self-perception of clients. Innocent as they might, explanations of human behaviour tend to limit the possibilities of change. Once assigned to a category, and the category is in the public domain, the person is the carrier of newly imposed restrictions on what he or she can be (Burman *et al.*, 1996; Sampson, 2001).

The obviation of power in theory construction itself can also have negative repercussions. What has been variously called the 'view from nowhere' or 'god's view' refers to the illusion that theories are independent of their creators. As such, they are only representations of something that exists 'out there', irrespective of our own subjective and socially constructed position. In perpetuating this chimera, we hide our power to define and categorize. When power is concealed, we feed into the mirage of detached truth. We present interpretations as facts, and we deny that power and social location play a role in our accounts of social events. This lack of reflexivity perpetuates the public's view that our renditions are uncontaminated by subjectivity. Such perception is instrumental in psychology's role as agent of social control. If power is nowhere to be seen, and science is all that we do, why should people suspect our motives, especially when many of us don't even realize that power contaminates our work?

As a result, we deprive people of the opportunity to question how we define them and how we treat them. As no power motives are seemingly involved, and as psychologists stand as representatives of science and professionalism, there is no need to interrogate the knowledge base or the subjectivity of the professional.

While some theories constrain and limit, others open up new horizons of opportunities. Some theories describe how people can plan, act, and change. Describing factors and processes that lead to personal and social change can be both instrumental and therapeutic on its own. Theories that explain how to promote personal, relational, and collective well-being at the same time can be very helpful in the process of emancipation. Similarly, theories that account for marginalized voices counteract explanations that derive exclusively from seats of privilege. Finally, theories that disentangle unjust discursive practices in our culture contain emancipatory potential; they disclose the many overt and covert ways in which people undermine each other and perpetuate systems of regulation. Once deconstructed, these practices are easier to critique, resist, and alter.

Research

Research can be oppressive or emancipatory, not only in its outcomes but in its very processes as well. We examine here both aspects of research. 'Research findings' do not come from nowhere, they come from an interaction of the values and assumptions of the researcher with the particular historical representation of the phenomenon under study. Chesler (1989), Ussher (1991), and Wilkinson (1997), among others, reviewed diverse strands of research that portray women as inferior to men, as more excitable, as less capable of working under pressure, and, of course, as more suited for house work. These conclusions were advanced as 'truths'. The way in which these conclusions were derived and protected power and privilege was never questioned. On the contrary, power and privilege were never meant to be discussed in the context of scientific research.

Chesler (1989:106) wrote that 'many female patients view themselves as "sick" or "bad" and commit themselves, quite voluntarily, to asylums or to private psychiatrists'. This distinct oppressive outcome has also been part of research with people with disabilities. As Woodill (1992) put it, 'few of us have escaped the researchers' scrutiny of their seemingly pathological fixation on the limitations and negative aspects of disability. We have been portrayed as sick, helpless, and incompetent; incapable of living independently' (2).

The research relationship itself can also be demeaning of participants. Oliver (1992) recounts the exploitation of people with disabilities in the research process. In their capacity as research participants, persons with disabilities often endure the disabling gaze of researchers who look for data more than dignity. Insensitive researchers engage in 'othering' of 'those who have been exploited and subjugated' (Fine, 1994:72). Several authors accentuate the need to amplify participants' voices, not only in the final report, but also in the very construction and negotiation of the research relationship (Goodley, 1996; Morris, 1992; Nelson, Ochocka et al., 1998).

We support the concept and practice of research partnerships. Establishing a collaborative research relationship is a central part of our vision. In such a relationship, partners decide together the means and ends of the investigation, bearing in mind the different skills that each partner brings to the table (Nelson, Prilleltensky, and

MacGillivary, 2001). There is no attempt to pretend equality in partnerships. Rather, there is a conscious effort to remember where people are coming from, what is their power position in the partnership, and what can be done to promote solidarity. In Part II we discuss methods for striking a research alliance with people who have not usually thought of themselves as equals to academics.

Action

Rose (1985, 1999, 2000) pointed out that theory is rarely divorced from social demands. In the case of psychology, instruments and concepts are devised to serve specific expectations. This is why it is important to attend not only to theory but also to the social demands shaping psychology.

> Psychology's role as an administrative science cannot be understood as the application of a psychological knowledge of normality, gained through theoretical reflection or laboratory investigation, to a domain of practical problems. On the contrary, it was through attempts to diagnose, conceptualise and regulate pathologies of conduct that psychological knowledge and expertise first began to establish its claims for scientific credibility, professional status and social importance (Rose, 1985:226).

Much to psychology's chagrin, Rose and others (Baritz, 1974; Danziger, 1990; Herman, 1995), document psychological applications to placate discontent, to foment conformity, and to support the status quo. We wish we could speak in the past tense, but collusion with systems of regulation persist. Critical psychologists try to operate in the name of resistance and emancipation, not conformity. However, we are still trying to learn the best ways to do that and we are still overshadowed by many practices rooted in the status quo.

Values, assumptions, and practices

In this section we introduce a framework for the evaluation of psychological approaches and for the construction of alternative practice. The framework, consisting of values, assumptions, and practices, is briefly depicted in Table 2.1. The framework lists the values required for the promotion of personal, relational, and collective well-being. Next to these values we pose questions for the evaluation of diverse approaches. We also mention a series of assumptions that distinguish psychological orientations, from research and knowledge to ethics. The third part of the framework addresses practices regarding problem definition, the role of agents and type of intervention.

Values

Values are principles that guide behaviour (Prilleltensky, 1997). They serve as reminders of what we regard important in personal, relational, and collective

Table 2.1 Framework for assessing psychological approaches

Domain	Questions
Values for	
Personal well-being	
Caring and protection of health	Does it promote the expression of care, empathy, and concern for the physical and emotional well-being of other human beings?
Self-determination	Does it promote the ability of individuals to pursue their chosen goals without excessive frustration and in consideration of other people's needs?
Relational well-being	
Human diversity	Does it promote respect and appreciation for diverse social identities?
Collaboration and democratic participation	Does it promote the peaceful, respectful, and equitable process whereby citizens have meaningful input into decisions affecting their lives?
Collective well-being	
Distributive justice	Does it promote the fair and equitable allocation of bargaining powers, resources, and obligations in society?
Support for community	Does it support vital collective structures that promote the well-being of the entire community?
Assumptions about	
Power in relationships	Who has more power in relationships? Are there attempts to share power?
Professional ethics	Does ethical framework employed invite input from consumers? Are service recipients part of ethical decision-making processes?
Research and knowledge	To what end is knowledge used? Is knowledge subordinate to morality or independent from it? What philosophy of science guides research?
The good life	What conceptions of the good life are promoted? Are these based on self-interest or cooperation?
The good society	What conceptions of the good society are promoted? Are these based on the pursuit of equality or personal gain at the expense of others?
Practices regarding	
Problem definition	What factors are included and excluded from problem definition? Are psychological as well as sociological and economic factors taken into account?
Role of client	Is client active or passive? To what extent does client participate in decisions affecting his or her well-being?
Role of helper	Is helper a true collaborator or a removed expert imparting advice?
Type of intervention	Does intervention focus exclusively on intra-psychic factors, or does it include systems affecting clients?
Time of intervention	Is intervention reactive or proactive? Does psychologist wait until victims of unhealthy environments seek help or does he/she try to prevent problems?
Focus of intervention	Does intervention focus only on reducing deficits or also on enhancing competencies?

domains. In order to attain holistic well-being, we need to attend to these three dimensions at the same time. Each individual finds him or herself on the receiving and giving ends of values. If values are seriously considered, they get translated into actions. These actions affect both the performer and the recipient of the behaviour. The performer may be a single individual or a group. At times, it will be difficult to identify the precise originator of a cultural practice or belief, but ultimately, it is *people* who construct, co-construct and reconstruct values in society (Crossley, 2000). The recipient of values is the person affected by the expression of values. When parents enact caring and compassion through nurturing, their children are the immediate recipients of the values. When a worker invites colleagues to be part of an interesting and rewarding project, he or she is enacting values of sharing, collaboration, and participation.

By definition, well-being is a holistic concept consisting of personal, relational, and collective domains. Each domain reflects distinct needs. Needs, in turn, are met by value-driven actions; actions aimed at the self, others, and the collective. Table 2.1 formulates questions associated with each value. These questions facilitate the evaluation of different psychological approaches.

The promotion of only one set of values is inadequate and insufficient to meet the vast range of needs required for well-being. In our recent book *Promoting Family Wellness and Preventing Child Maltreatment* (Prilleltensky, Nelson, and Peirson, 2001), we show how psychological and material resources, social programmes and government policies must attend to personal, relational, and collective needs. Our study found that liberal philosophies of personal responsibility focus primarily on the individual domain and lead to victim-blaming. On the other hand, countries with collectivist orientations support citizens in need with adequate resources. Our review shows that we have to provide resources, programmes, and policies that attend not only to the needs of the individual child, but to the needs of the family and the community as a whole. This could never be achieved without promoting social justice at the same time as individual well-being. To thrive, young people require more than caring and compassion, they require high-quality educational and recreational facilities and they require parents with decent jobs.

Assumptions

Values intersect with assumptions to produce modes of practice. We may be more or less conscious and articulate about our assumptions, but they influence our actions nevertheless. Power is exercized through assumptions, and, like values, assumptions can result in harmful or health-enhancing outcomes. Will our power as professionals threaten the voice of consumers? Will our position of expertise reshape the experience of clients in terms that are foreign to them?

Our questioning of assumptions is in line with Rose's call for critical reflection. According to him, it is 'a matter of introducing a critical attitude towards those things that are given to our present experience as if they were timeless, natural, unquestionable: to stand against the maxims of one's time, against the spirit of one's age, against the current or received wisdom' (Rose, 1999:20). This stance contests the merit of prevalent ethical and epistemological paradigms alike. Assumptions about research and knowledge have a great impact on our practice as theorists, clinicians, researchers and teachers. Do we subscribe to positivist models that study behaviour out of context, or do we try to understand psychological problems in their natural surroundings?

The epistemological orientation we espouse will have repercussions for the lives of the people we work with. If we explain psychological suffering exclusively in intra-psychic terms we obviate experiences of victimization and social alienation. Knowledge gives us the power to redefine the experiences of the subjects of psychological interventions. Whose knowledge do we regard as more valid, ours as experts or theirs as (in)experts? Foucault reminded us that 'knowledge and power are integrated with one another, and there is no point in dreaming of a time when knowledge will cease to depend on power . . . It is not possible for power to be exercised without knowledge, it is impossible for knowledge not to engender power' (Foucault, 1980:52). Our power as psychologists, then, generates different kinds of knowledge that are not necessarily reflective of truth, but of our power to define truth. To the extent that our version of truth may be coloured by our social location of privilege, its emancipatory effects are uncertain.

Presuppositions about the 'good society' and the 'good life' also inform practice. We use these terms in their philosophical sense of entities that are worth pursuing and justifying. In essence, these two constructs embody the social and political philosophy of citizens. A good life is a life of meaning, fulfilment and satisfaction. Similarly, a good society is one where personal lives can thrive. People usually have criteria against which they assess their lives. Each person has a preconceived notion of what is meaningful and worthy in life (Crossley, 2000). Autonomy may be celebrated by some, interdependence by others. Government intervention may be advocated by left-wingers, privatization by right-wingers. Our social location will influence what we think is 'right' and 'appropriate' for our clients.

Practices

Values and assumptions culminate in practice, practices that can have empowering or disempowering effects. Each time psychologists define problems, assign roles to themselves and their clients, and determine an intervention, they are enacting values and assumptions with multiple consequences. Problem definition is not just a professional act but a political one as well. When psychologists deflect human problems to the mental domain, the social domain remains unchallenged.

If the role assumed by the psychologist is one of a partner in solidarity, one in which there is respectful listening and attention to internal and external sources of oppression, it is more likely that the outcomes will be empowering. This is not so when the psychologist defines, in expert fashion, the ills of others, in disregard for the dissenting voice of the client, which is interpreted away as resistance.

Time, type, and focus of intervention also have potentially liberating or limiting effects. Comprehensive interventions have a better chance of positive outcomes than, for example, individual treatment alone (Prilleltensky, Nelson, and Peirson, 2001). Reactive interventions, by definition, do not come into play until people have experienced a great deal of suffering. Why wait when we can identify and prevent some of the risk factors leading to suffering and oppression?

The oppressive and emancipatory potential of values, assumptions, and practices

Values, assumptions and practices can be construed and enacted in emancipatory or oppressive ways. Table 2.2 denotes conditions under which they can promote liberation or collude with repressive forces.

Personal values like self-determination and autonomy, which are only a part of well-being, can become burdensome when they are the main values of a society. When happiness is ascribed to personal effort, unhappiness becomes a reflection of personal failure. In cases of misfortune, the conflation of self-determination with personal responsibility produces self-blame. Autonomy and assertion, however, can be used to empower people as well. When we invoke self-determination to instill hope, the belief in personal power can be empowering (Snyder *et al.*, 2000). But just as there can be reverence for personal values, so there can be a veneration for collective values. When the good of the collective is imposed as primary, as in the case of some communal societies such as the Russian kolkhoz (collective farm) and in Cuban society, calls for solidarity are used to renounce personal needs. Any set of values is subject to the risk of distortion and misappropriation for tyrannical ends. In and of themselves, values do not necessarily advance oppression or liberation; their effects depend on the context and the purpose for which they are invoked. According to Sen (2001:10),

> The same values and cultural norms can be extremely successful at one phase of development, but less so at another. What we have to look at is not the general excellence of one set of values over all others, but the specific fit of particular values

Table 2.2 Oppressive and emancipatory potential of values, assumptions, and practices in psychology

	Oppressive	Emancipatory
Values for		
Personal well-being	When belief in individualism leads to self-blame	When belief in self-determination leads to personal empowerment
Relational well-being	When participatory processes obstruct social action and mask inequality	When participatory processes afford voice and choice
Collective well-being	When the good of the collective comes at the expense of individual needs	When bargaining powers, resources and obligations in society are shared equitably
Assumptions about		
Good life	When success and failure are ascribed to personal merit alone	When meaning is ascribed to interdependence
Power in relationships	When power differentials are ignored or reproduced	When power differentials are acknowledged and dealt with
Practices regarding		
Problem definition	When pathologize	When deblame
Role of client	When promote passivity	When promote empowerment
Role of psychologist	When arrogate power	When share power
Type of intervention	When intra-psychic interventions ignore social conditions	When oppressive social conditions are addressed

with the nature of the problems that are faced in a given – but parametrically variable – situation. The contingent nature of the contribution that values make is important to seize.

The outcomes of practices can be rarely dichotomized into oppressive or emancipatory. However, certain discourses and procedures are more likely to lead to one outcome or another. When psychologists ignore social and political antecedents of problems, and when they arrogate power, they are more likely to abide by the reigning and oppressive status quo. Empowering practices, on the other hand, strive to raise consciousness about the societal origins of problems and seek to share power. Social ideals of equality cannot be pursued in relations that promote inequality. The way we do things is not just a means to an end, but an end in itself. Hence, we do not accept domination in therapeutic relationships, however minimal, strategic or momentary.

Implementation challenges

In the first two chapters of the book we have outlined our approach to critical psychology. Although we have presented views from various authors and orientations within critical psychology, we readily acknowledge that our philosophy may not represent all the varieties of critical psychology. Ours is an applied orientation that seeks to promote personal and social change to attain health and welfare. We resonate with Reicher's (1997) challenge for critical psychologists (94): 'If we are to be successful in being taken seriously, we must ask how critical psychology can supply not only a set of ideas but also a set of practices'.

We also readily acknowledge the danger of jumping to interventions before we are clear about our own limitations. The concepts outlined in this part of the book reflect our intellectual and political commitments. As such, they are circumscribed to our heritage, knowledge and identity. Our challenge is to promote action and to remain open to challenge at the same time.

We dedicate the next two parts of the book to training and applications. We use the framework of values, assumptions and practices for doing psychology critically in diverse mainstream settings.

Part II

Training

I have taught for the past 21 years in a small university in southwestern Ontario. The undergraduate student body, like the faculty, is predominantly white, middle class, and conservative. Moreover, the vast majority of undergraduate students in psychology are women. We have an MA Programme in Community Psychology (the only one in English Canada), which attracts students with a community and social change orientation, including students from diverse backgrounds.

At the undergraduate level, I teach primarily in the clinical and community areas of psychology. While there is typically a handful of students who resist the critical perspectives that I bring in to these courses, many of the students who self-select into these courses are excited to learn about critical perspectives. I find that many of the women students, and some of the men students, are quite interested in exploring feminism and gender issues, and I am aware that, as a male professor, I have an easier time introducing these issues than my female colleagues. I also find that bringing in speakers from disadvantaged backgrounds, going on field trips, and the mandatory field placement component to these courses keeps students in touch with issues of oppression on a very personal and emotional level. Many students report that these experiences are real 'eye-openers'.

As an undergraduate and graduate student in psychology, the research courses that I was required to take consisted primarily of statistics. I had an undergraduate course in social research methods and a graduate course in programme evaluation (the first time such a course was offered), but there was very little exposure to how research could be used to promote social change, to issues related to ethics and questions of power, qualitative methods, the epistemology underlying research approaches, or participatory research approaches.

As I began doing community research as a young, untenured academic, I quickly found that there was a lot more to research than I'd anticipated. I learned that I needed to develop collaborative relationships with people in community settings and to ask questions that were meaningful and useful to them, not just research out of theoretical curiosity. For example, in the research on mental health and housing needs, I remember sitting in the regional health department and talking with a group of public health nurses about the research. One of them asked me if this was going to be another one of those studies that was written up as a report only to sit on a shelf and gather dust, or if the study could actually make a difference in people's lives. Through this experience and others, I began to think a lot more about the action component of the research. In the end, we held a public forum to report the results of the research, and we invited the media and politicians who were running for office in the provincial election to attend. At the conclusion of the meeting, those in attendance decided to form a coalition to advocate for more desirable housing. The research participants became active partners for social change. I had discovered action research.

Also, in this study, one of the research assistants found that none of the people with mental health problems who lived in one custodial setting wanted to participate in the research. We learned that these people had previously been coerced into a study in which a researcher took them to a restaurant for a meal to observe and record their social behaviour and table etiquette, all without their informed consent. When one of the support workers for these individuals heard that they would not participate, this person offered to 'volunteer' people for the study, indicating who could be persuaded to take part in the study. I had to tell this person that we followed an ethical protocol of informed consent for research participation. I learned about the abuse of participants by researchers and professionals who are in positions of power.

During the time of this study, I met John Lord, a community researcher with a background in qualitative methods. I had no idea what qualitative methods were and was, in fact, sceptical that this was real research. After working with John on a couple of projects, I learned about the rich tradition of qualitative methods in other social science disciplines, the many different types of qualitative research, the rigour that is involved in qualitative data collection and analysis, and the valuable data that are gained from these methods.

Years later, John Lord, Joanna Ochocka, and I began working with three community mental health organizations on a research project that we came to call *Shifting the Paradigm in Community Mental Health*. We were interested in studying the change processes that were taking place within three community mental health organizations in our community. We worked with the executive directors of these three organizations to frame the questions and the initial methodology. We decided to have a Steering Committee, composed of representatives from each of the settings, to guide the research. This committee met monthly throughout the two years of the research and included significant representation of the people who used the services and supports of these organizations. These people asked tough questions and challenged us, particularly in the beginning. 'Why does the university hold the money for the study?' 'Is there money in the budget to employ psychiatric survivors or is it all going to well-paid professionals?' Two of the representatives of a self-help organization told us that an interview guide that we had constructed would not work in their context. For each of these challenges, we listened and worked together to find solutions that were mutually acceptable. As the study progressed, individuals got to know one another better and positive relationships developed. The challenges that we experienced were tests to see if we could be trusted. Would we try to maintain power and control or would we work in genuine partnership with others, sharing power and control? In the end, people with a history of mental health problems worked with us as co-researchers, co-presenters, and co-writers. Never in my wildest dreams would I have imagined that all this would occur. I had discovered participatory research, and I liked it!

When I was a graduate student in Clinical Psychology, I was required to take four terms' of work placement in the programme's Psychological Services Centre located on the campus of the University of Manitoba. Most of the 'clients' that I saw were people who were looking for support, kindness, and compassion. Once a client brought me a drawing of a spoon that she had done. When I showed it to my supervisor, this person laughed and said something to the effect that the drawing summed up the woman's problem quite well – an oral-dependent personality. While I didn't have the language or consciousness at that time to name that psychoanalytic interpretation as sexist stereotyping, my gut feeling was that it was quite a sickening thing to say. As someone who does sketching and likes art, I thought she was sharing something with me, a gift of hers, something special.

Experiences like this one along with exposure to a course in Community Psychology led some of us graduate students to push the clinical faculty for more opportunities for both academic and field training in community alternatives. I vividly remember in a meeting in which we presented our wishes to the faculty that one faculty member suggested that students were trying to 'finesse their way out of doing clinical work'. A committee of faculty and students followed up to generate recommendations for change. One faculty member, a community psychologist, was supportive of change but the other faculty member was quite unsupportive, stating that community psychology was a 'fad'. At that time, only token-level changes occurred in the programme. I completed the required four terms of clinical placement, along with a lot of community work for which I never received any formal credit. I worked with the Residents' Advisory Groups to the city council; I worked in a counter-culture crisis intervention and community health clinic; I worked for the provincial government in developing community mental health services in rural communities in southern Manitoba; and I worked in a halfway house for men who had spent time in the provincial prison. These were all 'extras' that I did on my own. A couple of years later, the programme did create a community stream, which addressed many of the needs that my peers and I had expressed earlier. I like to think that we sowed the seeds for the later change that occurred.

As a faculty member in the Community Psychology MA programme, I was co-ordinator of the programme's full-year placement course with my friend and colleague Steve Chris for ten years. The course consists both of a field placement and of weekly meetings to discuss those experiences and to build applied skills. One group exercise that Steve and I always found to be very useful was to ask the students early in the course the types of skills that they would like to learn. We would use the results of this exercise as the foundation for the placement groups. I also learned and re-learned on this course that skills in interpersonal relations, group facilitation, understanding systems and their politics are fundamental to critical practice.

Geoff Nelson

Introduction

Training opportunities for critical psychologists are currently very limited. At present, there are only a handful of critical psychology courses worldwide, including those in Australia (University of Western Sydney), Great Britain (Manchester Metropolitan University), Germany (Berlin University), and South Africa (University of Natal) (Ussher and Walkerdine, 2001). Few undergraduate psychology students in North America have exposure to critical psychology perspectives. Moreover, critical psychology is mostly taught as an academic discipline and the emerging books (for example, Fox and Prilleltensky, 1997; Sloan, 2000) and journals (*Annual Review of Critical Psychology, International Journal of Critical Psychology*) have an academic emphasis. Currently, materials and resources for training field practitioners are scarce.

This section of the book is written for both students and teachers. We focus on training for both undergraduate, graduate, and postgraduate students in psychology. In North America graduate students are those who have finished a Bachelor's degree and go on to a Master's or Doctoral degree. In countries such as England and Australia, they are called postgraduate students. In both cases, these are students who have finished a first degree in psychology. In this book we will use these terms interchangeably. In this section we tend to concentrate more on graduate or postgraduate education, as graduate courses in psychology have more explicit goals of training teachers, researchers, and practitioners. However, we do not neglect undergraduate education, as it reaches a large number of students who pursue a number of different work and career options (including work in human services and education), as well as providing a foundation for graduate education for a smaller, more select group of students. Moreover, we believe that undergraduate education in critical psychology provides a basic training in citizenship that involves an understanding and critical analysis of social issues and suggests possibilities for citizen participation and social action.

In this part of the book we devote three chapters to the following areas: (a) teaching, (b) research, and (c) practice in applied settings. Throughout these three chapters we emphasize that training in critical psychology is not just about theory, research, and epistemology. Rather, critical psychology focuses on issues of values and power at different ecological levels of analysis. We also want to emphasize that what follows is a 'work in progress'. Since critical psychology emphasizes a reflexive approach, we need to constantly critique and re-examine our values, ideas, and practices (Rappaport and Stewart, 1997).

In this part of the book, we examine and reflect on the context of training in critical psychology. Throughout the world, universities, which are hierarchically organized institutions with power imbalances at many different levels, are the primary vehicle for higher education. Those of us who espouse a worldview that is critical of mainstream society and psychology face persistent contradictions and challenges working in positions of privilege inside these 'ivory towers'. How can we train students in critical pedagogy when universities are bound to a system of grading that reflects a belief in meritocracy? How can we train students in emancipatory research in community settings when our colleagues in psychology departments value laboratory experimentation? And how can we train students in critical practice when universities value research and teaching over community service? We assume that everyone has critical impulses, but that such impulses often get squashed by prevailing power structures and social processes.

While there are formidable constraints and challenges to training in critical psychology in universities, we believe that there are also opportunities. Universities strongly embody western values of individualism and freedom. Once one passes the hoops of tenure, university professors have the 'academic freedom' to pursue a wide range of different ideas and topics in their scholarship and practice. In fact, the level of autonomy that university professors have is almost unparalleled in other work settings in different societies. At the same time, individualism has its limitations. In our experience, it is very difficult for an individual faculty to 'go it alone' in pursuing a critical psychology approach to training. Throughout Part II, we emphasize the need for developing contexts that are supportive of, and that provide, a culture of training in critical psychology. Programmes of study and interest groups are needed to provide students with a coherent experience in critical approaches, as well as to provide mutual support for students and faculty alike.

In all cases of training we highlight the need for developing partnerships, with students, research participants, clients, and community members. In our view, partnership is the main vehicle for reaching solidarity with those who are disadvantaged. While for the sake of clarity of presentation we have divided this section on training into three chapters, we want to emphasize that training in teaching, research, and practice are highly interrelated. Within a coherent programme context, the core concepts and values presented in Part I provide the foundation for, and bridge, the separate areas of teaching, research, and practice. To reinforce this coherence in our presentation, each chapter follows a similar format. Each chapter is organized around three main questions: (a) What is it (that is, critical psychology teaching, research, applied practice)? (b) How is it done? And (c) how can it be taught?

3

The Making of a Subversive Teacher

In a recent book entitled *The Knowledge Factory: Dismantling the Corporate University and Creating True Higher Learning*, Stanley Aronowitz (2000) argues that with the increased concentration of wealth and power in the hands of a privileged elite, universities and other institutions of 'higher learning' have become the handmaidens of corporate interests. Cutbacks to public funding for education have driven universities into so-called 'partnerships' with corporations, which have funded capital projects and schools of business and populated boards of governors with business moguls. Of course, the danger of this is that universities become beholden to and reflect these corporate interests in the culture of university education (Eglin, 1996).

Aronowitz (2000) distinguishes between education, training, and learning. Education, he argues, has become synonymous with the process of adopting the values, ideas, and belief systems of the prevailing social order, while training focuses on the skills required for fitting into 'useful careers' that meet the needs of the market place. For Aronowitz, true higher learning is '...the process by which a student is motivated to participate in, even challenge, established intellectual authority' (143). Similarly, in their book, *Educating for Change*, Arnold *et al.*, (1991) claim that 'the issue of power is central...education must empower all people to act for change...Education must be based on a democratic practice: by which we mean creating the conditions for full and equal participation in discussion, debate, and decision-making.' They further note that their book explores 'the political dimension of learning, and the learning dimension of politics' (Arnold *et al.*, 1991:1).

In the face of forces which are impinging upon universities and education, how does a critical psychologist 'teach to transgress' (hooks, 1994), to promote the type of higher learning of which Arnold et al. (1991) and Aronowitz (2000) are speaking? There are many barriers to teaching from a radical perspective, not the least of which is that the ruling apparatus keeps unequal power relations invisible in the daily work of universities (Smith, 1990). As Bannerji *et al.* (1991:7–9) stated:

> The way relations of power and knowledge are organized in and through the university make it possible to live these relations without reflecting on them...This 'not seeing' participates in the ruling practices which regulate the social relations in

which we live. Historically, universities have been, and continue to be, central to the production of such practices.

While university professors face many challenges that result from larger outside forces and the inertia of tradition, we also continue to enjoy some latitude in both what we teach and the way we teach it. In this chapter, we begin with a description of teaching and education that reflects the values and concepts of the critical psychology approach that we set forth in Part I. When we speak of teaching and education, we speak primarily about university-level teaching with graduate and undergraduate students. However, we will also discuss, to some extent, community education, as we believe that teaching in critical psychology should break down the walls that separate the university from the community. Next, we consider how this type of teaching is put into practice. We end this chapter with a section on 'training for teaching,' which is aimed at postgraduate level students and university professors.

What is critical psychology teaching/education?

The purpose and focus of teaching and education in critical psychology is fundamentally different from mainstream approaches to education. Teaching in critical psychology is concerned with transformation and change (O'Sullivan, 1999), rather than with educational 'authorities' (that is, teachers) imparting 'scientific knowledge' and 'truth' to passive students. Before discussing the key qualities of critical psychology teaching and education, we note three traditions that have informed this approach: (a) critical pedagogy, (b) feminist pedagogy, and (c) anti-racist education.

The foundations of critical psychology teaching/education

Critical pedagogy

Critical pedagogy has its roots in the work of the Brazilian educator, Paulo Freire, in his work with disadvantaged citizens in Latin America. In a very influential and widely cited book, *Pedagogy of the Oppressed*, and in subsequent publications, Freire (1970, 1975, 1994, 1999) linked educational processes and concepts with the political issues of oppression and liberation. Freire critiqued what he called the traditional 'banking' concept of education, in which students store up the facts that teachers deposit through a one-way transactional process. In this approach, the teacher is the authority and the active agent, while the student is the passive recipient of information. Alternatively, Freire introduced the concepts of conscientization and praxis. Conscientization is the process whereby students attain an insightful awareness of the psychological and socio-political circumstances oppressing them, while praxis refers to critical 'reflection and action upon the world to transform it' (1970:33). Tobbell (2000) recently captured the essence of Freire's contribution as follows (204):

Freire's work champions a philosophy of education which argues for 'critical and liberating dialogue' between educator and educand and so acts to encourage responsibility and autonomy in both parties and results in an appreciation of the dialectical nature of knowledge and thought. Freire's work is inspirational because although it focuses on the oppression and subjugation of human beings it brings with it the imperative of possibility to change systems and enables people to enable their own learning. Here is the crux of Freire's philosophy: he argues that education is not about knowledge per se but is about ideas, it is about engaging in dialogue to generate thought, explanations and understanding. He rejects the status of the 'expert' and instead argues for an exchange of ideas in which both parties benefit and develop. Education is expressed as a mutuality.

Within western countries, theorists of critical pedagogy have extended Freire's work into schools of education (Giroux and McLaren, 1986; McLaren, 1995; O'Sullivan, 1999). However, little of the work in critical pedagogy has been linked to psychology (see O'Sullivan, 1990 for an exception), and there has been little penetration of these ideas and practices into the teaching that goes on in most psychology departments.

Feminist pedagogy

A second tradition for critical psychology education and teaching is that of feminist pedagogy (hooks, 1994; Luke and Gore, 1992; Maher and Tetreault, 1994). Feminist pedagogy has arisen in women's studies courses out of the need to provide an alternative to the dominant androcentric, sexist educational system. Historically, university professors have marginalized women in both the content of courses and in course processes. Women students often feel silenced and not taken seriously in university courses (Rich, 1980); they are subject to sexist jokes and comments and sexual harassment (Bond, 1995); and women are at risk of date rape, sexual assault, and violence on university campuses (Koss, 1993).

In their review of feminist pedagogy in psychology, Forrest and Rosenberg (1997) identified several themes of this approach. Gaining a voice in the classroom and university is an important part of feminist pedagogy (Aisenberg and Harrington, 1988; Maher and Tetreault, 1994). Women are encouraged to speak out about their experiences and perspectives. Feminist pedagogies question educational dichotomies, such as mind/body, objectivity/subjectivity, and reason/emotion, which are typically used to exclude the body, subjectivity, feelings, and experiences from classroom discussion. In feminist pedagogy, women are encouraged to respond as whole persons, drawing upon their personal experiences and emotions, rather than in fragmented ways to their education. Feminist pedagogy also draws attention to power and authority in the classroom and strives to promote power-sharing (Kenway and Modra, 1992).

Relationships and community are also of central importance in feminist pedagogy and women's ways of knowing (Belenky et al., 1986). Thus, highly participatory processes are encouraged in feminist pedagogy. Attention to, and valuing of, diversity is another central component of feminist pedagogy (Bond et al., 2000). Recognizing that women are different by virtue of class, race, ethnicity, sexual orientation, religion, and a host of other characteristics draws attention to women's unique and diverse experiences. Finally, social action and change are often a key part of feminist pedagogy.

Anti-racist education

Multicultural, anti-racist, and diversity education is the third tradition underlying critical psychology education and teaching (Huygens, 2001; Lynch, 1992; Mukherjee, 1992; Ng, Staton, and Scane, 1995; Rossiter, 1995; Sleeter, 1991). Mukherjee (1992) and Watts (1992) have made a distinction between multicultural and anti-racist approaches to diversity. The multicultural approach focuses primarily on culture and its goal is to educate people about minority groups, to celebrate cultural differences and strengths, and to develop multicultural organizations and policies that reflect and support diversity. In contrast, anti-racist education focuses less on culture and more on inequity and oppression. The goal of anti-racist education is the empowerment of disenfranchised groups and overcoming systemic barriers to participation and access to valued resources. Whereas multicultural education is more liberal-reformist, anti-racist education with a socio-political emphasis is more transformative. As Mukherjee (1992:145) stated:

> Quite simply, the purpose of anti-racist change is to move our educational institutions from 'exclusive clubs' to 'inclusive organizations' in which: (a) there will be equity of results in academic achievement, curriculum, assessment and placement, staffing and community/school relations for all races and cultures; (b) there will be shifts in individual behaviours and attitudes; and (c) there will be willingness and ability on the part of everyone to recognize and challenge racism wherever it arises. In short, anti-racist education is not about equality of opportunity, sensitivity and dealing with individual acts of racism alone. More fundamentally, it is about voice, representation and participation in all aspects of the educational system for people who have been traditionally excluded from the curriculum and the institution; it is about challenging those dominant ideas, beliefs and assumptions that support such exclusion; and it's about actively confronting those individual behaviours and attitudes which perpetuate those dominant ideas, beliefs and assumptions.

The qualities of critical psychology teaching/education

While critical pedagogy, feminist pedagogy, and anti-racist education may have different roots, today they are quite interwoven. In most contemporary writings, there is considerable overlap of issues of class, gender, race, and sexual orientation in critical approaches to education (for example, hooks, 1994; Luke and Gore, 1992; McLaren, 1995; O'Sullivan, 1999; Rossiter, 1993, 1995). There are clashes and differences among these perspectives (Ellsworth, 1989; Giroux, 1988), but they also share a common focus on analyzing oppression and on using participatory approaches to create social change. In Table 3.1, we outline the qualities of critical psychology teaching/education according to the framework of values, assumptions, and practice that we described in Part I. For each dimension

Table 3.1 Qualities of teaching/education from a critical psychology perspective

Critical psychology tenets	Qualities of the content and process
Values	*Content:* Explore with students the balance among values for personal, collective, and relational well-being in different social contexts, and what changes in value priorities need to take place in order for vulnerable people to advance their interests. Subject prevalent social values to deconstructive analysis to determine whose interests they represent.
	Process: Foster values of personal growth, sense of community, and relational principles by identifying these as explicit objectives of the learning process and by developing collectively the means of achieving a facilitative learning environment. Identify contradictions between students' and instructors' stated values and behaviours and create safe space to discuss them. Afford students opportunity to respectfully challenge their own personal values, dominant social values, and the values of critical psychology.
Assumptions	*Content:* Analyze historical and socially-constructed nature of psychological concepts and discuss role of social power in according legitimacy to certain theories and not to others. Study the ties between concepts of gender, race, class, and ability in psychology and the voices they represent. Examine whose definitions are given legitimacy and whose are ignored. Explore how concepts might differ if they were defined by people in other cultures and subcultures.
	Process: Foster process of conscientization through denunciation and annunciation. Consider how power differences in the classroom facilitate or inhibit personal expression and dissent. Afford students a voice in co-determining with instructor aspects of course content and process of learning. Maintain equilibrium between process and outcomes.
Practices	*Content:* Study psychological phenomena from an inter-disciplinary point of view. Understand concept of cultural hegemony and forces inculcating social messages of conformity and acquiescence. Examine economic, social, cultural, anthropological dimensions of constructs like depression, normal development, adjustment, and anti-social personality.
	Process: Develop with students solidarity and social action projects that put into practice the material covered in the classroom.

of the framework, we note the qualities of both the content and the process of teaching/education. We briefly summarize this table below.

Values

Critical psychology teaching explicitly focuses on the values underlying psychological theory, research, and practice. While psychology is typically presented as a value-free, scientific enterprise, the implicit values underlying mainstream psychology, and society as a whole, are exposed and deconstructed. Alternatively, personal, relational, and collective values which inform the work of critical psychologists are considered. Critical psychology education encourages students to interrogate the values implicit within psychology and to consider the values that *should* underlie theory, research, and practice.

In terms of process, students and faculty reflect on their values, the difficulties of putting values into practice, and the contradictions between espoused values and actions. In this regard, it is crucial to create a safe atmosphere for such reflection, in case students and faculty feel judged for their challenges, doubts, and imperfections. Values clarification is a central component of critical psychology teaching.

Assumptions

Teaching in critical psychology also examines assumptions about power and diversity in mainstream psychology and society. Questions about why some topics and research approaches are deemed more worthy than others is examined, as is the broader social and historical context of psychology. Boundaries of what is considered in and out of the discipline are also questioned. More than anything else, critical psychology encourages students to pose questions, challenge assumptions, and reframe problems and practices towards the values of personal, relational, and collective well-being.

Critically examining assumptions involves a process of conscientization for students and the faculty. As we relate in the next section, power differences within the classroom must be uncovered and reduced. Moreover, students need a voice in the educational process about what and how they will learn. At the same time, the educational process must be purposeful and directed toward the goal of promoting student growth and critical awareness.

Practices

In critical psychology education, students should be encouraged to expand the boundaries of their analysis of issues by examining inter-disciplinary perspectives that span multiple levels of analysis. For instance, the social, economic, cultural, and anthropological dimensions of psychological issues should be considered as an alternative to the typical person-blame, micro-centred focus of psychology. Also, action strategies to address the issue at multiple levels of analysis need to be identified and discussed. In terms of process, field placements and action research projects are ways of connecting students with the real world of action.

How is critical psychology teaching/education practised?

In Table 3.2, we outline three outcomes of education in critical psychology and related educational processes to promote these outcomes. These outcomes and processes are organized according to different ecological levels of analysis and their related values.

The individual student

The first ecological level addressed is that of the individual student. At this level, critical psychology teaching should inspire personal reflection and consciousness-raising and promote the values of personal well-being. Self-determination, values clarification, and identity development are important ingredients of this personal change process. In contrast, mainstream psychology teaching emphasizes individual achievement and, indirectly, acceptance of the societal status quo. Gramsci

Table 3.2 Processes and outcomes of teaching and education in critical psychology at different ecological levels of analysis

Ecological level (and related values)	Key outcomes of education in critical psychology	Key educational processes in critical psychology
Student (personal)	• Personal reflection and consciousness-raising (self-determination, values clarification, identity formation)	• Student-centred learning • Sharing decision-making regarding course content and marking • Students as classroom facilitators • Personal reflection exercises • Valuing experiential knowledge and emotional expression • Connecting the personal and the political • Teacher as resource person and role model
Student in the classroom and the academic unit (relational)	• Developing supportive inter-personal relationships (caring and compassion, cooperation, respect for diversity, collaboration and democratic participation)	• Setting ground rules • Highly participatory and collaborative group processes • Peer feedback and respectful challenging • Human relations skills training • Attending to diversity • Building community within the academic unit
Student in the community and society (collective)	• Thinking globally, while participating in the local community (distributive justice, support for community structures, environmental steward)	• Individual and group projects in the community • Field trips • Bringing community members into the classroom and the university • Participation in campus and community events • Students speaking out and advocacy • Field placement and practical experiences

(1971) invoked the concept of cultural hegemony to explain how the public is inculcated in the values and beliefs about the dominant social order. Boggs (1976) describes cultural hegemony as follows (39):

> By hegemony Gramsci meant the permeation through civil society... of an entire system of values, attitudes, beliefs, morality, etc. that is in one way or another supportive of the established order and the class interests that dominate it...To the extent that this prevailing consciousness is internalized by the broad masses, it becomes part of 'common sense'.

Teaching in critical psychology strives to challenge cultural hegemony through critiques of mainstream perspectives and an examination of alternative perspectives. An important concept for individual change is the Freireian concept of conscientization, which involves two components, critique and reconstruction. Critique involves an analysis and awareness of how cultural hegemony operates. It is about challenging what is taken for granted as 'common sense'. It is also about making translucent 'invisible' power relations. Students speak of these as 'eye-opening' experiences. Psychological processes such as obedience to authority (of the teacher and psychological research), conformity, self-fulfilling prophecy, and learned helplessness, can be used to explain how students, the public, and disadvantaged citizens come to accept the hegemonic view of the world as immutable and ideal. If there was a test about what constitutes the public good, most of us would fail miserably, including those of us with university degrees. Lack of numerical and verbal literacy is bad enough, but there is another type of ignorance that has similar or even greater negative consequences: Moral and political illiteracy. This is the type of ignorance that results from not knowing how to challenge dominant ideas about what our society should be like. We learn more and more about how to control nature but fall short of resolving basic human predicaments. This is not because social problems are insoluble, but because there are powerful groups interested in keeping things the way they are.

Why is it that we acquiesce to the dogmatic tune of big business and fail to come up with compelling alternatives? It is because we have internalized a system of values and beliefs supportive of the established social order and the classes that control it; an order that venerates consumerism and apathy. These values become part of our 'common sense'. This common sense is achieved by defining problems in such a way that their solutions do not threaten the status quo. The dominant ideology defines social problems in terms of personal deficits. Thus, poverty is explained by individual deficits such as low intelligence or laziness. In fact, not personal but systemic changes such as a modest increase in corporate taxation would eliminate many social ills.

An understanding of how political illiteracy develops in one's life is critical for denouncing dominant ideology and perspectives. Reconstruction, on the other hand, involves the creation of alternative vision, values, and perspectives and taking action to change social conditions.

Consciousness-raising can also be the focus of community education. For example, Watts, Griffith, and Abdul-Adil (1999) link Freire's focus on conscientization and socio-political development with African-American spirituality in a community educational programme for young African-American men. The focus of their Young Warriors programme is on helping young African-American men to develop a critical awareness of the disempowering social conditions facing them and to take action to change such conditions. Their research has shown that the young men move through a number of stages of personal and socio-political development, beginning with an acritical view of the world and working towards a liberation stage in which the young men are involved in social action and community development.

Consciousness-raising in the classroom can be promoted in many different ways. We believe that learning in critical psychology should be student-centred rather than teacher-centred. That is, there must be ways for students to have some say over what they want to learn and how they want to learn it. Student-centred approaches are easier to implement in small, advanced, undergraduate seminars and graduate classes than in large undergraduate courses. In smaller classes, instructors can co-construct the agenda and format of the class with the students. This is an excellent way for creating ownership for the learning process. The role of the teacher becomes one of a resource person, facilitator, and role model. The expertise of the teacher should not be invalidated in critical teaching, but the authority of students over their experiences should be emphasized (Rossiter, 1993).

One obstacle that we face is the grading system, which creates a power imbalance between the professor and the students. In our graduate programme of study in Community Psychology at Wilfrid Laurier University we have discussed the issue of grading. While most students and faculty believe that grading is inconsistent with the values of our programme, we have decided not to advocate for abolition of the grading system (only the placement course is marked on a satisfactory/unsatisfactory basis). Students are concerned that this would put them at a disadvantage in competition for scholarships and applications for study at Ph.D. level and for jobs. Instead, we have tried to work within the grading system by using peer feedback, individualized learning contracts, and opportunities for improving one's mark. We try not to let the grading system be an obstacle to our mission of critical teaching and learning.

The assignment of small issue papers and personal reflection exercises are used to promote self-reflection and consciousness-raising. Classroom discussions are not limited to intellectual and empirical issues and debates, but often involve self-exploration, expression of feelings and opinions, and sharing of experiences. In our graduate programme, students report that the first term is an immersion in a world view that is either personally transformative or reinforcing of one's personal identity as a critical thinker and social change agent. For some, this transformation is quite emotionally jarring. We strive to maintain a balance between challenging each others' assumptions, while respecting individual choices and experiences. Since critical psychology teaching operates from a value-base, we realize that there is a danger of slipping into a dogmatic approach in which students feel coerced to adopt a certain point of view. However, this runs counter to the values of respect and self-determination. We expect that each student's journey will be different and that certain values and issues will be more dear to them than others.

The student in the classroom and academic unit

The second ecological level that is addressed in critical psychology education is that of the student in the classroom and the academic unit. The key quality of this level of critical teaching is the development of relational well-being (that is, supportive relationships among students and professors). The classroom and the academic unit (for example, a women's studies course) constitute the student's immediate community. Such settings should provide a safe and supportive environment for challenging mainstream ideas and practices and the exploration of oneself and the possibility of alternative world views.

Traditionally, classroom education has been socially constructed on a hierarchy of power. The professor controls the class agenda through construction of the course outline, which includes the topics that will be covered, how they will be covered, and how students will be marked. A lecture format is typically used, emphasizing the professor's voice and authority, with considerably less emphasis on student participation. Moreover, the vast majority of professors in universities across the western world continue to be white, middle-class men, even though most psychology students are women (see Pyke, 1991 for data on Canadian universities). Forrest and Rosenberg (1997) argue that larger social inequalities are reproduced in university classrooms. The use of sexist and patriarchal language, the focus on 'rational' argument as a way of knowing and learning, and the absence of critical material related to class, gender, race, and sexual orientation are some of the ways that this reproduction is enacted (Luke and Gore, 1992).

Feminist pedagogy, on the other hand, has emphasized the importance of community, relationships, and solidarity within the classroom. bell hooks (1994) has re-conceptualized power, so that it is based on relationships and 'power with,' rather than individualism and 'power over.' Moreover, hooks (1994) argues that much of what happens in education is that students learn to be obedient and find school boring. What she strives for as a critical educator is to bring excitement, passion, and joy into the learning process. Feminists, in particular, have paid considerable attention to the importance of classroom dynamics in critical education (for example, Lewis, 1992; Maher and Tetreault, 1994). It is through supportive relationships that women process their experiences and develop their knowledge (Belenky *et al.*, 1986).

Since discussion, expression of feelings, sharing of experiences, personal growth, and consciousness-raising are such an important part of critical pedagogy, professors, lecturers and teachers need to become experienced in group facilitation. We have found that setting ground rules for classroom discussions is important for establishing a climate of safety in which peers can listen to and respectfully challenge one another and their teachers. A major barrier to this type of education is that many instructors have little or no training in helping skills and group facilitation. Teaching staff would do well to take workshops which focus on basic interpersonal attending (active listening) and influencing skills and facilitation of classroom discussion (Ivey, Ivey and Simek-Morgan, 1997).

While having a course with a critical or feminist perspective can be a refreshing alternative to mainstream courses, a single course can be overshadowed by the 'chilly climate' that many women, minority, and gay and lesbian students experience within universities (Pyke, 1997). Having an academic unit (a women's studies course) or other alternative setting (a public interest research group) in which like-minded faculty can come together can reduce feelings of isolation and build solidarity and capacity for learning and action. hooks (1994) refers to such settings as 'sites of resistance'.

In our graduate programme in Community Psychology, we strive to create a positive climate throughout all the courses, the thesis process, and the extra-curricular life of the programme. This involves a great deal of attention to interpersonal and social processes within the programme. It begins with students participating as equal partners on the student admissions committee, establishing a buddy system to ease the transition into the programme, including students and staff in programme meetings and programme decisions, holding social events, addressing a variety of issues over the years (for example, women's experiences in the programme, marking, promoting diversity, creating ways of staying connected with programme graduates), and evaluating different components of the pro-gramme on a routine basis. While there are always issues to address and areas to work on, we have found that students, staff, and faculty to be generally satisfied with programme processes and outcomes (Alcalde and Walsh-Bowers, 1996).

The student in the community and society

The third ecological level is the student in the community and societal context, which pertains to the values of collective well-being. A very important part of critical teaching is for students to learn that they are citizens in a global community, who are impacted by community, social, and world issues, and who, in turn, can have an impact on such issues through local action. The phrase 'think globally, act locally' captures this theme. To promote citizenship, students need to learn about social issues within the classroom as well as to connect with community resources and networks of people for social change. Bennett and Hallman (1987) have emphasized the centrality of field training for undergradu-ate and graduate psychology students.

Activism can be promoted through a variety of different experiences. First, to break down the barrier between the community and the university, we have found bringing in guest speakers for colloquia and class presentations, and taking the class on field trips, to be useful for connecting students with social issues and community activists. Second, class projects can also be used to promote citizenship and activism. Teams of faculty and students can plan teach-ins and conferences, write articles for local publications, and speak out in public settings about important social issues.

Third, field training is very important. At the undergraduate level, we have a field placement programme in the Psychology Department at Wilfrid Laurier University, in which students are placed in a variety of different health, education, social service, and social change settings. A field placement coordinator and graduate students work with the students to process their learning in these settings. Also, faculty frequently have students critically reflect on their experiences through journals and assigned papers, in which they are encouraged to make links between course concepts and experiences in the field. At the graduate level, students participate in a year-long placement course, which promotes skill-building and provides individually-tailored experiences in social and community change activities. Individual supervision, group support, and mentoring from people in the field placement settings are critical sources of support for this field-based learning. Once again, professors, lecturers and teachers need to have extensive experience in community settings and their own clinical practice to be able to effectively provide students with an adequate grounding in community change approaches.

How does one train critical psychology teachers?

While a major part of the role of academics is teaching, unfortunately very few academics have any type of formal preparation to become teachers. Doctoral students who aspire to become teachers or community educators need some type of formal preparation for this role. Just as there is course work and applied experience for research and applied practice, so too should there be preparation for teaching. Rather than throwing inexperienced teachers into classes with little assistance, we believe that the best way to prepare critical psychology teachers is via a mentoring process. This can be done through a formal course in teaching or through informal seminars organized around topics regarding teaching (for example, philosophical bases of critical pedagogy, preparing notes, lectures and presentation skills, facilitating classroom discussion, use of case studies, and so on). Reading material related to such issues and having discussions about that material is important.

However, the heart of training for teaching is through experience. We have found that an excellent way to get graduate students started in teaching is through co-teaching experiences. We have involved our graduate teaching assistants in facilitating undergraduate classes. It is useful to plan the class jointly, to share the teaching duties in the class, and to have time after the class to reflect on the process and provide feedback to the trainee. Doctoral students should also have the opportunity to teach a course on their own with a faculty mentor or supervisor for support. The mentoring process can be beneficial for both the mentor and the apprentice. During his first year of teaching at Laurier, Geoff served as Isaac's teaching mentor, which both found to be an enriching experience. A similar approach is that of a 'buddy system' of new teachers, in which peers have an opportunity to discuss their teaching experiences, provide support, and give constructive feedback.

There are other valuable training tools for teaching. One is to visit the classes of, and observe, teachers who have an excellent reputation with their students. Another valuable tool is the use of role-playing and videotaping. Video-taped role plays of simulated lectures or class discussions can be mortifying for those of us who shy away from seeing ourselves on camera. But this is how our students see us. Having the opportunity for self, peer, and mentor feedback on the video-taped role plays can be a powerful learning experience. One can then take the feedback and use it in further role-playing. Obtaining student feedback is also very important for improving one's teaching skill. There are a variety of mid-course assessments that can be done through questionnaires or group interviews with students. Some students may be reluctant to give honest feedback if they feel that they may jeopardize their marks by being critical. In this case, peer consultants or mentors can be used to conduct the interviews.

While the above strategies are vitally important for preparing new teachers for the transition to teaching, training for teaching should not be viewed as a one-time experience. Rather, opportunities for training and professional development as a teacher should be available to teachers on an ongoing basis.

Conclusion

Teaching in critical psychology has its roots in critical pedagogy, feminist pedagogy, and anti-racist education. These different strands share an emphasis on a holistic, participatory, and social change-oriented approach to education. Moreover, critical psychology teaching/education focuses on multiple levels of analysis, ranging from the individual to society. Consciousness-raising for individual students, supportive classrooms and academic sites of resistance, and community and social change activities are the desired outcomes of a critical psychology approach to teaching/education. A number of different processes for critical psychology education were identified as important for promoting these outcomes. As well, suggestions were made as to how to train critical psychology teachers.

4

The Making of a Participatory Action Researcher

The type of research that we advocate in this chapter is not focused on the creation of 'knowledge for knowledge's sake'. We believe that research that claims to be value-neutral and objective runs the risk of reinforcing the societal status quo (Prilleltensky, 1994). Rather, we are concerned with research that advances knowledge that helps to create social change for the benefit of marginalized people (Kirby and McKenna, 1989; Nelson, Ochocka *et al.*, 1998). People who are poor and disempowered are rarely the beneficiaries of research. That is to say, research is done 'on' disadvantaged people, not 'with them'. Research should benefit not just researchers, but also those who remain silent through the process of research priority-setting. In this chapter, we begin with a description of research that reflects the values and concepts of the critical psychology approach that we set forth in Part I. Next, we describe how to conduct such research. We end the chapter with a discussion of training strategies for this type of research.

What is critical psychology research?

The purpose and focus of critical psychology research is different from mainstream psychological research in that critical psychology research is value-driven, attuned to issues of power, and oriented towards social change (Goodley and Parker, 2000). Before discussing the key qualities of critical psychology research, we first describe three traditions on which critical psychology research is based: (a) participatory action research, (b) qualitative research, and (c) feminist research.

The foundations of critical psychology research

Participatory action research

Participatory action research integrates participatory research and action research (Brown and Tandon, 1983; Brydon-Miller, 1997; Montero, 2000; Nelson,

Ochocka *et al.*, 1998). Participatory research has its origins in research with oppressed peoples in Latin America (Montero, 2000; Yeich, 1996) and continues to be used there (Lykes, 1997, 2000). In participatory research, oppressed people drive the research process, while researchers act as facilitators (Stoecker, 1999). Participatory research also has an explicit focus on social change (Tolman and Brydon-Miller, 2000). According to Hall (1993:xiv), participatory research is 'a way for researchers and oppressed people to join in solidarity to take collective action, both short and long term, for radical social change'. Similarly, Kirby and McKenna (1989) assert that 'research from the margins' should reflect the experiences and concerns of oppressed people, attend to issues of power, and serve as a catalyst for social change.

In contrast, action research has its roots in North American social psychology and has tended to focus on group and organizational change (Lewin, 1946). One of the developers of action research, Kurt Lewin, was a social psychologist who strived to blend social science with humanitarian values and practical action. Lewin emigrated to the USA to escape from Nazi Germany prior to the Second World War and was concerned about democracy, prejudice, and group/organizational processes. Coining the phrase, 'there is nothing so practical as a good theory,' Lewin argued that action research could both generate new knowledge and solve social problems. Like participatory research, action research involves key stakeholders throughout the research process. However, unlike participatory research, action research has tended to ignore power issues and to be closely allied with those who hold power in organizations (Brown and Tandon, 1983).

More recently, these two traditions of participatory and action research have been merged (Nelson, Ochocka *et al.*, 1998). Nelson, Ochocka *et al.* (1998) have defined participatory action research as 'a research approach which consists of the maximum participation of stakeholders, those whose lives are affected by the problem under study, in the systematic collection and analysis of information for the purpose of taking action and making change' (888). Moreover, they argue that participatory action research is based on values that are central to critical psychology (for example, empowerment, social justice). In participatory action research, researchers strive to engage participants as 'co-researchers' and 'co-analysts' in the creation of psychological knowledge (Smith, 1994). Recent examples of participatory action research include studies which give voice to experiences and strive to humanize social environments for psychiatric survivors (Nelson, Lord and Ochocka 2001a; Thesen and Kuzel, 1999; Wadsworth and Epstein, 1998) and people with disabilities (Balcazar *et al.*, 1998; Hutchison and Pedlar, 1999; Krogh, 1998).

Qualitative research

A second important tradition for research in critical psychology is that of qualitative research. While qualitative research has a rich tradition in several of the social sciences, most notably sociology and anthropology (Denzin and Lincoln, 1994), qualitative methods have not been widely used in psychology (Kidder and Fine, 1997). Psychology has been dominated by quantitative methods based on an epistemology of logical positivism, according to which psychological phenomena are reduced to quantified variables that presumably represent constructs that reflect an external reality. Such methods are considered to be objective and value-neutral. Moreover, research is designed to test hypotheses derived from theories regarding the relationships between these variables. Manipulation of variables in experimentally controlled research is used to examine cause–effect relationships, while correlational research, which examines naturally occurring relationships between variables, is often concerned with prediction.

While some qualitative research can be based on a version of positivist epistemology, most qualitative research is rooted in alternative philosophies of science that have been variously labelled as social constructivist, critical, or contextualist (Guba and Lincoln, 1994; Kingry-Westergaard and Kelly, 1990). These alternative epistemologies take issue with many of the assumptions of logical positivism. Critics argue that no research is objective and value-neutral (Guba and Lincoln, 1994). Researchers occupy a privileged status and social location in academic institutions, and they have historically had a monopoly on research and what gets counted as knowledge (Stam, 2000). What is an acceptable topic to research and how the research questions get framed are heavily value-laden. In contrast to this 'researcher as expert' approach, qualitative research can open up the field of play so that the voices of marginalized people are heard and the interpretation of findings is negotiated between the researchers and disadvantaged citizens (Denzin, 1994; Guba and Lincoln, 1994; Rappaport, 1990; Stam, 2000).

A fundamental question in choosing the research focus and framing the questions is 'who benefits from this research?' (Rappaport, 1990). Whether or not reality is assumed to be something that is real and absolute or something that is socially constructed and relative, qualitative research in critical psychology focuses on the experiences of disadvantaged people in multiple social contexts. Also, the meaning of those experiences to people is of central importance rather than the relationships between different facets of their experiences. Finally, critical, qualitative research emphasizes the possibility of change and the creation of a preferred reality, not just a focus on current realities (Guba and Lincoln, 1994; Kincheloe and McLaren, 1994).

Feminist research

Feminist research is a third important tradition for critical psychology research. Like participatory action research, feminist research has an explicit moral and political agenda of acknowledging the oppression of women and striving to eliminate sexism (Wilkinson, 2000). While there are a variety of different types of feminist thought, all feminist approaches value women and strive for social change that benefits women (Wilkinson, 1997). Feminist research has focused on sexist practices that are demeaning to women and how women as individuals and as a collective can resist and overcome the many faces of sexism, including the denigration of women's abilities and skills in comparison to those of men, unequal marital and opposite-sex relationships, violence against women (including sexual harassment, rape, verbal and physical abuse), political and economic inequality, and the patriarchal focus on women's bodies (including an emphasis on thinness and 'female beauty'). Morever, feminist research seeks to expose the values and assumptions underlying sexist research and to offer an alternative standpoint (Harding, 1991).

While qualitative methods, such as open-ended interviews, case studies, and oral histories (Reinharz, 1992), have been used in much of feminist research to hear women's voices and understand women's experiences (Olesen, 1994), some feminist researchers have advocated for epistemological, theoretical, and methodological pluralism (Morawski, 1997; Reinharz, 1992; Riger, 1992; Wilkinson, 2000). Reinharz (1992) has pointed out the value of survey research and experimental research for feminist psychology. Wilkinson (2000) has suggested that empiricist methods, like experiential and discursive (both qualitative) methods, have benefits and limitations in feminist research on breast cancer. For Reinharz (1992) and Wilkinson (2000), issues of epistemology and methodology are secondary to the moral and political goals of feminist research, which are to expose and eradicate sexism. Similarly, Rappaport and Stewart (1997) state that 'at its best, critical work is genuinely open to new (for psychology) methods of inquiry, such as various forms of qualitative and discourse analysis, without discarding mainstream quantitative methods on principle, as if they are irrevocably and inherently too sullied by association with the status quo to ever yield information of interest to a true "progressive"' (307).

Feminist research shares much in common with participatory action research. Feminist research is, by definition, highly action-oriented. Its raison d'être is social change. Feminist research also often emphasizes equal relationships between the researcher and the women who participate in the research (Lather, 1988; Lykes, 1997, 2000). Oakley (1981) has argued that the idea of women interviewing other women is a contradiction between the tradition of positivist methodology and the feminist standpoint of openness, trust, caring, engagement, reciprocal relationships, and solidarity among women. Thus, feminist research strives to overcome the traditional power imbalances between researchers and participants.

The qualities of critical psychology research

In Table 4.1, we outline the qualities of critical psychology research according to the framework of values, assumptions, and practice that we described in Part I.

Values

First of all, the type of research that we are promoting is driven by a moral or social objective. That is to say, critical psychology research is value-driven. The goal of this research is to collaborate with oppressed people to facilitate the achievement of their social aims (for example, justice, economic security, respect for diversity). Critical psychology research strives to find ways to advance these values both in the substance of the research and in the way the research is done.

Table 4.1 Qualities of research from a critical psychology perspective

Critical psychology tenets	Qualities of the content and process
Values	*Content:* Study what social conditions are most conducive to a balance among values for personal, collective, and relational well-being. Ask citizens what they would change in their societies to advance neglected values and priorities. Frame research topics and questions in action-oriented terms of how they will advance the interests of the vulnerable groups under study.
	Process: Promote participants' self-determination and democratic participation in research project. Formulate research agenda with community members by engaging in participatory process, attending to diversity of stakeholders and differing levels of power and ability to communicate their needs and values.
Assumptions	*Content:* Study how power suffuses social relations that perpetuate oppression, what social change strategies work under what circumstances, and what are social conditions most conducive to personal and collective emancipation.
	Process: Negotiate with multiple research stakeholders ways to reduce power differences by creating representative steering committees. Ensure voice and interests of participants are represented in research. Create climate of collaboration and foster sense of collective ownership to ensure that there is follow-up of research recommendations.
Practices	*Content:* Reframe problems and evaluate social interventions that are designed to enhance the personal, relational, and collective well-being of vulnerable groups.
	Process: Use participatory action research techniques. Identify with research participants goals and objectives for social change that would benefit their community. Ensure there is follow-up on recommendations for systemic change after data collection.

The research process should be highly participatory and action-oriented. When vulnerable groups play a major role in the research enterprise, they become agents of change, not just 'research subjects' who play a passive role. Moreover, in critical psychology research, oppressed groups and researchers work together to use the research findings to promote social change.

Assumptions

A second characteristic of critical psychology research is that it is highly attuned to issues of power. From an analytical perspective, critical psychologists view the social issues that they study through a lens of power relations. Issues such as violence against women, child maltreatment, and others are viewed in terms of the concepts of power and control. At the same time, critical psychologists recognize the socially-constructed power imbalances in the relationships between themselves as researchers and the disadvantaged people who are the objects of study. For this reason, critical psychology researchers strive to reduce the power imbalances between themselves and disadvantaged people, working as partners in the research (Nelson, Ochocka, *et al.*, 1998; Rappaport, 1990; Yeich and Levine, 1992). Whereas much of mainstream psychological research is focused on the individual and micro-systems, critical psychology research is ecological, systemic, and contextual (Kingry-Westergaard and Kelly, 1990).

Practices

The content of critical psychology research focuses on the personal, interpersonal, and collective experiences of oppression and empowerment of disadvantaged people. Professionals have often defined the 'problems' of disadvantaged people in such a way as to 'blame the victims'. Through an emphasis on individualism, problems have been construed, labelled, and reified as the 'deficits' of individuals, rather than as problems of the social environments in which disadvantaged people live. As we indicated in the two sections above, critical psychology carefully examines the values and assumptions of such positions and strives to reframe 'problems' in terms of alternative values, assumptions, and theories. As Rappaport and Stewart (1997:307) stated: 'In critical psychology, as in any academic/intellectual project, the power to frame the issues, define the terms of the debate, and set the agenda for discourse is to win the game before it happens'.

Since the substantive focus and the research process go hand in hand in critical psychology research, the inclusion of the voices of disadvantaged people in research partnerships in problem definition is essential. When we are approached by or when we approach disadvantaged citizens regarding a potential research project, we always ask questions like: What do you want from such a project? How could such a project benefit you and your organization? What are your concerns about such a project? What benefits could result from such a project? From these discussions, we begin to collaboratively identify the research questions that we want to examine. In this way, the research is guided by the lived experiences and concerns of disadvantaged people, who develop ownership over the project from the very beginning.

Since the research process is ultimately about collaboration among the people involved in the research, we believe that the concept of partnerships is useful for understanding the research process. Elsewhere, we defined partnerships for solidarity with disadvantaged people as 'relationships between community psychologists, oppressed groups, and other stakeholders that strive to advance the values of caring, compassion, community, health, self-determination, participation, power-sharing, human diversity, and social justice for oppressed groups. These values drive both the processes and the outcomes of partnerships that focus on services and supports, coalitions and social action, and research and evaluation' (Nelson, Prilleltensky and MacGillivary, 2001). In other words, it is through partnerships that the values which underlie our approach to critical psychology research are put into practice.

How is critical psychology research conducted?

In the previous section, we described the key characteristics of research in critical psychology. In this section, we examine in more depth the content and processes of critical psychology research at multiple ecological levels of analysis (see Table 4.2).

Individual

Content

The focus of critical psychology research at the individual level is on the transition from oppression through empowerment to the well-being of disadvantaged

Table 4.2 Critical psychology research content and processes at different ecological levels of analysis

Ecological level (and related values)	Research content	Research processes
Individual (personal)	• Examine oppression, empowerment, and well-being at the individual level	• Honour the stories of disadvantaged individuals and value their experiential knowledge • Hire and train researchers from disadvantaged groups • Write about personal experiences in research articles and reports
Group (relational)	• Examine the nature and impact of egalitarian and non-egalitarian relationships of disadvantaged people • Focus on self-help/mutual aid groups and informal social supports as important relational context • Study the qualities and impact of people who bridge between disadvantaged people and the dominant society	• Use research steering committees to ensure participation of people from oppressed groups • Build supportive research teams • Clarify roles and responsibilities of research partners • Clarify vision, values, and working principles of the research partnership • Emphasize clear communication and avoid use of professional and research jargon • Develop authentic relationships with people from disadvantaged groups
Community and society (collective)	• Examine how community structures and social policies contribute to oppression and well-being • Study how civic organizations, alternative settings, and social movement organizations contribute to social change	• Locate a group or groups to use the research findings for education and advocacy • Engage in action with members of disadvantaged groups to promote collective empowerment and eradicate oppressive structures and processes

people. At the level of the individual, well-being can be defined as the development of self-determination and personal empowerment, the experience of community integration, and access to the valued resources of employment, income, education, and housing (Nelson, Lord, and Ochocka, 2001a, b). Even if the focus of the research is on the individual, critical psychology research examines individual phenomena in their group, organizational, and macro-social context. Case studies and qualitative methods (Lord and Hutchison, 1993; Nelson, Lord, and Ochocka, 2001a, b), as well as more traditional methods using correlational and experimental designs (Rogers *et al.*, 1997), can be used to examine individual well-being and empowerment.

Processes

Part of the respect that disadvantaged people want is acknowledgement of the validity of their experiences and knowledge. Often times, professionals utilize research or professional knowledge and dismiss the experience of the people they serve (Trainor, Pomeroy, and Pape, 1999). Researchers do not have a monopoly on the 'truth' or 'knowledge' and can learn a great deal from disadvantaged people. In critical psychology research, there is an emphasis on mutual learning and valuing the experiential knowledge of disadvantaged people (Nelson, Ochocka *et al.*, 1998). We believe that it is an honour for researchers to hear the stories of disadvantaged people.

Furthermore, we believe that critical psychology research can benefit from hiring and training disadvantaged people as researchers (Ochocka, Janzen, and Nelson, in press). Disadvantaged people bring a great deal of experience of the issue under study that is beneficial to the research. As well, we believe that it is a moral imperative to hire and train people from disadvantaged groups so that they can share in the resources of a project. Since critical psychology research is reflexive (Smith, 1994; Stam, 2000), we believe that researchers should reflect upon and write about their experiences in the research process. In this way, they can share what they have learned about the process of conducting participatory action research. Researchers are typically encouraged to be 'objective' and to write up their findings in a very sanitized and highly orthodox fashion, conforming to particular style formats of journals and professional associations. However, this type of write-up usually does not reflect what really happens in the research and all the learning that could be passed along to readers.

Group

Content

Critical psychology research that focuses on the group level of analysis can examine the empowering and/or disempowering qualities of relationships, groups, and organizations and outcomes that result from relationships and settings. For example, Maton and Salem (1995) have identified some of the following characteristics of empowering settings: a belief system that inspires growth and focuses on strengths, opportunities for member participation and contribution, social support, shared leadership, and organizational power to effect community change. Research on the relationships and informal support processes that the disadvantaged experience in the context of self-help/mutual aid organizations is another important area of critical psychology research at the group level of analysis (Humphreys and Rappaport, 1994; Nelson, Ochocka et al., 1998). Also, research on 'bridgers' or 'boundary-spanners' (that is, people who have experienced disadvantaged conditions, but who are well-integrated into the mainstream) is needed, because such individuals play an important role in creating social change by bridging two different worlds (Bond and Keys, 1993).

Processes

The first step in a collaborative research project is to decide who should be 'at the table'. Based on the values of self-determination, collaboration, and democratic participation, we believe that the disadvantaged group that is the focus of the research should be strongly represented in the research process. In critical psychology research, it is important to find ways to help actualize substantial and meaningful participation of disadvantaged people in the research process. In our projects, disadvantaged people typically participate in one of two ways: steering or guiding the project and actually carrying out the research. We have found it useful to create different structures for these different types of participation (Nelson, Ochocka et al., 1998). A research steering committee can be formed to oversee the development and implementation of the project with representatives functioning somewhat like board members, making broad policy decisions. A research team, on the other hand, is responsible for carrying out the research, including collecting and analyzing the data. However, when people participate, it is important to clarify the roles and responsibilities of all the research partners.

One of the first tasks of both the steering committee and research team is to brainstorm the vision, values, and working principles for the research project. Developing shared values and principles among partners is critical for successful partnerships with disadvantaged people, yet few partnerships explicitly define the values from which they work or recognize the power imbalances between professionals and disadvantaged partners (see Nelson, Lord and Ochocka et al., 2001b). Our experiences are consistent with those of Lord and Church (1998:113) who state that: '...few partnerships are genuinely transformative. Most partnerships maintain unequal power relations between people with disabilities and service provider or government partners'. Talking about values at the beginning of the project is essential for addressing these inherent power imbalances. Unless there is value congruence at the outset, whatever research or action follows is likely to be fraught with conflict.

While conflict can be prevented by being on 'the same page', the translation of values into action has the potential to elicit conflict. Individuals often have different ideas of what the most important values are or the best ways to put those values into practice. Thus, it is important to develop working principles for decision-making and conflict resolution. In our experience, members of research steering committees indicate a preference for decision-making by consensus. With regard to conflict resolution, our experience is that it is important to address whatever conflict arises quickly and with clear and direct communication to minimize any potential damage that could ensue. The role of the community researcher with respect to issues of decision-making and conflict is to share power and to help facilitate conflict resolution.

Whenever we develop working principles in research with disadvantaged people, the themes of communication and supportive relationships are always of paramount importance. Clear communication entails regular and direct communication among all participants, speaking for oneself, and using language that is accessible and free of jargon (Nelson, Lord and Ochocka et al., 2001b). We have found that the structures of a research steering committee and a research team, which meet regularly to share information, are important vehicles for communication. However, it is also necessary to have methods of communication that go beyond the core research committees so that information can be shared more broadly. Steering committee members and research assistants play an important liaison role with their organizations, so that there can be more widespread sharing of information. Having periodic summary bulletins, news reports, and feedback sessions on the project are other valuable methods of communication. The more information is shared in critical psychology research, the more there is mutual ownership over the project.

When participants are asked about working principles for such projects, they often use words such as 'respect,' 'listening,' 'honesty,' 'integrity,' 'trust,' 'belonging,' 'cooperation,' and 'sense of humour' to describe what they want (Constantino and Nelson, 1995). In essence, they want to be treated as people, not objects, and they want professional researchers to act like people, not like experts who think they know everything. In our experience, developing supportive relationships among team members is essential for a successful research project. Developing reciprocal relationships among members involves getting to know one another on a personal level, going beyond titles or labels. We have found it useful in initial meetings to have people share some of their interests and hobbies, rather than talking about what their title is or what organization they represent. Celebrating birthdays and accomplishments and sharing sad experiences and stressors deepen the relationships among team members. Providing food at meetings and maintaining an informal atmosphere also encourage supportive relationships. In this vein, Stringer (1996:160) aptly characterized participatory action research as 'the search for understanding in the company of friends'.

Community and society

Content

Feminist, Charlotte Bunch (1987), has identified the goals of feminist organizing as material improvement in the lives of women, the establishment of group structures for further change, and increased control of social institutions by women. These goals can be easily applied to the empowerment of other marginalized groups. We believe that critical psychology research at the community and societal levels should focus on social structures and policies that promote individual well-being, as well as exposing the damaging impacts of oppressive structures and policies. In this regard, the area of social policy has been neglected in mainstream psychological research. In addition to social policy analysis, critical psychology research should focus on community-level settings, such as civic organizations, alternative settings, and social movement organizations. These middle-range settings mediate between disadvantaged people and larger social structures and have considerable potential for creating social change (see Chapter 9).

Processes

Research processes at the community and societal levels are important for the action component of participatory action research. In collaboration with disadvantaged people, critical psychology researchers need to develop strategies for communicating research results to effect community change. Sometimes this involves identifying advocacy groups or creating coalitions to lobby for change. The story about the mental health housing coalition, which we briefly recounted at the beginning of Part II, is an example of how research can be used to stimulate change (Nelson, 1994). The use of research for systemic advocacy is critical for eradicating oppressive social structures and for promoting collective empowerment.

How does one train critical psychology researchers?

In training critical psychology researchers, it is important to emphasize that critical research is more than a theoretical or technical exercise. Qualitative researchers are taught that 'the researcher is the instrument' (Lincoln and Guba, 1985), which implies that the researcher brings his or her subjectivity, values, assumptions, and experience to bear on the research problem. Given the importance that we have attached to partnerships between researchers and disadvantaged people, critical psychology researchers must be well-grounded in a critical perspective, aware of their values, politically astute, interpersonally skilled, and passionately committed to the issue under study. For these reasons, training in critical psychology research is best provided within the context of a course in a psychology programme of study that has a critical emphasis. At the graduate and postgraduate levels, there should be a graduate course or subject in research methods. However, the learning from theory, intervention, and placement courses feeds the learning in a research course.

We have found teaching courses or subjects in critical psychology research to be very demanding for the faculty and students. That is because we believe that students should be exposed to mainstream methods (for example, statistics, scale development, experimental and correlational research designs) *and* methods that are particularly pertinent to critical psychology research (for example, participatory action research, qualitative methods, feminist research, programme evaluation, quasi-experimental designs). This is a heavy load. We also find that graduate students come to us without much understanding of the philosophy of science underlying research methods. At the undergraduate level, a positivist epistemology is a given that is not presented, debated, or critiqued. Reading about, discussing, and learning about alternative epistemologies and critical psychology research methods involves a personal paradigm shift for students, one that takes time to process. Students are so well socialized at the undergraduate level in traditional approaches to psychological research that they are often perplexed when they are introduced to these alternative ideas and methods. For these reasons, it is important for critical psychology faculty members to push for undergraduate courses in critical, qualitative, or community research. This is beginning to happen at some universities and is necessary to prepare undergraduates with an inclination towards critical psychology for an undergraduate thesis or for graduate work in a programme that emphasizes critical perspectives.

People learn best through experience. For this reason, we believe that students must gain some experience with critical psychology research methods in their course work. This can take the form of mini-assignments in a research course or using the research methods that they are learning on a practical training course. The most important learning of critical psychology research methods, however, comes in the form a thesis experience, which can be at the undergraduate or graduate level. We do not believe that students should follow the research interests of the faculty. Rather, we argue that students should pick a topic or issue about which they are passionately concerned. It is through the thesis process that students can have an integrated learning experience in which they are able to link values, theories, research methods, and action on an important social issue. We see the role of the thesis advisor as one of mentor or coach who helps the student to frame the problem and research study, develop a research plan, and analyze and feed back the data to the setting. Having a thesis support group can also be useful for sharing experiences and ideas and for giving and getting peer support.

Conclusion

In this chapter, we have identified some of the key characteristics of critical psychology research and some of the important steps and issues in the research process. For the purposes of this presentation, we have strived to clarify issues in critical psychology research to help the reader understand how critical psychology research is similar to, and different from, more mainstream psychology research. Critical psychology research can use many of the same research strategies that are employed in mainstream research, and it should be no less rigorous, scholarly, or concerned with the development of knowledge. However, unlike mainstream research, critical psychology research is done with disadvantaged people toward the goal of creating beneficial social change for them.

In striving to outline what critical psychology research is and how to do it, we may have underemphasized what a messy business this type of research truly is.

The guidelines that we offered in terms of the processes of conducting critical psychology research are not offered as a step-by-step recipe. Improvisation, creativity, and being willing and open to respond to challenges to one's integrity are essential. Above all else, we are calling for a personal paradigm shift for researchers, a shift toward inclusion, power-sharing, and supportive relationships with disadvantaged people in the research process.

Collaborating with disadvantaged citizens is a sound alternative to objectifying participants and mystifying knowledge, and the framework of values, assumptions, and practices that we have presented direct us toward an ideal goal. But ideal goals require the actions of grounded agents, agents who struggle with conflicting values, interests, and power. We are, after all, imperfect human beings who strive to do what we believe is best in an imperfect and messy world in which value and ethical dilemmas abound. We can neither interpret ethical dilemmas' 'objectively,' nor can we remain 'unaffected' by vested interests (Rossiter, Prilleltensky, and Walsh-Bowers, 2000). However, we can be self-reflective about our thoughts, actions, and choices and open to dialogue with others about new and better ways of thinking and practising critical psychology research. Critical psychology researchers must live with the tension of how to best combine their wisdom and humility.

5

The Making of a Critical
Practitioner/Activist

Since much of critical psychology has been academic in nature, there is a need for training students of critical psychology in action-oriented strategies (Austin and Prilleltensky, 2001). In this regard, we agree with Bennett and Hallman (1987) who have argued that supervised field experience should be a central part of the training component for critical psychology practitioners/activists. As we noted in the previous chapters in this section, critical approaches to teaching and research are oriented towards social action and social change. In this chapter, we consider training for skills in applied practice. We begin by identifying the key features of critical psychology practice/action. In so doing, we briefly review the foundations of critical psychology practice/action and its values, assumptions, and practices. We then describe what we believe are the core competencies and skills for applied practice/action in critical psychology. Finally, we discuss strategies for training in critical psychology practice/action.

What is critical psychology practice/action?

Critical approaches are most often associated with collective approaches to social and political action. However, we agree with Fook (1993) and others (for example, feminist therapists) who have argued that a critical perspective can inform practice at the individual and group levels as well. We begin this section by identifying the foundations of critical practice/action at multiple levels of analysis.

The foundations of critical psychology practice/action

Individual practice

As we argued earlier in the book, mainstream psychology has a narrow, individualistic orientation, in which the social and political context of human concerns is sheared off any analysis or intervention for human concerns. Moreover, this individualistic bias has permeated the applied areas of psychology. For example,

63

clinical, counselling, and health psychology have traditionally focused on changing individuals, rather than changing their social environments.

However, there are a number of critical, alternative approaches to individual practice that are emerging. Feminist therapy (Brown, 1994), empowerment approaches (Dunst and Trivette, 1989; McWhirter, 1994), critical casework (Fook, 1993), and narrative therapy (Morgan, 2000) all attend to the structural roots which underlie some clinical problems. Therapists and health promoters working from these critical frameworks collaboratively explore oppressive life conditions and experiences (for example, sexual abuse, homophobia, stigma, powerlessness) with their clients and strive to encourage a process of personal empowerment and participation in social change (Lord and Hutchison, 1993). We elaborate on these approaches in the next chapter on critical approaches to clinical and counselling psychology.

Group processes and organization development

Critical practitioners/activists have long emphasized the importance of groups as an important context for personal and social change. Freire's (1970) critical pedagogy is based on a small-group format, in which the teacher and students engage in a dialogue about the social and political conditions which affect group members. Consciousness-raising in groups has also been a tradition of feminist (Kravetz, 1987) and Black pride (Watts, Griffith, and Abdul-Adil, 1999) interventions. Also, self-help groups for people with disabilities and psychiatric survivors (for example, Chamberlin, 1990) have been critical of mainstream services, have provided alternative sources of support, and have advocated for social change. All of these critical approaches that have used a small group format have emphasized the importance of power-sharing and mutual learning in the educational process, rather than a one-way, leader-centred, hierarchical approach with power vested in the leader.

While organization development has historically been based on humanistic values and has utilized a systems approach to change (Lewin, 1951; McGregor, 1960), as Goldenberg (1978) has noted, it has often been closely aligned with management rather than workers or consumers. More recently, organizational change theorists such as Senge (1990) have emphasized the importance of creating a shared vision and values and using participatory decision-making processes to promote organization development. In innovative human service organizations, such as those for people with disabilities (Racino, 1991) or psychiatric survivors (Nelson, Lord, and Ochocka, 2001b), the vision and values of the organization is critical to guiding the everyday actions of organizational members. Participatory decision-making processes in which the voices of consumers are emphasized serve to distribute power throughout the organization (Shera and Page, 1995). A variety of strategies, such as process consultation, action research, and team-building, can also be used to facilitate organizational change.

Community development and social action

Heller *et al.* (1984) and Rothman and Tropman (1987) have made a distinction between two approaches to social intervention: community (or locality) development and social action. Community development is a cooperative, consensus-building approach that assumes that the majority of the population would, if educated, be supportive of change; there is agreement regarding underlying values; untapped resources within the community are available; and decision-making is pluralistic. Citizen participation is the foundation of community development. Citizens come together because of some issue or concern; they network and build relationships; they assess needs and develop programmes to meet those needs; they develop an organizational base; and they make linkages with other systems, settings, and funding sources. Community development is often used by disadvantaged groups and their allies to create local community change.

In contrast, social action is a confrontational, conflict-oriented, direct action approach that assumes that there is a major part of the population that is antagonistic to change; there is a clash in values between the 'haves' and 'have nots'; resources are scarce; and decision-making power is concentrated in the hands of elite groups. Social action is associated with social movement organizations which have, as a goal, broad social change and redistribution of power and resources. Community organization is used to create a coalition for change, and advocacy and direct action strategies are designed to disrupt the status quo and put pressure on elite groups to change. The targets of social action are usually governments and large corporations, while the agents of change are disenfranchised groups, including low-income people, working-class people, aboriginal people, people of colour, women and children, and people with disabilities.

The qualities of critical psychology practice/action

In this section, we consider the values, assumptions, and practices that are associated with the practice of critical psychology (see Table 5.1).

Values

Elsewhere, Isaac (Prilleltensky, 2001) has developed a framework for value-based praxis. Value-based praxis is the unity of reflection, research, and social action that is founded on the set of values that we set forth in Chapter 2. We believe that values such as collaboration, democratic participation, self-determination, respect for diversity, and social justice provide a firm foundation for the promotion of personal, relational, and collective wellness. Such values can profitably be used to guide the development of social policies and programmes, particularly for the benefit of people who have experienced oppression.

Since values are central to the practice of critical psychology, they should be of paramount importance in training for applied work. In their description of the graduate programme of study in Community Psychology at the University of Waikato in New Zealand, Thomas, Neill, and Robertson (1997) outlined a set of values and principles, similar to what we have set forth in this book, as core competencies and knowledge for students in this programme. In the graduate programme in Community Psychology at Wilfrid Laurier University, values also

Table 5.1 Qualities of applied practice from a critical psychology perspective

Critical psychology tenets	Possibilities for action
Values	*Content*: Collaboratively develop with students a vision and values that underlie training in applied areas and skills. Such values should provide a foundation for the promotion of personal, relational, and collective well-being.
	Process: Engage in discussion of values and values clarification with trainees. Applied skills training should be viewed in the service of the values of individual members and the collective. Care should be taken by faculty and students alike to strive to live the values and to avoid both dogmatism and relativism regarding the enactment of values in daily life. The vision and values should be the ethos of the training programme.
Assumptions	*Content*: Training in applied practice should emphasize the central role of power in the social world. An examination of the concepts of power, oppression, liberation, and well-being and how these concepts can be applied to real world phenomena should figure prominently in applied training.
	Process: Encourage trainees to reframe presenting problems in terms of power inequalities and dynamics. Also, emphasize transformative change and the need to be creative and 'think outside the box'. Challenge dominant ideologies of person blame and focus on strengths and capacity for change in partnerships with disadvantaged groups.
Practices	*Content*: Critical practice and action require generic assessment and intervention skills, including programme planning and evaluation, consultation, individual and group process facilitation, community development and organization, and social policy. Some specialized knowledge of the content area is also required.
	Process: Need to develop mechanisms to enable the linking of professional practice and political action to sustain critical work in applied settings.

occupy a central role in the process of training M A-level students (Alcalde and Walsh-Bowers, 1996). A mission statement, displayed prominently in the hallway of our department, was developed collaboratively by faculty and students and was recently revised. This mission statement serves as a tangible reminder of the values of the programme. Values and social ethics also figure prominently in feminist therapy training and practice (Lerman, 1994).

We believe that values should occupy a central position in the training of critical psychologists in applied skills. Applied skills are the tools for change, whereas values constitute the worldview from which one uses the skills. In focusing on skills without attention to values, applied psychology training courses run the risk of producing professional technicians who end up perpetuating the status quo in their practices. The many graduate students that we have trained comment that the most important part of their training was socialization into a set of values that stand the test of time and act as guide posts for work in whatever settings they find themselves.

We have a couple of caveats regarding values clarification and education based on our experiences as teachers and trainers. First, it is important not just to preach the values, but to practice the values in training programmes. Students are highly attuned to hypocrisy, and there are all too many stories of how we as teachers and trainers have failed to live up to the values we believe in. It is not critical that we be perfect or pure, as we are all human beings with shortcomings, blind spots, and personal agendas. What is important is that faculty consciously strive and struggle with students to enact our espoused values in the process of training. Second, as Isaac has stated in his article on value-based praxis, 'we need a *set* of values that is internally consistent, that avoids dogmatism and relativism, and that promotes congruence between means and ends' (Prilleltensky, 2001:753). We need to be clear in what we believe in, but open to dialogue and change. Presenting values as moral absolutes is dogmatic and stifles discussion and personal exploration of values. Faculty and students alike need a safe spot for values clarification where they are not judged, but listened to and respected. The other extreme of presenting values in relativistic terms is 'wishy-washy' and leads people to wonder what values are important or where the teacher is coming from. Dialogue about values in applied critical psychology training is essential.

Assumptions

Training for applied work in critical psychology pays keen attention to power imbalances and power dynamics. Before one even considers an intervention, critical practitioners/activists consider questions like: Who is benefiting from current and past arrangements? Who is suffering as a result of those arrangements? Often problems are socially constructed in such a way as to take existing power imbalances for granted. Using the language of 'power' and 'oppression' brings a new framework to the analysis of human problems.

'Reframing the problem' in terms of power inequalities is an important first step in any type of intervention (Seidman and Rappaport, 1986), because it challenges the dominant mythology of 'blaming the victim' for problems. Reframing also suggests that radically different strategies must be tried to create change. Innovative and creative solutions must be considered to tackle problems that are embedded within in both immediate and larger social and political contexts. Critical practitioners realize that they must think laterally to create change. In critical practice, potential solutions must be transformative, rather than ameliorative. Ameliorative solutions are at best reformist and do not address the systemic roots of problems. More of the same or improved versions of past practices are not likely to lead to significant change. Moreover, interventionists operating from a critical perspective realize that there are no single, magic solutions. Every strategy is at best a partial solution and one that will likely lead to new problems that need to be addressed in a continuous cycle of social problem-solving in social action (Sarason, 1978).

Critical practice also assumes that liberation, resistance, and a shift to well-being are possible. Rather than focusing on people's deficits and assuming the worst of people, critical practitioners focus on the strengths, resilience in the face of adversity, and potential for change for people who have experienced injustice. Critical practitioners/activists assume that transformative change is possible when people have a voice, community, and access to valued resources.

Practices

To some extent, practices and practice competencies in applied critical psychology vary with the type of setting and population with which one works. Those who work in schools must understand child development, educational systems, and intervention strategies for children, while those who work in healthcare settings need to be knowledgeable about health and health problems. While some degree of specialized knowledge is required for any area of applied work, our position is that critical psychology practitioners/activists should be generalists. Like Humphreys (1996), we believe that rather than focusing narrowly on one approach, such as psychotherapy, that applied practitioners should have a broader based set of skills including programme planning and evaluation, consultation, individual and group process facilitation, community development and organization, and social policy. In the following sections, we elaborate on some of the skills, and training opportunities to develop those skills, that should comprise applied training in critical psychology.

Another point that we think is important for critical practice/action is the distinction between professional practice and political action. As M.B. Smith (1990) noted, psychology has traditionally drawn sharp lines between so-called professional objectivity and advocacy. In contrast, critical psychologists believe that professional practice and political positions are inextricably intertwined. In the process of working with individuals, groups, or communities in any number of different settings, issues of power, oppression, and liberation quickly become apparent to the critical psychologist. While critical psychologists typically do not have a problem integrating their personal and political selves, the settings in which we work often have a problem with this integration. Professional licensing and regulatory bodies and bureaucratic rules and procedures and the people who enforce them often try to stifle innovation and silence workers from being more vocal about their views. For example, in a study of occupational therapists working in the mental health field, Townsend (1999) found that the good intentions of workers to enact an empowerment approach with clients was often overruled by bureaucratic obstacles. Unfortunately, professional practitioners do not have an equivalent to the principle of academic freedom that protects (at least to some degree) those of us who work in academic settings.

To engage in political action and systemic change, practitioners must carefully assess how supportive the settings are in which they work and find strategies that are workable within their context. Finding supportive colleagues, both in and outside the setting, and being strategic about which issues to pursue are some of the coping mechanisms that are important for sustaining workers in their roles as social-change agents. Taking the initiative and taking risks is important, but there is also a need to weigh the costs to oneself. One strategy that we have found useful is the formation of coalitions for social change. Often times, people who work for a state-funded organization, such as a school or a hospital, are afraid to speak up too loudly, or they are cautioned by their colleagues and superiors to be quiet, lest there be government reprisals or public backlash against the organization. However, workers can come together with like-minded allies, in coalitions to agitate for change. In this way, they are able to speak for themselves or for a coalition of organizations, groups, or individuals, without having to worry about work-related complications.

What are the core competencies and skills for applied practice/action in critical psychology?

Applied critical psychologists can play a number of different roles. The roles of direct service worker, participant observer, researcher–evaluator, consultant, facilitator, trainer, interventionist-change agent, and planner–conceptualizer each require somewhat different skills (Lykes and Hellstedt,1987; Stenmark, 1977; Thomas, Neill and Robertson 1997). However, in practice there is often considerable overlap and blending of these different roles. In this vein, Julnes *et al.* (1987) have suggested that conceptualization, intervention, evaluation, and description are skills rather than roles. Similarly, Thomas, Neill and Robertson (1997) have suggested that there are three broad sets of competencies and skills that cut across these different roles: technical skills (for example, research, evaluation, grant-writing), collaboration skills (for example, networking and partnership skills), and personal effectiveness skills (for example, communication and interpersonal skills). Like Rappaport (1977), we believe that it is useful to conceptualize roles and skills in terms of different ecological levels of analysis, ranging from the individual to society. In this section, we consider the core competencies and skills for critical psychology practice/action at different levels of analysis (see Table 5.2).

Individual

Competencies and skills at the individual level include both intrapersonal skills of the critical psychologist and interpersonal skills for working with individual clients (McWhirter, 1994). Training in critical psychology needs to focus on personal reflection, consciousness raising, values clarification, and identity as a critical practitioner/activist for the trainee. Since the therapist or counsellor is the agent of change in individual-level interventions, training must start with the individual. For example, psychoanalytic training has emphasized that the trainee should undergo his or her own psychoanalysis to become more fully aware of his or her blind spots.

Intrapersonal growth is key to the development of competent practitioners. McWhirter (1994) has suggested that self-esteem, ways of coping with anxiety and irrational beliefs, and creative self-expression are some of the intrapersonal skills that are important for practising an empowerment approach to counselling. Similarly, Baird (1999) has argued that applied training needs to focus on issues

Table 5.2   Skills and training processes for critical psychology practice/action at different ecological levels of analysis

Ecological level (and related values)	Applied skills for critical psychology practice/action	Key training processes for applied skills in critical psychology
Individual (personal)	• Personal reflection and consciousness-raising (self-determination, values clarification, identity formation) • Communication skills (basic attending and influencing), assertiveness, leadership skills, ability to set boundaries • Assessment and intervention skills for working with individuals in different settings	• Personal reflection exercises which encourage emotional expression, connecting the personal and the political, and self-understanding • Values education and clarification • Sequential training in basic attending and influencing skills (human relations training) • Field placement, practical, and internship experiences with supervisor providing role modelling, mentoring, and resources • Peer feedback and respectful challenging
Group and organization (relational)	• Skills in group process facilitation and different group intervention methods • Skills in organization development, including process consultation, action research, team-building, programme planning, partnership processes	• Opportunities for practice of group facilitation • Group-based training and support groups • Field placement, practical, and internship experiences with supervisor providing role modelling, mentoring, and resources • Peer feedback and respectful challenging • Building community within the academic or professional unit
Community and society (collective)	• Skills in community development and community organizing • Skills in social action, coalition building, and advocacy • Skills in social policy analysis and formulation	• Individual and group projects in the community • Exposure to community and social issues through field trips, guest speakers, and practical placements • Encouragement of participation in campus and community events • Field placement, practical, and internship experiences with supervisor providing role modelling, mentoring, and resources • Peer feedback and respectful challenging

of stress and self-care of psychologists, and he has suggested a number of strategies for physical, emotional, cognitive, and financial self-care.

Interpersonal skills, which have been called human relations skills, communication skills, or consultation skills, are also very important for the practice of critical
psychology (Parsons and Meyers, 1984). Ivey, Ivey, and Simek-Morgan (1997)
have outlined a training programme for what they have called basic attending and
influencing skills. Attending skills are those that enable a client to speak freely

about his or her thoughts and feelings and include body posture and language and active listening on the part of the helper. Influencing skills are used later in the helping relationship to assist the individual in making a change in his or her life and include skills in confrontation, interpretation, and reframing problems. Other important interpersonal skills include assertiveness, leadership skills, the ability to set personal boundaries and avoid or deal with manipulation, effectively giving and receiving feedback, and attending to diversity in its many and varied forms.

While these intrapersonal and interpersonal skills are often discussed in the context of clinical training or working with individuals, we believe that they are fundamentally important to critical work with groups, organizations, communities, and society. Many of these skills are the basic building blocks for a variety of different interventions at different levels. Also, depending upon one's area of focus, there are more specialized skills that need to be acquired for working with individuals. For example, school psychologists should be well-informed about different assessment methods. Even if one largely rejects the utility of traditional testing and assessment, the decision not to use such an approach should be based on a sound understanding of testing and assessment.

Group and organization

Work with groups and organizations is also basic to the practice of critical psychology. Trainees need to develop an understanding of what happens in groups and how to facilitate groups. Group processes or dynamics deal with issues such as morale, climate, patterns of participation, influence, leadership, conflict, and cooperation, to name a few. While most people work in groups at least some of the time, few people are trained in or understand group processes. People know when groups are working well, and most people have had negative experiences in groups where they can recount what went wrong. However, few people understand the basics of group processes. In addition to learning as a participant–observer, trainees need to learn how to facilitate groups and to encourage healthy group processes. Developing ground rules for group meetings, having a clear and mutually agreed upon agenda, encouraging participation and sharing leadership, actively listening to and recording suggestions, testing for consensus regarding decisions, making process observations and comments, managing conflict, moving the process and discussion along towards action, respecting time lines, and promoting fun and laughter are some of the important skills for facilitating groups.

Change agents often work with organizations, either as insiders or outsiders. Insiders need to be good leaders and have good management skills. Skills that are consistent with the values of critical psychology and that are important for organizational leadership include networking and partnership building, bringing people together to identify a common vision and values, using highly participatory strategies, and distributing power and decision-making throughout the organization (Senge, 1990; Shera and Page, 1995). External consultants require similar skills in being able to take the pulse of the organization, collaboratively identify with the changes needed by stakeholders, and utilize strategies, such as process consultation, action research, and team-building, to create organizational change

(Alpert and Meyers, 1983; Parsons and Meyers, 1984). In addition to these skills in collaboration and organizational change, skills in programme planning, implementation, and evaluation are also important for critical work with organizations.

Community and society

Just as working with individuals is a building block for working with groups and organizations, being able to understand what is happening in groups and organizations is a foundation for understanding what is happening in communities and societies. The main difference is that community and social systems are more complex and multi-layered than groups and organizations. In community development, the critical psychologist must not only be able to form partnerships with low-income and disadvantaged groups who are, based on experiences, deeply mistrustful of would-be helpers, but he or she must also be able to engage and form partnerships with numerous other stakeholders and systems (Jones and Silva, 1991; Powell and Nelson, 1997).

Applied critical psychologists also need to develop skills in social action, coalition-building, political advocacy, and social policy to create broader social change. Unfortunately, there are few shining examples of social change agents within psychology who can serve as inspiring heros and role models. In this regard, training programmes for critical psychologists need to ally themselves more closely with social movement organizations in which students can get exposure to and work with experienced social change agents. The Highlander School in Appalachia (Bell, Gaventa, and Peters, 1990) and the School of Human Services in New Hampshire (Osher and Goldenberg, 1987) are examples of formal settings which have trained social activists. Skills in advocacy include learning to advocate with vulnerable people rather than for them, understanding the various dilemmas and choice points in advocacy strategies, and organizing broad-based coalitions for social change (Glidewell, 1984). Also, critical psychologists need to be trained to understand the process of social policy formulation, to analyze social policy issues and positions, and to influence social policy (Iscoe, 1984; Weinberg, 2001).

How does one train critical psychology practitioners/activists?

Having outlined some of the general competencies and skills required for the practice of critical psychology, we now turn to the question of how these competencies and skills can be developed. In Table 5.2, we summarized some of the important training processes for the development of competence in applied critical psychology. Field training is essential and should take place at many different levels, beginning with undergraduate field placements and service learning (Bennett and Hallman, 1987; Chapman, 1999; Elias, 1987; O'Sullivan, 1997), then moving to graduate placements (Bennett and Hallman, 1987; Gensheimer and Diebold, 1997; Lykes and Hellstedt, 1987), and finally to doctoral level internship training (Baird, 1999; Weinberg, 2001). While the level of competence and skill and the length and intensity of the training experiences increases from one level to the next, the processes of training are similar in nature.

We believe that applied training in critical psychology should be guided by several principles. First, consistent with the value of self-determination, student trainees should direct their own learning. This begins with a period of self-reflection and consideration of possible field placements and concludes with an evaluation of the field experience and lessons learned (Lykes and Hellstedt, 1987). Students should drive the training process with lecturers and professors acting as mentors, coaches, and resource people who provide guidance and support. Second, training should occur within a context that is supportive of the student trainee's learning. Student trainees need to feel safe and secure in their development of competencies and skills in applied critical psychology. Several different parties in the field training can play a supportive role. Typically, there is a faculty supervisor who is available for regular support and problem-solving, and often there is a site supervisor or contact who also provides support to the trainee. There needs to be some liaison and communication between the trainee, the university supervisor, and the site supervisor. In our experience, meetings of these three people can be organized at key points in the placement process, usually at the beginning, part-way through the placement, and at the end of the placement. Support groups or a placement group can also provide a supportive context for learning with peers. Peer feedback and consultation is an additional source of support. Finally, the overall climate of the training programme sets a tone for field training. The degree to which the field training course is congruent and fits with the other courses and the level of collaboration and support that trainees experience throughout the programme are important.

One final principle of field training in critical psychology is that it should be process-oriented and competency-based. Competency-based means that the goal of the training process should be to develop those competencies and skills that we outlined in the previous section. Process-oriented means that training is organized sequentially to address different phases of training (Lykes and Hellstedt, 1987). The initial phase of pre-entry involves a process of personal reflection and placement evaluation (Cherniss, 1993). During this phase, students identify the skills that they want to develop, reflect on their interests, and 'shop around' for the type of placement that suits them. During the second phase of contracting and entry, students identify their personal learning objectives and the tasks and resources needed to meet those objectives. These objectives can be included in a placement proposal or contract, which also outlines the roles and responsibilities for the different parties (student, faculty supervisor, site supervisor) and the objectives for the setting. The third phase is the work phase in which the student carries out the tasks delineated in the contract with the assistance of the supervisors. The final phase is one of evaluation of the experience and the extent to which the goals of the placement were fulfilled and separation from the setting.

Conclusion

In this chapter, we have focused on training in applied skills in critical psychology. Practice and action in critical psychology lag behind theory and research (Austin and Prilleltensky, 2001). We identified the values, assumptions, and practices of critical psychology practice/action and some of the foundations upon which these qualities are based. We want to emphasize that critical practice/action spans the boundaries of working with individuals, groups, organizations, and larger social systems. To span these boundaries, applied critical psychology training needs to follow more of a generalist rather than a specialist model. We identified some of the core competencies and skills required for this boundary spanning, as well as the types of training processes that are needed to build such competencies. We know that there are many dilemmas in the practice of critical approaches to psychology. Thus, we consider the ideas that we have set forth in this chapter as a work in progress. We look forward to seeing more emphasis on training for practice and action in critical psychology and to the dialogue that emerges from that work.

Part III
Applications

When I was an undergraduate student, I worked in two different clinical settings for children and youth in Urbana-Champaign, Illinois. The first programme was a token economy for youth who were in trouble with the law. Many of these children had what is called 'conduct disorder', manifesting a variety of delinquent behaviours – aggression, bullying, lying, stealing, and cheating. Others were 'followers', who were lacking in life and social skills and became involved in law-breaking activities by virtue of their association with peers who were more active leaders in those activities. The second programme was a residential children's mental health centre, where many of the children seemed like younger versions of the kids in the token economy. Many of the younger and older kids came from low-income families, in which the parents had many problems of their own. While in these residential treatment programmes, both the younger and older kids appeared to improve. However, once they 'graduated' and were sent back to their homes and schools, things often unravelled very quickly. The kids reverted back to the types of problems that they were experiencing when they first entered the treatment settings. What I learned from my experiences in these two settings was that systemic intervention is needed; changing individuals without changing their circumstances is not likely to be successful.

In my first job as a psychologist with the Child Guidance Clinic of Winnipeg, I worked in two inner-city schools with a high percentage of aboriginal students. Aboriginal students were often referred to me because of academic underachievement, absenteeism, and also problems of substance abuse. I got to know a number of these youngsters and some of their families quite well. I wasn't properly prepared to work with aboriginal people in my clinical training. I don't recall having a reading or class discussion about aboriginal mental health and I never saw an aboriginal client in the clinical programme's training centre. Relying on my instincts, I found that many of these students were in need of a mentoring relationship with an adult. Ideally, such a programme could have been organized through a partnership between the aboriginal community and the Child Guidance Clinic with aboriginal elders or adults as mentors. But in the absence of that, I befriended several of these students. Some of the 'therapy' that I did involved taking these students out for lunch, going out for a ride in my car, or visiting their homes. These activities helped to build relationships with these youngsters, who began to open up to me. I remember that when one of the schools once brought in an aboriginal medicine man for a school assembly, the aboriginal students that I knew (some of whom were supposed to have an attention deficit) were completely quiet and engrossed with what they saw.

From these different clinical experiences, I learned that the problems of some of the therapy clients that I had seen were structural in nature. But the therapies in which I was trained did not address these structural problems of class prejudice, stigma, and racism. I also found that these individuals were seeking a supportive, trusting relationship with someone, not necessarily a therapist. Finally, many of the people that I saw needed more than 'talk' therapy; they needed a more 'hands-on' approach to help guide them through problems in their families and communities. Liberation workers have called this a process of 'accompaniment', which I think captures the essence of the type of helping approach that can be potentially empowering and transformative if it deals with the socio-political processes that impact on individuals.

I have been quite active volunteering in community development activities, particularly with low-income neighbourhoods. A key principle of this activity has been to work in solidarity with disadvantaged people and to encourage their participation in community development. I have played a variety of different roles in these activities, including organizer, facilitator, consultant, advocate, and researcher. I have worked with three different low-income neighbourhoods. Two of them, the Langs Farm Village Association and the Highfield Community Enrichment Project, have developed and maintained vibrant neighbourhood organizations which are controlled by local residents. While I am no longer active with these settings, as one of the founders or 'historical figures', I get invited back for annual meetings or consultations. I am always amazed at the level of activity and growth in these settings.

Another major involvement of mine has been with community mental health organizations. I was an active board member of the Waterloo Branch of the Canadian Mental Health Association for 10 years and contributed to the development of its programmes, and I have consulted with a mental health self-help organization in the development of a loan fund to help consumers start their own businesses. I have also worked with colleagues in research and evaluation capacities with community mental health and housing organizations. A goal of all this work in community mental health has been to transform services towards a new paradigm of empowerment and community integration and to develop alternative consumer-controlled settings that embrace the values of empowerment and social justice.

I have always found work in community settings to be very rewarding, but also very messy. Progress in community development is often slow and uneven with a fair share of false-starts and setbacks. Conflicts and challenges are par for the course. In the work that colleagues and I have done with mental health consumer/survivor organizations, we have had to overcome suspicion and anger because of our position as professionals. A consumer/survivor friend of mine related that whenever she hears the word 'research', she thinks of the CIA-funded studies of hallucinogenic drugs and 'psychic driving' that were inflicted on mental patients in a Montreal hospital. Through listening and letting people tell their stories, I have learned a great deal about what consumer/survivors have experienced. And through sharing power and resources, my colleagues and I have been able to develop authentic partnerships with consumer/survivor organizations. Sometimes the process is uncomfortable. But when this happens I have come to believe that these moments are important opportunities for learning about my blind spots and things that I may take for granted.

In spite of the difficulties of doing community work, I am constantly impressed by community members who step up and take the initiative to make changes in their communities. Often times, it is people who have experienced many disadvantages who lead the way for change. It has been a privilege for me to work with so many talented people in so many different settings over the years in the quest to make some kind of positive changes in communities.

Geoff Nelson

Introduction

We use the framework of values, assumptions and practices to formulate critical psychology applications in diverse settings. In each setting we distill the implications of critical psychology for the content as well as the process of practice. Thus, for example, we examine the role of values in informing the content as well as the process of applied community work. Similarly, we review the inherent assumptions of clinical practice and offer alternatives based on the pursuit of well-being and the resistance to oppression. Critical modes of therapy and problem definition are suggested throughout the entire section.

Although unique tasks are expected of psychologists in different settings, there is a need to think systemically about mental health and about oppression. Thus, for example, oppression taking place in the home, in the form of wife or child abuse, is related to oppressive cultural norms such as the high degree of violence in society. Another example is the stress occasioned by social factors such as unemployment, discrimination, or poverty. The symptoms provoked by these factors will manifest themselves in various forms in various places, but the underlying issues of oppression and social injustice are common throughout many problems. Critical psychologists, we think, should be able to ascertain the power dynamics upholding inequality and systemic exclusion in multiple contexts.

Disempowerment is a pervasive phenomenon that exists across many layers of well-being. It happens in intimate relationships, in families, at work, and through the media. In every case, critical psychologists search for the links in powerlessness and resistance across levels of analysis. We ask the question: how is the exploitation of power and advantage in families related to norms of gender discrimination in society at large? In the same vein, we ask what can be done at the social level to stop child abuse happening within families; and what can be done at the cultural level to prevent eating disorders affecting women's bodies. From the micro to the macro setting, we ask what needs to change in families so that males will not exhibit aggressive behaviours in sports. Multiple causality and multiple points of interventions should become part of our modus operandi. Our objective in this part of the book is to show how to bridge across levels and places in thinking and in action.

In the next few chapters we describe how psychologists can practise critical psychology either in mainstream or alternative settings. We will draw on existing critical practices such as feminist therapy, just therapy, and community psychology. The message is that critical psychology is an integrative approach that can be applied wherever one works. Existing critical approaches focus on one population (feminist therapy deals primarily with women) or one mode of helping (therapy as opposed to individual work *and* community action). Our approach is integrative of populations and modes of action and tries to provide a coherent frame of reference. It does not position one mode against another. Rather, it integrates the best qualities of approaches invested in promoting sincere partnerships with community members who are trying to resist domination.

We offer guidelines for practice in clinical, counselling, school/educational, health, work, and community settings. In each place we take the side of the one with the weaker voice and with the most to lose. It is a high calling, for it is easy to get co-opted into serving power. Reflexive practice and critical feedback from peers are the only antidotes we know of that can fend off that risk. Throughout the next few chapters we try to keep that in mind.

6

Clinical and Counselling Settings: Making a Difference with Disadvantaged Clients

Epidemiological studies have reported the one-year prevalence rates for adult mental health problems (Offord *et al.*, 1994; Regier *et al.*, 1984) and children's mental health problems (Offord, Boyle, and Szatmari, 1987) to be in the vicinity of 20 to 25 per cent. However, these studies are likely to have underestimated the scope of these problems because of segments of the population excluded from study (for example, homeless persons, people in institutions), diagnoses excluded (for example, sexual dysfunction), and problems related to self-report and memory of past events (Albee, 1990). Also, this epidemiological research focused on clinical levels of problems and did not count the number of cases in which problems do not reach clinical levels but are nevertheless personally distressing (for example, anxiety, depression). Suffice it to say, however, that mental 'disorders' and social and emotional problems are widespread.

Like Albee (1990), we believe that many, but not all, so-called mental health problems reflect some form of oppression. A critical approach to clinical and counselling psychology pays particular attention to issues of oppression that surface in the mental health field, including the oppression of women, psychiatric survivors, poor people, minorities, and gay, lesbian, and bisexual persons. We begin this chapter by first considering the traditional practice of clinical and counselling psychology. We then highlight various critiques of clinical and counselling approaches. The remainder of the chapter focuses on alternative approaches that are potentially transformative and empowering.

Describing and critiquing the status quo

The traditional practice of clinical and counselling psychology

Clinical psychology and counselling psychology are based on common assumptions, and both use similar approaches. The major difference between the two is that clinical psychology supposedly focuses on more severe problems that reach clinical levels, while counselling psychology is concerned more with problems in living or with normal life transitions (for example, career choices). Clinical and counselling psychology have become part of the mainstream of western society. Talk shows, newspapers, and popular magazines routinely provide coverage on different 'disorders', and diagnostic terms like 'anorexia' and 'ADHD' (attention deficit hyperactivity disorder) have become part of our everyday language. Moreover, psychotherapy by mental health professionals has proliferated since the end of the Second World War (Humphreys, 1996). We see cartoons in which 'psychiatric help for 5 cents' is offered (in Peanuts), or we find Lassie (sheepdog) reclining on a couch with an analyst behind her after the frame in which a drowning Timmy cries to Lassie to 'get help'. Columnist, Ann Landers, routinely advises US readers to seek counselling. Survey research has found an increase in consultation with social workers, counsellors, and psychologists for mental health problems from 1957 to 1996 (Swindle *et al.*, 2000), and *Consumer Reports* has conducted a study on the use of psychotherapy (Seligman, 1995).

So what is the essence of this growing cultural phenomenon? Textbooks in clinical and counselling psychology (for example, Ivey, Ivey, and Simek-Morgan, 1997; Nietzel, Bernstein, and Milich, 1998) typically emphasize the roles of assessment/diagnosis and treatment/therapy. The focus of diagnosis is on the occurrence of various signs and symptoms (thoughts, emotions, and behaviours) that are presumed to reflect an underlying diagnostic condition, as defined in the Diagnostic and Statistical Manual (DSM) of the American Psychiatric Association (currently in its fourth edition). While the DSM now has several dimensions, including one that focuses on psychosocial and environmental problems, the major emphasis remains on the first dimension, clinical syndromes. Clinicians and counsellors use a variety of standardized tests (for example, clinical tests, such as the MMPI, interest or vocational tests), projective tests (for example, the Rorschach inkblots), interviews, and observations to arrive at a diagnosis. Sometimes referral to a medical professional or some other specialist is used in the assessment process.

Clinical and counselling practice proceeds logically from diagnosis to treatment. Clinicians and counsellors have a wide variety of therapeutic approaches available from which they can choose. While there are many different schools of therapy, the three main current approaches are psychodynamic, humanistic, and cognitive-behavioural (Nietzel *et al.*, 1998). Within each of these schools, there are variations and a multitude of specific techniques that can be used to treat particular problems. In addition to individual therapy or counselling, there are couple, family, and group therapies. These approaches are often based on the three major theoretical perspectives identified above, but they have also incorporated some form of a systems perspective in which the dynamics of the couple, the family, or the group are viewed as particularly important in the development, maintenance, or treatment of the presenting problem (Goldenberg and Goldenberg, 1983).

Since Eysenck's (1952) claim nearly 50 years ago that there was no evidence demonstrating the effectiveness of psychotherapy, there has been an explosion of research on the processes and outcomes of therapy. Early on, researchers noted that the question 'Is psychotherapy effective?' is not the best research question. Rather, they argued that a better research question is 'What treatment, by whom, is most effective for this individual with that specific problem, under which set of circumstances?' (Paul, 1967:111). In the last 20 years, there has been an ascendency of the behavioural and more recently cognitive-behavioural school of therapy. The behavioural and cognitive-behavioural school has produced the greatest amount of research on the effectiveness of different techniques to treat a broad range of both clinical problems (for example, anxiety, depression) and lifestyle problems (for example, obesity, parenting) for adults (DeRubeis and Crits-Christoph, 1998) and children (Kazdin and Weisz, 1998). To their credit, behaviourists and cognitive-behaviourists have linked research and practice and have tackled some of the most difficult and intractable clinical problems (for example, children with autism, adults institutionalized for severe developmental and/or mental health problems) much more than proponents of the other therapeutic approaches.

As Larner has noted (2001), there has been more and more emphasis in recent years on 'evidence-based practice' that favours short-term, solution-focused, results-oriented behavioural and cognitive-behavioural approaches. There are now more constraints on therapeutic practices than there were in the 1960s and 1970s when there was a proliferation of different therapeutic approaches. As Cushman and Gilford (2000) have argued, this trend has been influenced by larger societal changes that have been manifested in health care systems. In the USA, 'managed care–that is, large for-profit corporations specializing in the management and control of health care delivery through the exercise of bureaucratic rationalism–has become the dominant force in mental health care' (986). In managed care, employers provide employees with insurance benefits that cover some of the costs of some mental health services, that are available from a managed care provider. Who benefits from this relationship? The goal of the managed care provider is to make a profit, and the goal of the employer is to have productive employees. Within a managed care framework, the therapist becomes more of a technician following a pre-determined, 'manualized' treatment approach. A therapeutic alliance between therapist and client is emphasized, but only because such an alliance is believed to enhance the *compliance* of the client with the treatment regime (Cushman and Gilford, 2000).

We do not dispute the fact that there are effective therapeutic approaches for many mental health problems or that there is value in research that enhances 'evidence-based practice'. Evidence is important. At the same time, we recognize that positivistic outcome research does not provide the full picture of clients, therapists, treatments, and effectiveness (Larner, 2001). In practice, effective therapy involves the blending of the clinical wisdom of the therapist (the art of therapy) with the best available evidence (the science of therapy) to help the individual client (Larner, 2001). A critical approach draws attention to the life experiences of clients, including experiences of oppression and the potential for treatment to be damaging, irrelevant, or masking some of the larger problems that many people face. Like Cushman and Gilford (2000), we believe that what is missing in the current discourse of 'evidence-based practice' and 'managed care' is an explication of the moral values that underlie this approach. In the next section, we elaborate on the criticisms of mainstream clinical and counselling psychology that flow from the alternative, value-based approach to critical psychology that we are advancing in this book.

Critical appraisal of clinical and counselling psychology

Clinical and counselling psychology have been roundly criticized from a number of different sources on a number of grounds. Community psychologists have argued that clinical psychology is overly focused on the individual and micro-system levels of analysis; that clinical and counselling psychologists have become preoccupied with psychotherapy, ignoring other potential helping roles and interventions; and that the need and demand for clinical and counselling inter-vention far outstrips the availability of trained psychotherapists (for example, Albee, 1990; Prilleltensky, 1994; Sarason, 1981). These critics have shown that in political efforts to gain equal status with psychiatry, clinical psychology began practising in the 'master's house'–the VA (Veterans Administration) hospital and other hospital-based psychiatric settings–in the post-Second World War period.

In spite of tensions and efforts by psychiatry to curtail the activities of clinical psychologists, including psychotherapy (Humphreys, 1996), clinical psychology has allied itself to a large degree with psychiatry. Even today, there is a debate among clinical psychologists as to whether they should be given psychoactive drug prescription privileges, a move which would further wed clinical psychology to psychiatry. Parenthetically, drug treatment is favoured under managed care, because it is usually a less costly alternative to therapy and counselling. Within the traditional approach, tremendous financial benefits accrue to the pharmaceutical industry and the psychological testing industry. As a consequence of buying into a narrow medical model of mental health, clinical psychology has saddled itself with all the trappings that go with that model. Clinical psychologists have adopt-ed the DSM approach to diagnosis and use it as a template for abnormal psychology textbooks, as well as for practice.

Feminists have been highly critical of the DSM and clinical judgement, which, they argue, reflect a patriarchal mental health establishment with male mental health professionals having the power to label women as 'abnormal' (Caplan, 1991; Chesler, 1989, 1990; Hare-Mustin, and Maracek, 1997). Caplan (1991) has told the story of her unsuccessful opposition to the inclusion in the DSM of the dubious diagnostic categories of 'Late Luteal Phase Dysphoric Disorder' (PMS/PMT) and 'Self-Defeating Personality Disorder', both of which attach a mental illness label to women. To make her point of bias against women, Caplan proposed another category, 'Delusional Dominating Personality Disorder', that would label men in the same way that the other categories label women. What is clear from her story is that the entire process of deciding what diagnostic categories are included is intensely political.

Further evidence of the predominantly male mental health establishment's biases against women is provided in an early study by Broverman and colleagues (1970). The researchers asked clinicians to describe the qualities of a mentally healthy man, woman, and person. The clinicians ascribed stereotypic male quali-ties to the mentally healthy man and stereotypic female qualities to the mentally healthy woman. What was most interesting was that stereotypic male qualities were ascribed to the mentally healthy person, thus demonstrating the catch-22 of clinical judgement for women clients. If women did not conform to a traditional sex role stereotype of the passive, obedient wife, and stay-at-home mother, cook, and cleaner, they were deemed to be mentally unhealthy women (as depicted in the 1970 film *Diary of a Mad Housewife*). But if women did conform to this traditional female role, they were deemed not to be mentally healthy people. No matter how women behaved, they were 'abnormal'.

Feminists have also asserted that conventional therapies typically do not attend to the unique life stressors that women have experienced, that are sometimes the core issues underlying their presenting problems in therapy (for example, anxiety, depression) (Chesler, 1989). One clear example is sexual abuse. Child sexual abuse typically involves a female victim and an adult male perpetrator (Bagley and Thurston, 1998; Offord et al., 1994). It is only recently that child sexual abuse has been named, found to be widespread, and shown to have devastating consequences (Bagley and Thurston, 1998; Paproski, 1997). Moreover, sexual abuse of women is not limited to childhood. Throughout their lives, many women have experienced rape, sexual assault, and sexual harassment (Bond, 1995; Koss, 1993).

Similarly, violence against women, which is widespread (Browne, 1993; Walker, 1999), has been ignored and denied by male therapists. Pressman (1989) recounts a session with the renowned family therapist, Salvador Minuchin, in which he dismisses a woman's fear about her husband's violent temper, even when the husband admits losing his temper with his two girls and wife, putting his fist through a wall, throwing a shoe at a wall, and disclosing his own father's abusive behaviour when he was a child. Pressman argues that psychodynamic therapy blames women who have been the victims of spousal violence and that family systems therapy, in its emphasis on circular causality, blames family interaction patterns for such violence. Neither approach holds men responsible for their violent actions. Moreover, violence against women is accompanied by psychologically damaging verbal and emotional abuse (Lecovin and Penfold, 1996).

Some women seeking help have also been physically and sexually abused by male therapists (Masson, 1988; Penfold, 1992; Seto, 1995). Clinicians' failure to acknowledge that there is a power imbalance between therapists and clients together with the lack of sufficient training and organizationally-sanctioned and supported opportunities for open discussion of ethical issues in clinical practice, in general, and therapist sexual abuse of clients, specifically, perpetuates both blatant (for example, physical or sexual abuse) and subtle abuse (for example, minimizing client self-determination and input into the therapy process) of clients (Prilleltensky, Rossiter, and Walsh-Bowers, 1996; Prilleltensky, Walsh-Bowers, and Rossiter, 1999; Rossiter, Walsh-Bowers, and Prilleltensky, 1996; Walsh-Bowers, Rossiter, and Prilleltensky, 1996).

Gay, lesbian, and bisexual people are another oppressed group that has resisted traditional clinical and counselling approaches. Under earlier versions of the DSM, people with a gay, lesbian, or bisexual orientation were deemed to be suffering from a mental illness. The diagnostic category of homosexuality as a mental illness was dropped from the DSM not because of new research findings or because of professional enlightenment (although there were clinical psychologists and psychiatrists who actively opposed the inclusion of homosexuality), but because gay and lesbian people were politically active in pushing for its removal (Bayer, 1981). Gay, lesbian, and bisexual people have also noted that clinical and counselling interventions have historically ignored the widespread violence, prejudice, and rejection that they experience in their families, schools, work settings, and communities (Kitzinger, 1997). Moreover, in promoting various 'conversion therapies', clinical and counselling psychology has colluded with mainstream heterosexist, homophobic values in the oppression of gay, lesbian, and bisexual people.

Psychiatric survivors have also been very vocal in their opposition to diagnostic labelling and the power imbalances that they have experienced with mental health professionals in institutions (Burstow and Weitz, 1988; Chamberlin, 1990). Many people who have been institutionalized for mental health problems are now calling themselves 'consumers' or 'survivors' of the mental health system, because they object to psychiatric labels that dehumanize, objectify, and stigmatize them. While labelling is not likely a cause of major mental health problems, it can lead to harmful consequences for individuals, such as discrimination with regard to employment and housing (Page and Day, 1990) and public perceptions of danger (Dallaire et al., 2000). Rosenhan's (1973) well-known pseudo-patient study showed that psychiatrists are likely to diagnose 'schizophrenia' and other major categories and to prescribe medication to individuals based on limited information that does not remotely suggest 'schizophrenia.' Moreover, the pseudo-patients in his study experienced the stickiness of diagnostic labels, with mental health professionals interpreting much of their behaviour in terms of the label.

Iatrogenic problems, including abuse, neglect, and coercive 'treatment' in institutional settings have been well-documented (Burstow and Weitz, 1988). Poor people with serious mental health problems who are admitted to institutions have been particularly vulnerable to this extreme power imbalance (McCubbin and Cohen, 1996). Hollingshead and Redlich's (1958) classic study of social class and mental disorder found that people from the lowest social classes were most likely to be judged as having the most serious mental disorders (for example, schizophrenia) and to be admitted to public institutions where they receive custodial care and ECT (Electro Convulsive Therapy), whereas people from higher social classes tended to be diagnosed as less disabled and received psychotherapy. A more recent study by Harris, Hilton, and Rice (1993) found that many of the problems experienced by people admitted to a psychiatric hospital were economic in nature.

Clinical and counselling psychology have also been problematic for people from different ethnic, cultural, and racial groups. O'Nell (1998) has provided a case study of a Native American man who was diagnosed as having depression and alcoholism using DSM criteria. He notes, however, that the DSM formulation lacks sensitivity to the unique world view and cultural context of this man. Moreover, such a diagnosis would lead to a mainstream treatment approach that the client would likely not accept or benefit from, because it does not take into consideration his culture and world view of healing. The problem with this approach is that it is based on a universalist approach to psychological knowledge, when a more contextual approach is needed (Dudgeon, Garvey, and Pickett, 2000; James and Prilleltensky, in press). Finally, the issue of racism and how it contributes to the subjugation of ethnic, cultural, and racial groups is not a primary focus of traditional therapies.

In summary, we have highlighted serious problems with diagnosis and therapy/counselling that have been identified and resisted by different critical voices. These problems in the practice of clinical and counselling psychology occur in the larger context of their alliance with psychiatry and their practice under the auspices of managed care providers. With such strong ties to psychiatry, employers, and for-profit managed care corporations, clinical and counselling psychology have come to emphasize mainstream, western, capitalist values of individualism, instrumentality, conformity, and efficiency (cost-effectiveness) (Cushman and Gilford, 2000). We see clinical and counselling psychology, as traditionally practised, as firmly supporting the societal status quo. In the next section, we turn to a consideration of alternative approaches that challenge the status quo.

Shifting the paradigm in clinical and counselling psychology

In the light of these criticisms, it is quite evident to us that clinical and counselling psychology needs a shift in perspective for many so-called mental health problems.

Partnerships for practice

In Table 6.1, we provide an overview of the values, assumptions, and practices for critical clinical and counselling psychology.

Values

Beginning with values, traditional clinical and counselling psychology, as we have shown, is rooted in the individualistic values of personal growth, protection of health, and caring and compassion. (Under managed care there appears to have been a shift in emphasis away from personal growth and towards health protection). In ignoring the larger social and political context, traditional approaches often unintentionally blame the victims of oppression for their oppression. We argue that critical clinical and counselling psychology needs to attend also to relational and collective values to situate problems in their socio-political context. That is, clinical and counselling psychology needs to consider social ethics, as well as the ethics of individual practice (Prilleltensky, Rossiter and Walsh-Bowers 1996). Feminist ethical codes (Lerman, 1994) and the work of Prilleltensky, Rossiter and Walsh-Bowers (1996) provide more inclusive frameworks for clinical and counselling work to incorporate values of empowerment and social justice.

Assumptions

Moving to the assumptions of critical clinical and counselling psychology, there is an assumption that some clinical problems reflect oppression and have structural

Table 6.1 Critical clinical and counselling psychology: Partnerships for practice

Critical psychology tenets	Qualities of the content and process
Values	*Content:* The traditional clinical values of personal growth, protection of health, and caring and compassion need to be accompanied by attention to diversity, collaboration, support of community infrastructures, and social justice. *Process:* The therapeutic process needs to emphasize personal, relational, and collective values to avoid an individualistic bias that 'blames the victims.'
Assumptions	*Content:* Assume that the causes or consequences of some clinical problems reflect political and psychological oppression. Assume further that experiences of oppression will require structural as well as personal solutions. Clinicians practising from a critical perspective are aware that the language and practices of traditional helping approaches focus on social control, mask experiences of oppression and ignore the role of structural factors. *Process:* Focus on clinical problems with structural causes (for example, sexual abuse, violence against women, sexism, racism) or structural consequences (for example, labelling, stigma, and disenfranchisement of people with serious mental health problems). Identify and name structural causes (for example, sexism) and consequences (for example, discrimination). Help 'clients' to frame their problems in terms of structural causes, to engage in a critique of social, political, and economic arrangements, and to take personal and collective action to overcome victimization.
Practices	*Content:* Encourage 'clients' to pursue personal and collective empowerment. Be attuned to issues of victimization and abuse and demonstrate sensitivity towards gender, race, ethnicity, sexual orientation, and other 'differences' that are devalued by society. Participate in social movement activities and model for 'clients' how to become involved in social change. *Process:* Work in a highly participatory and collaborative manner with 'clients,' sharing power over the therapeutic process. Attend to internal experiences and concrete realities faced by 'clients'. Work with 'clients' in natural settings and accompany them, if they so desire, to obtain resources and support from other sources or to advocate for themselves. Encourage 'clients' to move beyond therapy to develop supportive social networks and to participate in self-help/mutual aid groups and other community organizations focused on mutual support and social change.

causes and/or consequences, which require structural solutions (Fook, 1993). Thus, critical clinical and counselling psychology pays particular attention to clinical problems that are rooted in unjust life conditions described in the previous section (for example, sexual abuse, violence). Clinicians and counsellors can help their clients to reframe their problems in terms of structural conditions and consequences. A critical clinical and counselling psychology also challenges the assumptions of traditional clinical approaches by shifting the discourse from a medical model language of diagnosis and therapy to a critical language of oppression and empowerment (for example, Gammell and Stoppard, 1999).

Brickman and colleagues (1982) have made an important distinction between individuals' attributions for the causes of problems and responsibility for solutions to problems that we believe is important for clinical and counselling interventions from a critical perspective. In our view, individuals are not responsible for the causes of their oppression; rather, structural causes and consequences are responsible. However, individuals must take some responsibility for their own process of personal empowerment, or else they will remain passive victims. By this point, we are underscoring the importance of the *agency* of the client. We are not suggesting that clients are responsible for solving social problems.

Many texts in which critical approaches are proposed begin with a discussion of whether it is possible to pursue critical approaches at the level of the individual (for example, Brown, 1994; Fook, 1993). These authors note that while critical approaches are most often associated with collective approaches to intervention, such as community development and social action, that critical approaches can also inform practice with individuals. Critical psychologists should not ignore the pain and suffering of individuals who are marginalized, but they must be careful to avoid promoting adjustment to unjust social conditions.

Practices

The values and assumptions of critical psychology have important implications for the practice of clinical and counselling psychology. The main goal of this approach is to catalyze a process of personal empowerment and liberation and collective empowerment and social change (Fook, 1993; McWhirter, 1994). This is the goal of feminist therapy (Brown, 1994; Chesler, 1990), culturally-sensitive therapy (James and Prilleltensky, in press; Paproski, 1997), and therapy and counselling that is sensitive to the issues and experience of gay, lesbian, and bisexual people (Perez, DeBord, and Bieschke, 2000; Schneider, 1991).

Moreover, critical clinical and counselling psychologists should engage with clients in a collaborative support process in which therapists and clients share power. Carl Rogers called his humanistic approach 'client-centred therapy.' He emphasized the importance of the client directing the therapeutic process, the personal qualities of the therapist, and the relationship between the therapist and client as critical for client growth and change. Research on client-centred therapy has shown the importance of Rogers' (1961) original formulation of therapist empathy, warmth, and genuineness as important factors for promoting client self-disclosure, affective experiencing, and personal growth (Truax and Carkhuff, 1967).

Similarly, research has demonstrated that the 'therapeutic alliance' or 'working alliance' is critical for positive client outcomes (Horvath, 1994; Horvath and Symonds, 1991), regardless of the specific therapeutic approach that is followed (Raue, Goldfried, and Barkham, 1997). For example, Webster-Stratton and Herbert (1993) have argued that the therapeutic process and relationship between therapist and clients are critical for behavioural family interventions for children with conduct problems, and Raue et al. (1997) have shown that the therapeutic alliance is important for cognitive-behavioural therapy for adults with depression. Moreover, basic attending and influencing skills, which have their roots in the work of Rogers, are now widely taught to lay or volunteer helpers, professional helpers, and even clients in marital and family therapy (Ivey et al., 1997). Relationship-building and power-sharing are key aspects of the practice of critical clinical and counselling psychology.

Critical alternatives

What are the key qualities of critical alternative approaches to therapy and counselling? First, critical approaches are attuned to the intersection of multiple sources of oppression. For example, in addition to confronting issues of sexism, feminist therapy has begun to address issues of racism, ableism, and homophobia (Brown, 1994; Herbert and McCannell, 1997; Ora Prilleltensky, 1996). As we noted earlier, critical approaches encourage disadvantaged clients to reframe their problems in terms of structural conditions and consequences. Practitioners of alternative approaches need to beware of the potential social control functions of therapy and counselling in case they further contribute to the client's powerlessness. Second, as we noted earlier, critical approaches emphasize that the client is in control of the therapeutic process. The essence of empowerment-oriented approaches is that clients share power with therapists and therapists are highly encouraging of client self-determination and collaboration in the therapeutic process (Doherty, 1995; Dunst and Trivette, 1989; McWhirter, 1994).

A third characteristic of critical alternatives is that they de-emphasize pathology and diagnoses and emphasize the strengths of the individual (Saleebey, 1992; Van Uchelen et al., 1997). Clients are not diagnostic entities, but whole persons with strengths and resources that can be used as a foundation for growth and change. Moreover, there is a focus on the potential of recovery from traumatic experiences (Herbert and McCannell, 1997; Paproski, 1997) and serious mental health problems (Anthony, 1993). Fourth, critical approaches to therapy and counselling have a systemic focus. Systemic therapies strive to change couple, family, and social support systems. However, unlike traditional systemic approaches, critical approaches emphasize the issue of power in systems. Thus, critical systemic approaches strive to equalize power within couple and family systems.

Fifth, critical therapists and counsellors should be willing to work with clients in natural settings. As Fook (1993) has argued, therapists and counsellors need to accompany and advocate with clients, if they are asked to do so, in situations that clients find stressful and oppressive. For example, empowerment approaches to support coordination for people with serious mental health problems involve support coordinators working side-by-side clients in the community and helping them to integrate into natural community settings and gain access to the basic resources of housing, income, employment, and education (Nelson, Prilleltensky and MacGillivary 2001). Tangible, 'hands on' support is necessary for some disadvantaged clients.

The summer after my first year in graduate school, I (Geoff) worked in a storefront crisis intervention and community health clinic in the downtown area of Winnipeg, Manitoba. Many of the people who walked in, phoned, or used the crisis services had serious mental health problems. One person that I befriended was a man who had been diagnosed with 'paranoid schizophrenia'. He told me that when he was hospitalized he was used in the psychiatry grand rounds as an example of this diagnosis. What I liked about this storefront clinic was that everyone treated him as a person rather than focusing on his mental health problems. I persuaded him to help with painting the interior of the clinic and later assisted him in getting a job.

Not everything went so smoothly for this man. Once he decided to go off his medication. As a non-medical model programme, the staff and I saw this decision as his choice, even though we doubted that it was a good choice. After being off the medication for a week or so, he became more paranoid, and his appearance was very disheveled. I remember visiting him at his apartment, with him telling me that he needed to go back on the medication. Another programme might have forced him to take his 'meds', but I think it was a better learning experience for him to make the decision to go off, and then back on, the medications himself. I learned about the importance of informal support and de-professionalized approaches to helping.

Finally, critical therapists and counsellors need to realize that many disadvantaged clients need to develop social support networks and friendships, and that therapy cannot be a substitute for such relationships. One promising alternative in this regard is self-help/mutual aid groups and organizations (Humphreys and Rappaport, 1994). Psychiatric survivors, women, and many other disadvantaged groups report tremendous feelings of solidarity in self-help organizations (for example, Chamberlin, 1990). While not typically called self-help, collective approaches to healing by aboriginal people certainly embody many of the values and strategies of self-help (Connors and Maidman, 2001; Herbert and McCannell, 1997), and the feminist therapy institute, for which Chesler (1990) has advocated, could also be construed as a self-help approach. We say more about self-help groups in Chapter 9.

New approaches to clinical and counselling use terms like 'empowerment' counselling or case management (Dunst and Trivette, 1989; McWhirter, 1994) and 'community counselling' (Lewis et al., 1998). There is some question about whether empowerment and community approaches to clinical and counselling are new and unique approaches, or whether they provide additional dimensions to existing approaches. For example, feminist approaches to therapy have been tied to psychoanalytic (Kaschak, 1992) and cognitive-behavioural or social learning approaches (Hurst and Genest, 1995; Pressman, 1989). At this point, we believe that uniquely critical approaches and critical perspectives which are integrated with existing therapeutic approaches are both possible. Below we provide one example of a uniquely critical approach and one example of how critical perspectives can be incorporated within existing approaches.

One particularly promising critical approach is narrative therapy (Freedman and Combs, 1996; Morgan, 2000; White and Epston, 1990). According to its proponents, dominant cultural narratives about some segments of the population are oppressive. The media and everyday discourse are saturated with derogatory narratives, such as 'the drunken Indian', 'castrating women', 'the dangerous "psycho" mental patient', 'people on welfare who are "ripping off the system"', and so on. The goal of narrative therapy is to expose these narratives, to encourage clients to critique and reject these scripts for themselves, and to assist clients in constructing their own stories that run counter to dominant cultural narratives. One technique that is used in narrative therapy is to 'externalize the problem' (White, 1989). Rather than internalizing the oppression of the dominant cultural narrative, clients are urged to separate themselves from particular problems. The role of the therapist is to collaborate with the client in attacking the problem.

Another important aspect of narrative therapy is its focus on the client's strengths. In 're-authoring their lives' or transforming their identities, clients need to take pride in themselves and their strengths (Rappaport, 1993). The language of 'gay pride', 'black and proud', or 'survivors' (of abuse, violence, psychiatry, and so on) is a key part of this identity transformation. Identity transformation is enhanced by making connections with people who have been through similar life experiences (Lord and Hutchison, 1993). As individuals move forward in their process of personal empowerment, clinicians and counsellors should provide information on self-help and social movement groups and organizations in which they can become involved. Taking such a step will not only move toward collective empowerment and action, but it can further solidify changes in individual identity. Rappaport (1993) has argued that self-help organizations provide alternative narratives that can be incorporated into the personal stories of individual members. Creative artistic expression (through painting, music, dance, drama) is another therapeutic means by which people who have been marginalized can demonstrate their strengths and transform their identities (Community Education Team, 1999; Thomas and Rappaport, 1996).

Critical perspectives have been integrated with couple and family therapy and counselling. The addition of critical perspectives deconstructs traditional notions of what constitutes a 'normal' marriage or family, beginning with the assumptions that fathers are essential to families (Silverstein and Auerbach, 1999) and that heterosexual relationships between a mother and father constitute the only valid forms of marriage and families (Kitzinger, 1997). Feminist approaches to couple therapy focus on the promotion of egalitarian couple relationships (Knudson-Martin and Mahoney, 1996; Rabin, 1994), and power inequalities between partners are examined in the assessment process (McCannell, 1986).

A major focus of feminist therapy with couples and families concerns an examination and treatment of abuse and violence by men against their partners and children. In contrast to traditional approaches that ignore power differences between men and women, feminist approaches utilize both individual (for men and women) therapy and couple/family therapy in which men are held responsible for the abuse that they have perpetrated (Pressman, 1989; Silovsky and Hembree-Kigin, 1994). Recently work has been conducted with adolescents (Community Education Team, 1999; Pitman, Wolfe, and Wekerle, 1998) and couples in the early stages of marriage (Holtzworth et al., 1995) to prevent male violence against women in intimate relationships.

Conclusion

In conclusion, we have pointed out problems with the traditional practice of clinical and counselling psychology. First, diagnosis is not a neat, clean, scientific process, as its proponents and managed care providers would have us believe (Larner, 2001). It is really quite a messy process with moral, political, and cultural dimensions. Use of the DSM highlights the diagnostic label rather than the unique experiences, life context, and wholeness of the individual who gets labelled. Labels can mask sources of oppression, such as violence or abuse, and they have created further oppression and stigma (for example, the labelling of gay, lesbian, and bisexual people). Second, therapy and counselling approaches can be problematic. Therapy can be used to try to adjust people to unjust social conditions and to mask or ignore sources of oppression that the client has experienced or is experiencing. Moreover, there is evidence of iatrogenic problems created by therapy and counselling (Morgan, 1983; Walsh, 1988). Third, we argued that the current context of managed care in mental health reinforces a clinical and counselling psychology approach that is likely to uphold rather than challenge the societal status quo.

In this chapter, we also identified the values, assumptions, and practices that we believe should guide critical approaches to clinical and counselling psychology. There is no one singular critical alternative that challenges the status quo, but rather several strands or voices of dissent from which alternative practices are emerging. People who have been oppressed because of their class, gender, ability, race/ethnicity, sexual orientation, or mental health have begun to construct approaches that are geared to personal and collective empowerment and social change. These approaches can be new and unique, as is the case with narrative therapy, or critical perspectives can be integrated within existing therapeutic approaches, such as feminist couple and family therapy. What therapists who use these approaches have in common is a critical mind-set about values, power, and systems. Critical perspectives challenge the hegemony of dominant cultural narratives, professional practices in psychology, and the current 'managed care' approach to mental health services. We therapists have much to learn from our 'clients' and their experiences of life and the role of psychological services in their lives.

In closing, we want to emphasize two points. First, critical alternative approaches are not for everyone. While mainstream mental health services have often not been helpful for disadvantaged client groups, we recognize that some clients might be better served by more mainstream approaches. All clients should have a range of services and supports from which to choose. Second, research is needed on critical approaches to therapy and counselling. While narrative therapy is conceptually and ideologically appealing, there is currently little research to support its effectiveness. Research on critical alternatives should not be limited to the randomized controlled trials that characterize positivist research on mainstream approaches. Qualitative methods, case studies, and process research are also needed. Finally, critical perspectives call into question what is a desirable therapeutic outcome. The traditional focus on symptoms, behaviours, and cognition as outcome domains is limited. A broader view of health and mental health for disadvantaged clients suggests that outcomes of self-determination and empowerment, community integration, and acquisition of valued resources are other vitally important outcome indicators for critical therapeutic approaches (Nelson, Lord, and Ochocka, 2001b).

7

Educational Settings: Learning a New School of Thought

Behavioural, emotional, and academic problems of children and youth in schools are widespread. An epidemiological study of children in Ontario found that 26 per cent of children experience one or more of these problems (Offord, Boyle, and Szatmari, 1987). Moreover, the researchers reported that at the very least 12 per cent 'have clinically important mental disorders, and at least half of them are deemed severely disordered or handicapped by their mental illness' (Offord, 1995:285). Similarly, the Institute of Medicine (IOM) (1994:487) reported that at least 12 per cent of children in the USA 'suffer from one or more mental disorders – including autism, attention deficit hyperactivity disorder, severe conduct disorder, depression, and alcohol and psychoactive substance abuse and dependence'. As critical psychologists, we are highly critical of such diagnostic labels and what gets counted as 'disorder'. At the same time, however, we know that individual misery and suffering of children is widespread.

Using this figure of a prevalence rate of 12 per cent for behavioural, emotional, and developmental 'disorders' in children around the world, Kramer (1992) argued that 'the total number of cases of mental disorders in children under 18 years of age would increase from 237.8 million in 1990 to 261.5 in the year 2000, an increase of ten per cent. In the more developed regions, the number of cases would increase from 37.8 million to 38.2 million' (Kramer, 1992:15). Moreover, early manifestations of behavioural, emotional, and academic problems can progress into major problems in adolescence, including substance abuse, pregnancy, AIDS, delinquency, depression, suicide, and school drop-out (Dryfoos, 1990).

Problems of this nature and scope manifest themselves in schools across the world, and school or educational psychologists are called upon by teachers, school administrators, and parents to assist with these issues. In this chapter, we propose some ways in which the values and concepts of critical psychology can inform how such problems are viewed and what can be done about them. We note that some English speaking countries like the UK use the term educational psychologists, whereas in North America the term school psychologist is more common. Here we will use the terms interchangeably.

We begin with a brief review and critique of the traditional practice of school psychology. Next, we consider partnership practices and alternative interventions that are potentially transformative and empowering. The fundamental question that the critical psychologist practising in the school must ask himself or herself is: 'Am I working for the school as an agent of social control, or am I working with disadvantaged children and families for personal, educational, and social change?'

Describing and critiquing the status quo

The traditional practice of school/educational psychology

For the most part, school psychologists are expected to deal with the problems presented by 'exceptional children'. Children with behavioural, emotional, or academic problems are assessed to determine what internal factors (for example, genetic, organic, cognitive) or micro-level factors (for example, family, peer group, teacher–child interaction) may be causing or contributing to the problem (Kaplan and Kaplan, 1985). A variety of assessment strategies are used to diagnose these problems, including intelligence tests, cognitive and achievement tests, personality tests, classroom observation, reports from teachers and parents, and interviews.

Once a diagnosis is arrived at, the school psychologist meets with the teacher(s) and parents to communicate the results and begin to develop a plan of action to remediate the problem. Intervention strategies include direct work with the child (remedial assistance, psychotherapy), classroom modifications (an alternative or modified academic curriculum, classroom behaviour management strategies, teaching assistance), intervention involving the parents (more routine parent–teacher communication, suggestions for parents to assist their child at home), placement (in a special education setting or mental health setting), and referral to another mental health or educational specialist for further assistance (family therapy, tutoring). The goal of assessment and intervention is ultimately to help the child better adjust to school, and the typical roles of the school psychologist are diagnostician, therapist, and referral agent.

Critical appraisal of school psychology

Many writers have been critical of the traditional practice of school psychology (for example, Nelson, 1983; Prilleltensky, 1994; Sarason, 1982). In adopting a narrow, medical model approach to the practice of psychology in the schools, school psychologists, no matter how well intentioned, 'blame the victims,' typically the child and the family, for problems in living that the child experiences in school. Diagnostic labels stigmatize the child and emphasize how he or she is different from other students, and these labels tend to be 'sticky,' following the child as he or she moves through the educational system. Moreover, these labels can potentially create negative 'self-fulfilling prophecies' of how the child will behave or achieve. Segregated services further remove children from the mainstream of the school and peer relationships. Moreover, it is children from the lowest social classes who are at greatest risk for behavioural, emotional, and academic problems and who are over-represented in special education programmes (Brooks-Gunn, Duncan, and Britto, 1999).

Another problem with this medical model approach is that there is great power imbalance between the professional psychologist and the students and his or her parents. The psychologist speaks with the voice of authority, backed up with psychological test results, while the voice of the child is rarely heard. Parents may be permitted input into decision-making, but seldom do they have control over decisions that affect their child. The expertise of the parent(s) and child(ren) and their ideas for problem-solving are typically minimized. Sometimes the not-so-hidden agenda of the school is to remove the child from his or her regular classroom, as opposed to helping the child.

One other major problem with the medical model approach is that the potential contributing role of the school system or larger external systems are never called into question. In adopting person-centred and micro-system analyses of the problems and intervention strategies, the school system is vindicated (Prilleltensky, 1994). Schools are a major social institution that reflect the values of the dominant culture. As we noted in Chapter 3, some proponents of critical pedagogy have argued that schools reproduce and perpetuate existing power inequalities related to class, gender, and race (Apple, 1982; Giroux, 1988; McLaren, 1995). Given the cherished western values of individualism and competition, one can argue that schools are 'rigged' to maintain inequalities. The purpose of grading practices, streaming, and the diagnosis and treatment of children with exceptional problems is to separate the 'winners' from the 'losers' in North American society. What can school psychologists who do not buy into this agenda do to promote transformative change? In the next section, we consider a variety of alternative ways of thinking and practising.

Shifting the paradigm in school/educational psychology

If we could totally reconstruct educational psychology from a critical perspective, what might it look like? Just beginning to dream about this kind of transformative change is liberating. But once we get past our fantasies of packing up our testing kits and storing them away, what might school psychologists actually do to respond to the suffering of children and families? Critical school psychologists need to move beyond critique to action to change schools. But psychologist Seymour Sarason (1982, 1990, 1996), who has written extensively about schools based on his experiences and observations, has asserted that schools are relatively 'intractable'. That is, schools are very hard to change. Sarason (1996) argues that the reason reforms have typically not been successful is that they do not address issues of power imbalance.

> Reform efforts have left untouched existing power relationships within the classroom, among layers of the school system's hierarchy, between the schools and the university where educators are selected and prepared, and between school and parents-community . . . Changing power relationships is a necessary (but not sufficient) condition for

establishing contexts of productive learning for students and teacher, not only students. Teachers cannot create and sustain contexts of productive learning for students if those contexts do not exist for teachers (Sarason, 1996:253–4).

In this section, we consider promising strategies for untracking this intractability.

Partnerships for practice

In Table 7.1, we provide an overview of the values, assumptions, and practices for critical psychology partnerships in the schools.

Values

Traditionally, schools and school psychology emphasize the values of individualism, competition, and unequal distribution of resources (schools and students in

Table 7.1 Critical psychology in schools: Partnerships for practice

Critical psychology tenets	Qualities of the content and process
Values	*Content:* With students, staff, teachers, and parents, develop a vision and values for each school and the school board that attends to personal, relational and collective well-being. Critique traditional values of individualism, competition, power hierarchies, and unjust allocation of resources. Supportive relationships and structures enable students, staff, teachers, and parents to feel good about themselves, their relationships, and their school.
	Process: Ask students, staff, teachers, and parents what they require to meet their own personal and relational needs and what they can do to help others within the organization to meet their own individual and collective needs. This process acknowledges that all members of a school community have personal needs and are expected to contribute to the collective well-being at the same time.
Assumptions	*Content:* Assume that many problems that students experience are structural in nature and will require structural solutions. Also, assume that past practices and tradition are a major obstacle to overcome in innovation and change emphasizing structural solutions based on an alternative value system.
	Process: Work with students, staff, teachers, and parents to reframe problems, emphasizing students and families in their larger social and political context. Develop mutual support strategies to assist in making this personal paradigm shift to emphasize risk-taking, active participation, and collaboration among stakeholder groups.
Practices	*Content:* Shift from reactive, individualistic practices which focus on diagnosis and labelling of students and 'treating' their deficits towards preventive and health promotion activities, school change, community development, and social change.
	Process: Work in a highly participatory and collaborative manner with students, staff, teachers, and parents to implement new practices in schools and the community. The importance of policies and structures to support this innovation cannot be over emphasized.

the most advantaged communities have the best resources). Alternatively, a critical psychology perspective is based on an alternative value framework that we have elaborated throughout this book.

Elsewhere, we have outlined the key steps in a partnership approach for working with stakeholders in schools and the community in the development of alternative interventions (Nelson, Amio et al., 2000). In line with the values of self-determination, collaboration, and democratic participation, we believe that disadvantaged people, including parents and youth, must be front and centre in partnerships for school programmes. Teachers, school administrators, and other service-providers are also key stakeholders who should play an active role in the partnership process. Moreover, parents and youth from disadvantaged circumstances must have a strong voice in the partnership. This means that critical school psychologists, teachers, and other professionals must create a climate that is welcoming and supportive for the participation of disadvantaged people. Barriers to the participation of stakeholders (for example, the timing of meetings, the costs of child care) need to be identified and strategies to reduce them need to be implemented (see Nelson, Pancer et al., under review).

The participation of different stakeholders in schools is essential for developing a vision and values that guide the particular intervention that is planned. Individual stakeholders need to identify personal, relational, and collective values that are important to their well-being as well as to that of others who will participate in the intervention. But it is not enough to have the values listed. Working principles must be developed to ensure that the values are put into practice in the partnership process. Procedures for decision-making and conflict resolution that are consistent with identified values need to be put into place (Nelson, Lord, and Ochocka, 2001a, b).

Assumptions

Professionals who work in schools are guided by the assumptions that problems are the exception to the norm; that such problems are caused by individual or micro-systemic factors; that professionals are the 'experts' in solving problems; and that schools are basically good. In contrast, a critical perspective suggests that problems experienced by students in schools are widespread; that such problems often result from a number of factors, including structural arrangements; that all stakeholders, including the most disadvantaged people, have strengths and expertise; and that schools are often a big part of the problem for teachers and students. For these reasons, the participation of different stakeholders in schools is essential for formulating alternative interventions.

Critical school psychologists should encourage stakeholders to dream about the type of changes that they would like. As Sarason (1982) has observed, people who work in schools are often prisoners of traditional practices and seldom question basic assumptions about whether schools, as they are currently arranged, are the best places for learning to occur. We believe that stakeholders need to question the assumptions upon which schools are deeply embedded before they can consider critical alternative interventions. One place to start is questioning the place of professional expertise. Professionals need to listen to disadvantaged people, appreciate their strengths, and benefit from their experiential knowledge. The pooling of knowledge and experience of the different stakeholders is an important place to start in designing any school intervention (Nelson *et al.*, 2000).

Practices

Reframing the problem in school intervention means a shift from reactive, individualistic practices which focus on diagnosis and labelling of students and 'treating' their deficits towards preventive and health promotion activities, school change, community development, and social change. The various stakeholders need to plan alternative interventions collaboratively. This includes defining the dimensions of the problem, planning the intervention, and evaluating the intervention (Nelson *et al.*, 2000). This collaborative approach encourages innovation and builds ownership for the intervention (Peirson and Prilleltensky, 1994; Prilleltensky, Peirson, and Nelson, 1997). In a way, planning the intervention becomes an important intervention in and of itself, because of the relationships that develop among the different stakeholders.

When I (Geoff) was first hired as an Assistant Professor at Wilfrid Laurier University, the Community Psychology programme proposed a resource exchange programme with what was then called the Waterloo County Board of Education. The basic idea was that the Chief Psychologist of the school board and I would exchange some duties; no monetary arrangement was involved. My exchange partner taught one course per term that I would normally be required to teach, and I worked a day and a half per week with two schools (an elementary school and a middle school) in one community. While it was assumed that I would do the typical duties of a school psychologist, such as individual assessment and consultation, one of the goals of the exchange was to work at a broader level with the schools and community to address some of the issues that the community was experiencing. We also wanted to have a research and student training component to our activities in this community.

Fortunately for me, the behavioural consultant and special education departments of the school board de-emphasized individual assessment and emphasized consultation and programme development. While I was involved in some of these individual-level activities, much of my time was devoted to other activities in the school and community. Both schools were located in a low-income neighbourhood with public housing. There were numerous referrals from teachers regarding children with emotional and behavioural problems. In addition to consulting with teachers about classroom management, I developed a social skills training programme for children, using university students as the trainers. A graduate student and I then worked with teachers to implement this programme for all children in their classrooms, so that the programme was more inclusive and less stigmatizing. The guidance counsellor from one of the schools and I also developed a parent education programme for parents in the community.

But many of the problems had their origins in the community. Residents reported vandalism by teenagers, who 'hung out' on the streets or a convenience store with nothing to do. There was also a senior citizens' complex in the neighbourhood. Youth harassment of seniors and vandalism of the complex led to strained relationships between these two groups. Community-level solutions were necessary to address these problems and build the capacity of the neighbourhood. The principals from the two schools (both of whom lived in the neighbourhood), two representatives from the Mennonite church in the community, community psychology faculty, and a couple of neighbourhood residents began a community development process, which led to the creation of a neighbourhood association and, eventually, a community centre. Parents and youth were asked what they would like to see in the community and programmes were developed based on identified needs. Parents formed a board for the association and different funding sources were secured. While the project had its 'ups and downs' with regard to funding in its early years, it is now a thriving neighbourhood association. The latest addition to the association is a community health centre with health promotion activities and primary care located in and run by the neighbourhood. The project has become a model for similar initiatives in the region.

One other programme that was developed involved an exchange between the seniors' centre and the middle-school. Middle-school students were recruited to befriend seniors. Students assisted seniors by reading to them (if their vision was impaired), helping them to walk, writing letters for them, and playing games with them. Seniors also shared some of their interests and talents with students. Initially, the seniors' centre was very wary about the idea of an exchange programme, but with experience, young and old people came together to bridge differences and create community.

Many graduate students from Laurier became involved in this project through work placement, thesis research, and sometimes paid employment. Several research projects were undertaken to examine the impacts of the different programmes that were generated by community members. What started out as a school exchange broadened into psychology working in partnership with low-income community members and other service-providers to improve the entire neighbourhood. One of the main lessons I learned from being the principal exchange person from the university was that school psychology can move beyond the boundaries of individual assessment and intervention to community development and prevention.

Critical alternatives

In this section, we highlight different intervention approaches that can be used by critical educational psychologists. The success of implementing any of the interventions that we describe in this section is predicated on the ability of the school psychologists to mobilize different stakeholders and create partnerships for change (Nelson *et al.*, 2000). We begin this section with a discussion of interventions that focus on individual students.

Interventions that focus on individual students

These interventions tend to emphasize personal or individual values, such as self-determination, protection of health, and caring and compassion. What distinguishes this approach is its focus on the *prevention* of behavioural, emotional, and academic problems and the promotion of health and competence (Nelson, Prilleltensky, and Peters, 1999). In contrast to traditional practices that are reactive and focus on those students who have already manifested some problem at school, prevention/promotion approaches have a population-wide or school-wide focus on children who are not manifesting problems. It is a more inclusive, less stigmatizing approach that avoids labelling individual children.

To complement schools' emphases on academic and cognitive learning, social decision-making, social problem-solving, and social and life skills training are some of the approaches that have been used to promote students' social and emotional learning (Elias and Tobias, 1996). Formalized curricula have been developed for these programmes and teachers have been trained to use these approaches in their classrooms. Social problem-solving involves a series of steps that are taught to pre-school, primary, elementary, or middle-school students to help them cope with and resolve interpersonal conflicts. These steps include defining the problem and identifying feelings, formulating a goal of what the student wants, stopping and thinking before acting, thinking of several possible solutions, anticipating the consequences of those solutions, and choosing a solution and trying it out. There is a great deal of literature demonstrating that students can learn these problem-solving skills and some research which has also found positive impacts on students' social behaviour and social adjustment (Weissberg and Elias, 1993). These programmes clearly reflect the value of children's self-determination in their emphasis on problem-solving and decision-making.

While such programmes tend to focus on individual students, there has always been an emphasis on the role of the teacher. In their original work on problem-solving, Shure and Spivack (1988) highlighted the importance of teachers 'dialoguing' with their students about interpersonal conflicts as they occur. The learning that takes place through the standardized curriculum is applied and practised in real-life situations in the classroom and the school. More recently, programmes with primary-elementary-school and high-school students have included a focus on changing the classroom climate and norms, training parents, changing school norms and discipline policies, and providing service-learning opportunities for students in the school and the community (Elias and Tobias, 1996; Hawkins, Catalano, and Associates, 1992; Peters, 1990). Moreover, such programmes have evolved from single-focus, time-limited interventions to multi-focused programmes which address a number of different life issues faced by students from grades K to 12 (ages 5 to 17) (Graczyk *et al.*, 2000; Weissberg and Elias, 1993). Such efforts aim to humanize classrooms and schools.

A number of programmes have also been designed to promote health or prevent specific problems, such as suicide or substance abuse. Elias (1995) has argued that many of these programmes are offered as short-term, discrete, disconnected pieces without any firm theoretical or empirical foundation. He suggests that programmes designed to protect and promote health should be based on a common theoretical framework. For example, the social problem-solving or social decision-making approaches described earlier can be applied to a variety of health-related issues.

In support of Elias' (1995) position, Botvin *et al.* (1990) developed a programme for students in grades 7 to 9 (ages 11–14) that consists of two general skills training components (personal skills and social skills) and a problem-specific training component for drug abuse. The personal skills component focuses on decision-making and problem-solving, identifying and resisting media influences, and self-control skills for coping with anxiety, anger, and frustration, while the social skills component deals with communication, assertiveness, dating relationships, and effective social interaction and conversation. The substance abuse specific component deals with knowledge and attitudes concerning substance use and skills for resisting influences from the media and peers regarding substance use. Specific teacher and student curriculum materials and exercises have been developed for the programme. A large-scale prevention study involving 6000 grade 7 (ages 11–12) students from 56 schools in New York State randomly assigned whole schools to experimental groups, which received this Life Skills Training programme, or control groups (Botvin *et al.*, 1990). Students in the programme showed significantly less smoking, marijuana use, and problem drinking than control students at the end of Grade 9 (ages 13–14), significantly less marijuana use and excessive drinking at the end of Grade 10 (ages 14–15), and less smoking, heavy drinking, or marijuana use at the end of Grade 12 (ages 16–17). Consistent with the argument of Elias (1995), Botvin, Schinke, and Orlandi (1995) have suggested that the strategies found to be effective in preventing substance abuse can be applied to the prevention of AIDS (acquired immune deficiency syndrome), STDs (sexually transmitted diseases), and unwanted pregnancy.

Hawkins, Catalano, and colleagues (1992) have reported a similar approach, which also includes a focus on changing the norms of classrooms and families that are conducive to refraining from substance use. The results of their research not only shows positive preventive impacts on the students, but also positive changes in the families and schools. Other research on substance abuse prevention has found that interactive programmes are more effective than strictly information-oriented programmes (Tobler and Stratton, 1997). From our perspective, programmes to prevent substance could go even further. For example, Prilleltensky, Nelson, and Sanchez Valdes (2000) described a smoking prevention programme which included critical consciousness-raising about the role of tobacco companies in promoting addiction. A social action component against tobacco companies encouraged children to speak out against these companies.

To promote the value of caring and compassion, a variety of mentoring and support interventions have been developed for students in schools (Barrera and Prelow, 2000). Mentoring programmes involving adults or older students as mentors to younger students have been used in and outside of school to increase the social support of children and adolescents (Barrera and Prelow, 2000). Another intervention approach related to the value of caring and compassion is the implementation of school-based support groups. Such groups typically focus on a concern or experience that some students have in common, such as living with a parent with alcoholism, experiencing the death of a parent or the divorce of one's parents. Irwin Sandler and colleagues have developed and evaluated a number of school-based support programmes for children facing these issues and reported positive impacts of such programmes (for example, Wyman *et al.*, 2000).

While the preceding prevention programmes are very important, critical school psychologists cannot and should not ignore children and families who are already experiencing difficulty (Prilleltensky, 1994:159–60). As we noted in Chapter 6, it is important that clinical or reactive (after the problem has developed) methods for such children and families adopt a systemic perspective. School psychologists must examine micro-systems, as the family and classroom, which may be contributing to such problems, and work collaboratively with parents and teachers to develop systemic interventions to address the problems (Dunst, Trivette, and Deal, 1988). MacLeod and Nelson (2000) found that the degree to which reactive family interventions focus on family strengths and encourage parent participation are associated with better outcomes than professionally-driven, expert approaches. Moreover, the contribution of larger systemic influences needs to be examined to place the 'problem' in context.

The interventions that we have described in this section cannot be developed in a vacuum. Most of these successful individual-level programmes have been well-resourced and have received administrative support. Time for teacher and parent training and support is critical. Programmes that teachers perceive to be an 'add-on' have little chance of working. Resources need to be built in to ensure the success of these interventions (Peirson and Prilleltensky, 1994).

Interventions that focus on the classroom and school

While the preceding individual-level interventions touch on the classroom and the school, a number of different school intervention strategies focus more explicitly on changing classroom and school environments. Such interventions tend to emphasize the relational values of collaboration, democratic participation, and human diversity. The goal of such intervention is promoting structural change within schools.

Organization development (OD) is one approach that seeks to change power relationships in schools. OD strives to improve human relations through cooperative and team approaches to decision-making and problem-solving. The pioneering work of Richard Schmuck and colleagues (Schmuck, Runkel, and Langmeyer, 1969) demonstrated that organization development interventions can improve school climate and promote innovation. Another important finding from research on OD in schools is that the power between principals and teachers becomes more equalized through such interventions (Bartunek and Keys, 1982). While original applications of OD typically did not involve students, teachers were observed to utilize OD practices in their classrooms with students, leading to greater student participation and satisfaction (Schmuck et al., 1969). More recent OD interventions have involved students as partners in the change process (Cherniss *et al.*, 1982; Prilleltensky, Peirson, and Nelson, 1997).

Over the past two decades, there have been many efforts at transforming educational and school environments (Fullan and Stiegelbauer, 1991; Oxley, 2000). Overall, reform is typically directed at changing *traditional* school structures (large, bureaucratic, hierarchies), processes (centralized and top-down decision-making), and goals (which emphasize student achievement) towards *alternative* structures (smaller, less rigid, more horizontal structures), processes (collaboration, shared decision-making, mentoring guidance, active learning, participation), and goals (which focus on multiple skills and intelligences, curiosity, critical thinking, and problem-solving, and social, emotional, and health outcomes) (Oxley, 2000). A number of different strategies have been used to make this shift.

One strategy is to create a 'school within a school'. For example, Felner and Adan (1988) noted the difficulties that many students experience in making the transition from primary or middle-school to high school and strived to make a structural change in high schools so that they would provide more support to entering students. The school was reorganized so that grade 9 (ages 13–14) students remained with the same group of students in the same part of the building for most of the day; they had a small group of teachers; and the home-room teachers handled many of the guidance-related issues for these students. Effectively this intervention created a smaller, more supportive environment within the context of a larger, more impersonal school. Compared with students in a control group, the students who participated in this new arrangement reported more positive attitudes towards school, had fewer absences, and had better marks.

School-wide and classroom-based anti-bullying and violence prevention programmes are another example of a structural change within schools that is very much needed to stem the rising tide of violence in schools. Emphasizing skills in conflict resolution, encouraging peers to speak and act against violence and bullying, are all important for violence prevention (Pepler *et al.*, 1995). But preventing violence in schools is an uphill battle when we live in societies that condone and glorify violence. We agree with Gil (1996) who has argued that violence prevention programmes will have limited success unless they are accompanied by a transformation in social values and social policies that strive to promote equality. Intervention is also needed at the community level, as many youth are exposed to violence in their homes and community settings other than schools.

While OD and school transformation projects are important ways of improving schools, another approach to school change is the creation of alternative schools (Cherniss and Deegan, 2000). Alternative schools are meant to be fundamentally different from mainstream schools in their structures, processes, and goals. A more flexible, individualized approach to education is designed to improve the 'fit' between students and school. For example, Trickett and colleagues (Gruber and Trickett, 1987; Trickett *et al.*, 1985) have examined the processes and outcomes of an alternative high school in a low-income community. While the project experienced difficulties in shifting power from teachers to parents and students, positive outcomes were reported for classroom environments and the social and academic development of the students.

Regarding the value of diversity, Bond (1999) has discussed the implications of gender, race, and class for organizations. It is quite disappointing that so little research has been devoted to interventions designed to make schools more inclusive and friendly environments for people from diverse backgrounds. While there are few noteworthy examples, much more attention needs to be devoted to promoting the value of diversity in schools.

One area where there has been some progress is with students with disabilities and special needs. In the past, schools were far from welcoming to students with special needs and the wishes of their parents to see them supported in mainstream education. Schools excluded students with developmental disabilities, who were relegated to distant institutional settings, segregated schools, or special classes. With the growth of the disability rights movement and pressure from parents, legislation has been enacted in many jurisdictions to ensure that students with disabilities are provided with an education appropriate to their needs in their home communities (Sarason, 1984). While there have been many problems with the implementation of such policies, this legislation has been a step forward in promoting the inclusion of students with disabilities. Critical psychologists can play a proactive role by working with parents and disability organizations to promote inclusion and community within schools.

To combat sexism, psychologists have developed programmes that strive to promote egalitarian relationships between men and women students and prevent violence against women. For example, Wolfe, Wekerle, and Scott (1996) have developed and implemented a successful programme to prevent violence against women in high schools. Bond (1995) has made suggestions about how sexual harassment of women can be prevented through the creation of empowering organizational climates. While most of the literature on social problem-solving in schools has not focused on gender, Turner, Norman, and Zunz (1995) have noted risk factors and protective mechanisms that are unique to girls and have made suggestions for gender-specific programming for girls.

To prevent racism, Mukherjee (1992) has proposed a number of different strategies to transform schools. Training and hiring teachers from minority backgrounds, including information about the history and culture of minorities in the curriculum, and developing anti-racist school board policies are some of the suggestions that he has made. The Young Warriors programme for black male students that was briefly described in Chapter 3 is another example of an intervention that strengthens diversity and pride of an oppressed and stereotyped group (Watts, Griffith, and Abdul-Adil, 1999).

There is a glaring gap in the literature on making schools more welcoming and safe places for gay, lesbian, and bisexual students. As issues of sexuality begin to emerge in middle-school and high school, this can be a particularly stressful period for gay, lesbian, and bisexual students. These young adults must struggle with their identities in the context of a homophobic family, peer group, school, and society. Critical school psychologists need to collaborate with schools and members of the gay and lesbian community to address problems faced by gay, lesbian, and bisexual youth and to transform schools into more inclusive settings for such youth (Garnets and D'Augelli, 1994).

Interventions that focus on the community and society

While individual and organizational change strategies are important, such strategies do not address larger systemic influences on the problems that children and families experience. Since disadvantaged communities and socioeconomic inequality play a key role in educational 'success' (broadly defined), social and community interventions are necessary.

Children who live in low-income communities do not enter school with the same preparation and advantages that are enjoyed by children from middle- and upper-class communities. The playing field at school is not level. So the question becomes, what can schools and communities do to provide children from low-income backgrounds with a greater advantage and chance of 'success' in school and in life? In the USA, Head Start is a major federal policy initiative that began in the 1960s and which continues today. Head Start is a pre-school education programme for children from low-income communities. While the programme has been criticized as being insufficient in both time and scope to address the problems faced by children from low-income families, there is evidence that these programmes do have many long-term positive impacts (McLoyd, 1998; Schweinhart, and Weikhart, 1989). Moreover, efforts to extend educational assistance into the child's early school years (Project Follow-Through) have found more positive impacts than pre-school experience alone (McLoyd, 1998).

But pre-school education is no panacea for the problems of poverty and racism (Wiley and Rappaport, 2000). Prilleltensky and Nelson (2000) have recently reviewed interventions for families that reflect collectivist values. At the community level, there is a need to develop strong community infrastructures that address the needs of low-income families. One valuable invention at this level is that of 'full-service schools' (Dryfoos, 1994). Such schools entail a school–community partnership which brings a range of family support services, pre-school education and childcare, community development, and job training into schools that meet the multiple needs of children and families. As recent reviews have shown, multi-component programmes have been found to have both positive short-term and long-term impacts on children and families (MacLeod and Nelson, 2000; Prilleltensky and Nelson, 2000).

While the very language of 'full-service schools' suggests an intimidating bureaucracy, some of these multi-component programmes are driven by parents and community members. For example, the Yale-New Haven project, which involves two elementary schools in black, low-income neighbourhoods, is based on four key elements: '(a) a representative governance and management group, (b) a parent participation program and group, (c) a mental health program and team, and (d) an academic (curriculum and staff development) program' (Comer, 1985:155). A three-year longitudinal evaluation of this project found significant improvement on measures of school achievement and social competence for children participating in the intervention compared with children in control schools (Cauce, Comer, and Schwartz, 1987). In Canada, the 'Better Beginnings, Better Futures' initiative in Ontario is based on a community development philosophy in which low-income parents have control over the direction and management of the project (Pancer, 1994; Peters, 1994).

As Prilleltensky and Nelson (1997, 2000) have argued, there is a need to go beyond community interventions to social interventions that strive to achieve distributive justice. In North America, few citizens are aware of the impacts of global capitalism, and government policies which support it, in creating further socioeconomic inequality within countries and between 'have' and 'have-not' countries' (Macedo, 1994). Multinational corporations are engaging in a full-scale frontal assault on health, education, and social policies across the world (Barlow and Campbell, 1995). The needs of low-income families are neglected in neo-liberal, Social Darwinist, 'blame-the-victim' policies that are driven by a corporate agenda, including welfare 'reform' (reduction), mandatory drug testing of people receiving social assistance, and other punitive measures.

Education, consciousness-raising, and advocacy are sorely needed to exert counter-control against this worldwide shift to the political right. While difficult to achieve in the context of government-funded programmes, there are some hopeful examples of education and advocacy. In the 'Better Beginnings' project, some of the most actively involved women leaders and youth have learned valuable lessons about how government works and the need for advocacy. In the face of having their projects de-funded after the demonstration period, parents, youth, and residents organized advocacy activities which were instrumental in securing ongoing funding for this project.

Advocates for social change need to become aware of inequalities of power and resources and the forces that drive them at an early stage. One avenue that has yet to be explored involves education of high-school youth in global issues and social change. Partnerships with volunteer, non-profit social change organizations can be pursued for students in co-op programmes, and consultation with high-school history and politics teachers regarding such initiatives could potentially harness youth energy and talents towards critical analysis and social change, rather than consumption of mass media and commercial products. There is a great potential for social activism of youth, if opportunities can be created for education, consciousness-raising, and participation (Pancer and Pratt, 1999).

Conclusion

In conclusion, our goal for this chapter was to provide direction for critical school psychologists. After briefly highlighting some of the well-known and understood problems associated with the traditional 'gatekeeper' role of the school psychologist, we presented a highly action-oriented approach for critical school psychologists to promote child and family well-being, to create school change, to develop strong community infrastructures for children and families, and to agitate for social change. This approach addresses different levels of analysis and different values. To shift the school psychology paradigm will require a shift in roles for psychologists from diagnostician, therapist, consultant, and referral agent to prevention/promotion programme planner, organization developer and systems-change agent, and community collaborator, educator, and activist. The approaches that we have presented are quite idealistic and the barriers to moving in this direction are significant (Sarason, 1990). The challenge for critical school psychologists is to develop partnerships with different stakeholders so that some of these ideas (and other ideas for social change in schools) can be translated into action. In this regard, we outlined some of the key tasks and issues involved in the creation and implementation of such partnerships.

8

Health Settings: Fighting Inequality to Enhance Well-being

Health is central to well-being. It is a precursor as well as a consequence of well-being. We conceptualize well-being in broad terms that include psychological and physical health. As previously defined in the book, well-being is a satisfactory state of affairs, brought about by the combined presence of values, resources, programmes and policies. Each one of these four components contributes to health. Indeed, health is one of the central values guiding our work. We regard health as an intrinsic as well as an extrinsic value. It has merit on its own accord, but it is also instrumental in bringing about self-determination, personal growth, and opportunities in life.

Resources, the second component of overall well-being, are also crucial for health. Psychological and material resources, such as social support and economic security, are meaningful correlates of health (Marmot and Wilkinson, 1999; Taylor, 1995). Social programmes such as support for single parents and for the unemployed, as well as policies for universal health care are pivotal in the attainment and maintenance of healthy lives (Wilkinson, 1996).

The way the World Health Organisation (WHO) defines health is reminiscent of our notion of well-being. According to the WHO, health is more than the absence of illness; it comprises positive physical and emotional features that enable individuals and groups to pursue their goals in a context of equality and justice (Tones, 1996). We resonate with this inclusive definition, for it encompasses values of self-determination, caring and compassion, personal growth, democracy, equality and justice.

Health can be promoted, maintained, and restored in micro (for example, close personal relations, family), meso (for example, school, work), and macro spheres (for example, community, society). From a critical psychology perspective, each one of these contexts is suffused with power differentials that privilege the powerful and discriminate against the weak (Petersen, 1994). Freund and McGuire (1999) claim that power is a strong determinant of health. In their view, there is a strong connection between the two, illustrated by

the power of workers over their work pace; the power of people to control the quality of their physical environments; the power of various groups or societies to shape

106

health policy or to deliver what they consider healing; the power of people of different statuses to control, receive, and understand information vital to their well-being; and the power of the mass media to shape ideas about food and fitness (Freund and McGuire, 1999:7).

Power is cardinal to the entire enterprise of critical psychology. As discussed in Part I of the book, power is instrumental in the promotion of well-being, in resisting oppression and in striving for liberation. For critical psychologists, a special challenge is to focus on the health of disadvantaged groups such as children, low-income women, gays, lesbians, people with disabilities, and citizens in developing countries. Following a critique of existing practices in health psychology, we explore interventions that link inequality with health. We will see that economic, political, and psychological inequality have deleterious effects on the health of the disadvantaged.

Describing and critiquing the status quo

The traditional practice of health psychology

Psychologists working in health settings such as hospitals and clinics, or interested in health promotion, have come to be known as health psychologists. The field of health psychology has gained much recognition within psychology and allied health professions in the last 25 years. It is a growing field with a few journals, international conferences, divisions or committees in the major psychological associations, and extensive literature. A sign of growth is perhaps the existence of a critical health psychology movement within the field (see Murray and Chamberlain, 1999; Stainton-Rogers, 1996, and special issue of *Journal of Health Psychology*, 2000). Taylor offers a useful definition of the field of health psychology. According to her

> Health psychology is the field within psychology devoted to understanding psychological influences on how people stay healthy, why they become ill, and how they respond when they do get ill. Health psychologists both study such issues and promote interventions to help people stay well or get over illness (Taylor, 1995:3).

The services offered by health psychologists include coping with physical illness, pain management, psychosocial rehabilitation after accidents, promotion of healthier lifestyles, support groups for sufferers of chronic disease, and the like. These activities fall into two broad categories: clinical services in medical settings (Belar and Deardorff, 1996; Bennett, 2000), and health promotion programmes in community settings (Bennett and Murphy, 1997).

In working with individuals, health psychologists are expected to help with a variety of issues, ranging from reactive to proactive interventions. Reactive interventions with indicated populations address problems with sufferers of illness. An example of such intervention is pain management. Proactive interventions with high-risk populations are meant to prevent deterioration likely to occur due to the vulnerable status of group members. Diet and exercise programmes for overweight individuals is an example of this type of work. Proactive universal interventions, in turn, address the needs of people who are not known to be at risk. Instruction guides for use of condoms to prevent HIV (human immuno-deficiency virus) illustrates the last type of intervention (Nelson, Prilleltensky, and Peters, 1999; Winett, 1995).

Health psychologists often engage in reactive interventions in medical settings. Services offered directly to patients or through consultation with other profes-sionals include coping with acute or chronic pain, compliance with medical treatments, training to overcome physical limitations after trauma, preparation for surgery and stressful medical procedures, and psychosocial rehabilitation (Belar and Deardorff, 1995; Bennett, 2000).

Proactive interventions occur usually in worksites, community health centres or educational institutions. They tend to take the form of programmes to stop smok-ing or drinking or to improve diet. Work with groups and organizations can also be reactive or proactive. Health psychologists can work with patients in support groups or exercise programmes, and they can assist worksites to improve the social climate and reduce stress and conflict. Many health psychologists assist organizations to improve the health of their employees through lifestyle changes and exercise. Psychologists participate in health-promotion campaigns through research, education, and intervention. They may facilitate the dissemination of information through regional health authorities or contribute to the development of public policy. Many of the interventions described in the chapter dealing with community settings apply here as well, as community psychologists are involved in the pursuit of physical and mental health primarily at this level.

Critical appraisal of psychology in health settings

Institutional settings like hospitals prescribe and perpetuate roles for all the players within it. The sick role of the patient diminishes his or her power and self-determination, whereas the expert role of physicians increases their ability to make decisions for others. In such a hierarchical place, all the actors are at risk: some, like patients and low-status workers, for reduced ability to control their lives and environments; others, like high-status professionals, for abusing power and engaging in patronizing behaviour. The dominance of the medical profession, for instance, 'is expressed and reinforced through the micro level of medical encounters. In the hospital, the "consultant's round" has long been an expression of power over medical students, nurses, and patients' (Hardey, 1998:83–4).

In the interaction between patients and medical professionals, the power (and occasional arrogance) of the latter diminishes the self-determination of the former in multiple ways. First, by prescribing treatments without consulting with patients. Second, by failing to communicate in clear language the nature of the problem. Third, by minimizing concerns unrelated to the physical ailment. Fourth, by creating distance and fostering asymmetrical relationships among themselves and patients. Fifth, by patronizing patients and making decisions on their behalf; and finally, by restricting the control of patients over their environments and life choices. Numerous studies demonstrate the control of physicians over the content, length, and nature of interaction with patients (Curtis, 2000; Samson, 1999; Weitz, 1996). It has also been found that many physicians promote stereotypical roles for women and that they react in a defensive manner when challenged by their female patients (Hardey, 1998). In this context, the psychologist is at risk for abusing his or her relative high status, and for being discounted by medical practitioners who run hospitals and assume ultimate decision-making powers with respect to patients.

We assume that the physical ailments presented by clients are real enough, and that proven strategies of coping and behaviour modification need to be applied. But all of this takes place in a context suffused by power differentials where the perspective of the client or other health professional, such as physiotherapists or social workers, may be lost due to their relative lack of power. There is, then, the physical construction of illness and the social construction of illness (Freund and McGuire, 1999). In the social construction of illness, we have to give the sufferer an opportunity to express his or her narrative. We concur with Murray that 'narratives are not simply a personal means of self-care but an opportunity to engage with others to critique the adequacy of master narratives within official discourse' (2000:345). Furthermore, Murray argues that 'in discussing the role of narrative in socially shared belief systems it is important to consider their ideological dimensions. This is a crucial task which a critically informed health psychology needs to tackle' (2000:345).

The chosen method of helping is not determined only by the best available scientific evidence. It is also mediated by the meaning of the condition negotiated among patient and multiple professionals. Thus, for example, a patient may complain about pain in a certain place, but tests do not confirm the complaint. This leads to professionals questioning the legitimacy of the complaint, and to suspicions of malingering. If a lawsuit is pending against an employer or the state, diagnosis becomes even more complicated. Professionals then assume the role of social-control agents and engage in police work.

The point of this hypothetical situation is to show how complicated the assessment and choice of treatment can become. When we combine all of the contextual factors implicated in diagnosis and treatment, a fairly complicated picture emerges. A critical appraisal of the situation would take into account power differentials in problem formulation, risk of diminished self-determination of patients, potential labelling of the patient, and access by the patient to needed resources. In synthesis, critical psychology adds another dimension to helping. Selection of the best cognitive or behavioural strategy is not enough. Patient participation and empowerment in the choice of method of help are also crucial.

However helpful clinical interventions might be, health psychology has been criticized for concentrating too much on individuals and for preferring a reactive mode of intervention. According to Winett, 'to be effective health psychologists need to adopt an intervention orientation more diverse in terms of timing and level than their apparent preference for tertiary prevention with clinical, individual-level interventions' (1995:344). We resonate with that view. Studies show that remedial interventions for high-risk conditions such as obesity, high cholesterol, and smoking are not very effective (Smedley and Syme, 2000; Wilkinson, 1996). Once entrenched, these patterns of behaviour are hard to change. In any case, even when they are effective, they do not address the constant flow of new cases with such adverse conditions.

The critique leveled against health psychology is not only that it responds late to conditions, but also that it addresses individuals and not societal structures. The proactive approach that centres on individuals at risk is incapable of reducing incidence, or the number of new cases of a problem. As Wilkinson noted,

> Sometimes it is a matter of providing screening and early treatment, other times of trying to change some aspect of lifestyle, but always it is a matter of providing some service or intervention. This applies not just to health, but also to studies of a wide range of social, psychological, developmental and educational problems. What happens is that the original source of the problem in society is left unchanged (and probably unknown) while expensive new services are proposed to cater for the individuals most affected. Each new problem leads to a demand for additional resources for services to try to put right the damage which continues to be done. Because the underlying flaw in the system is not put right, it gives rise to a continuous flow, both of people who have suffered as a result, and of demands for special services to meet their needs (1996:21).

In the meso context of hospitals, clinics, and work settings, power and control affect health in significant ways as well. In the Whitehall studies, Marmot and his colleagues followed the health of thousands of British civil servants for three decades (Marmot, 1999; Marmot et al., 1999). The participants were all middle-class people who enjoyed relative affluence. Although all of them could be considered middle class, the 25-year follow-up study showed that those in lower positions had a four times higher mortality rate than those in administrative positions. There was a clear correlation between level of control over the work environment and several measures of disease, with those lower on the scale of control experiencing poorer health. When participants were divided into four employment grades, there was a distinct and gradual escalation in health from the lower grade to the higher grade. As Marmot (1999:12) noted,

> There are abundant data showing a link between poverty and ill health. These results from Whitehall have influenced us in coming to the view that inequality is also important. The problem of inequality in health is not confined to the poorest members of society but runs right across the social spectrum. In Whitehall the social gradient was seen not only for total mortality, but for all the major causes of death, including coronary heart disease and stroke.

The studies conducted by Marmot and others suggest that the work environment affects health through three psychological mechanisms. The first relates to levels of demand and control, whereby higher demands and lower levels of control affect health negatively. The second mechanism refers to the effort-reward imbalance, and the third to the level of social support (Marmot et al., 1999).

From a critical psychology perspective, we see that the amount of power experienced by workers is directly related to health and mortality. How this power is attained, and how it may be challenged and redistributed is a key concern for critical psychologists. The struggle to distribute power and control equitably within hospitals and work settings defines a key job for the critical health psychologist.

Hospitals and work settings are laden with power conflicts. It would be a mistake to intervene in these types of organizations without considering the effects of the political environment. Unless the health psychologist recognizes the political role that he or she might be fulfilling, undesirable consequences may ensue. Interventions to improve the working climate may mask underlying conflict, to the direct benefit of management. Surely reducing stress is a good cause, but diverting attention away from the root causes of that stress is not. As we can see, the health psychologist is caught in a bind, much like the organizational psychologist who is asked to improve working conditions. On the one hand, research clearly suggests that reduced stress is good for health. But on the other hand, superficial attempts to alleviate conflict may divert attention from more fundamental roots of discomfort.

Marmot and colleagues (1999) clearly showed that lack of control at work is related to increased levels of illness. Launching initiatives that restore employee control across the board is a good health intervention for as long as it is not temporary or superficial. The health psychologist has the difficult job of discerning whether an intervention will benefit workers unequivocally or only temporarily, and whether or not the net effect of the programme is worker appeasement.

The macro-economic and psychosocial environment where we live have direct repercussions for health and quality of life. Consider the following examples provided by Wilkinson (1996). A child born and raised in Harlem has less chances of living to 65 years old than a baby born in Bangladesh. Also in the USA, life expectancy is 7 years longer for whites (76 years) than for African-Americans (69 years). In lower social classes, infant mortality in Sweden (500 per 100,000) is less than half the rate in England (1250 per 100,000). Because of more egalitarian income distribution, the life expectancy of Japanese people increased by 7.5 years for men and 8 years for women in 21 years. This dramatic increase took place between the years 1965 and 1986. Japanese people experience the highest life expectancy in the world (almost 80 years) in large part because, in that period of time, they became the most advanced society with the narrowest income differences. Communities with higher levels of social cohesion and narrow gaps between rich and poor produce better health outcomes than wealthier societies with higher levels of social disintegration.

When probability of death between ages 15 and 60 is compared between richer and poorer countries, the former have outcomes that are about three times better than the latter. Reasons for death include infections – perinatal, nutritional, maternal, cardiovascular – cancer, respiratory disease and other external causes (see Marmot, 1999:6). Lack of shelter and sanitation are major causes of killing diseases around the world. Feuerstein (1997) reports that, between 1988 and 1991, in 34 of the 47 least developed countries, only 46 per cent of the population had access to safe water. The atrocious effects of poverty on health have been documented extensively. They remind us that health is not only the effect of healthcare but of living conditions (Smedley and Syme, 2000).

Within countries, the poor, the unemployed, refugees, single parents, ethnic minorities and the homeless have much lower rates of health than more advantaged groups. This applies not only to poor countries, but to rich countries as well. Homeless people in western countries, for example, are 34 times more likely to kill themselves than the general population, 150 times more likely to be fatally assaulted, and 25 times more likely to die in any period of time than the people who ignore them on the streets (Shaw, Dorling, and Smith, 1999). There is no question that the macro-environment influences health in potent ways.

But the body of knowledge compiled by Marmot and Wilkinson (1999) clearly indicates that, in addition to economic prosperity, equality and social cohesion are also powerful determinants of health. Indeed,

> In the developed world, it is not the richest countries which have the best health, but the most egalitarian...Looking at a number of different examples of healthy egalitarian societies, an important characteristic they all seem to share is their social cohesion...The epidemiological evidence which most clearly suggests the health benefits of social cohesion comes from studies of the beneficial effects of social networks on health (Wilkinson, 1996:3–5).

As Wilkinson observed, social cohesion is mediated by commitment to positive social structures, which, in turn, is related to social justice. Individuals contribute to collective well-being when they feel that the collective works for them as well. Social cohesion and coherence are 'closely related to social justice' (Wilkinson, 1996:221). The critical psychologist faces a serious challenge in trying to incorporate these lessons into his or her practice. We distil below some of the implications for action.

Shifting the paradigm in health psychology

Partnerships for practice

Table 8.1 provides a synopsis of how critical psychology values, assumptions and practices may guide partnerships for the promotion of health.

Values

Partners should note how the value of self-determination needs to be contextualized in the light of disability and chronic illness. The much esteemed value of autonomy needs to be rethought, and replaced, by the value of interdependence. The value of diversity, in turn, reminds us that there are many ways of being, and that living with a disability is just another way. Although justice is not usually invoked as a prerequisite of health, it is closely associated with well-being. Partners should be always reminded that there cannot be health in the absence of justice.

Table 8.1 Critical psychology in health settings: Partnerships for practice

Critical psychology tenets	Possibilities for action
Values	*Content:* Balance prevalent, emphasis on autonomy with concern for caring and compassion and interdependence. Consider power differentials in hospital settings and their impact on patients' empowerment and self-determination. Social cohesion, collaboration and democratic participation at community level benefit population health.
	Process: Show caring and compassion for citizens seeking service, respect their social identities, and foster their ability to pursue personal goals in light of chronic illness or disability. Involve community members in civic and health-related activities. Create partnerships with community groups to achieve justice in health care.
Assumptions	*Content:* Ensure that definitions of problem and health include voice of citizens seeking help and is not circumscribed to professional opinion. Consider role of corporate profit-making in health problems. Promote focus on strengths and competencies of person as perceived and described by person seeking help. Beware of the pursuit of pathology prevalent in hospital settings.
	Process: Act as resource collaborator instead of removed expert. Engage citizens in active roles throughout the process of help or self-help. Consider alternatives to medical treatments such as health-promotion activities related to diet and lifestyle. Promote non-professional interventions such as mutual-help groups. Afford people seeking help meaningful opportunities to present their point of view concerning their health. Renew informed consent often and solicit input from patients as to direction and aims of helping relationship. Respect privacy of patients in medical settings.
Practices	*Content:* Consider approaches that go beyond reactive and indicated interventions and that are proactive in nature. Address social and economic origins of ill-health and maldistribution of resources and health in society.
	Process: Collaborate with advocacy and social justice groups in addressing the health needs of the entire population. Create solidarity partnerships with community groups affected by ill-health. Promote political education and social action leading to health promoting cultures and organisations.

Assumptions

Psychologists need to advocate for definitions of problems that include the voice of the person or group affected by a condition. Otherwise, the pursuit of pathology tends to prevail. Dominant discourses of pity need to be challenged. Ora Prilleltensky, Isaac's wife, worked as a psychologist in a rehabilitation hospital. She researched the topic of physical disabilities and volunteered in disability advocacy organisations. Sometimes, she uses a wheelchair herself. Ora has a physical disability that limits her mobility. Recently, we spent a weekend with friends in their summer house. Ora had walked to the beach with her female friend, and we, the male partners, followed. We took the wheelchair for Ora to use later. My friend's son wanted to use the wheelchair, which proved to be quite an attraction for the kids – they loved wheeling themselves in it. The child, who is nine years old (and able bodied), sat in the wheelchair and started rolling it towards the beach. My friend, his dad, told him humorously: 'everyone is going to have *pity* on you'.

Although it was said half jokingly, the statement spoke volumes about our culture's discourse about people with disabilities. Pity can be disempowering and objectifying. Norms that define people with disabilities by their disability and by pity are widespread. Pity is radically different from caring, compassion, support, and empathy. My friend, who also happens to be a psychologist, was perpetuating, however innocently and jovially, an oppressive stereotype about health and well-being; a stereotype that puts people with disabilities in the box of 'pity'.

By engaging community members themselves in definition and action on health problems we de-medicalize afflictions, thereby increasing the chances of empowerment for health. Table 8.1 also points to the need to consider alternatives to medical treatments in the form of mutual-help groups and non-consumerist lifestyles.

Practices

Power's omnipresent character is highlighted in Table 8.1. Power differentials across the medical divide have to be carefully attended to by critical health psychologists. Our own potential to abuse power in a setting that accentuates the privilege of professionals must be monitored. Patient or client collaboration is a good antidote to arrogance. Advocacy is a key feature in health settings. Patients have to negotiate their treatment with professionals who are not always sensitive to the psychological condition of the person seeking help. But advocacy should extend beyond the walls of the clinic or the hospital. In our discussion of roles for critical psychologists we distinguish between individual, group, community, and societal interventions (Winett, 1995).

Critical alternatives

Table 8.2 describes potential interventions for critical health psychologists. The interventions vary along timing, population, and ecological levels. Across the top of the table we can see different units of interventions: individuals, groups and organisations, and community and society. Each unit of intervention is guided, respectively, by a set of personal, relational, and collective values. These sites of intervention parallel those discussed in the previous chapter dealing with educational settings.

The three rows in Table 8.2 distinguish among clinical interventions for people who already have problems (reactive/indicated), programmes for people who are at high risk of developing health complications (proactive/high risk), and health promotion initiatives for the population at large (proactive/universal). The table informs the discussion that follows.

Interventions that promote individual well-being

Opportunities for helping are present at the individual, group/organization, and community/societal levels. At each level, we propose to use the partnership

Table 8.2 Ecological levels, values, and potential critical psychology interventions in health settings

Timing and population of intervention	Values for personal well-being (self-determination, protection of health, caring and compassion)	Values and ecological levels	
		Values for relational well-being (collaboration, democratic participation, and respect for diversity)	Values for collective well-being (support for community structures, social justice)
	Individual well-being	Group and organisational well-being	Community and societal well-being
Reactive indicated	• Self-determination in rehabilitation • Power sharing in treatment plans for coping with illness and chronic pain	• Assertiveness training for hospital patients dealing with professionals • Communication training for professionals dealing with vulnerable patients	• Securing access of minorities, refugees and the poor to all health services • Lobbying for funding of health services in deprived areas
Proactive high risk	• Smoking cessation with emphasis on exploitation of community by tobacco companies • Diet and exercise programme for overweight people with emphasis on ill effects of consumerism	• Exercise programme for disadvantaged populations at high risk for heart disease • Organisational interventions to reduce stress in patients and staff	• Self-help/mutual aid and support groups for people caring for disabled family members • Community wide programmes to improve diet, lower alcohol consumption and increase exercise
Proactive universal	• Self-instruction guide on breast examination • Self-instruction guide on HIV prevention	• Organisational development to improve working atmosphere • Bill of rights and responsibilities for patients and staff in hospitals	• Critique and boycotts of media and corporations making profits at expense of population health • Promote social cohesion and egalitarian social policies

model presented in previous chapters. A partnership ensures that clients and all other professionals are heard. Furthermore, it implies that decision-making power will be shared, and that the wishes of medical patients will be given proper priority.

Individuals affected by physical ailments become psychologically vulnerable. We consider here the case of chronic pain, which is an issue often handled by health psychologists (Bennett, 2000; Curtis, 2000). The pain may be excruciating and may lead to deterioration in work and family life. At times, pain patients endure the indignity of being told that 'it's all in your head' (Eimer and Freeman, 1998; Nicholas *et al.*, 2000). The treatment of chronic pain is very difficult and optimal outcomes require the full participation of the patients. Empowerment is crucial if the person is to become his or her own 'case manager'. The subjectivity of pain defies easy and categorical assessment by objective measures. Patient participation in diagnosis and treatment has to be nurtured and elicited. However, vulnerable patients may have a proclivity to rely on expert advice, an inclination reinforced by medical professionals (Lupton, 1994). We see a role for the critical health psychologist in ensuring that patient empowerment is taken seriously. This may go against habitual ways of practice for physicians as well as for nurses and physiotherapists. Moreover, active participation may go even against patients' beliefs that they do not know enough to be of help.

Psychological methods of treating pain include relaxation, hypnosis, cognitive, and behavioural therapies. Pacing, problem solving, and other life skills are also helpful (Eimer and Freeman, 1998). As in other cases of psychological help, the critical psychologist would want to ensure that the technique being used is acceptable to the client and that he or she is fully aware of potential risks or side effects. The client should remain an active partner throughout the decision-making process of choosing and implementing treatment.

Rehabilitation is another common domain for health psychologists. Many professionals hold the assumption that independence is a venerable end. We challenge that assumption. We heard of professionals wishing to teach rehabilitation patients to do certain things that others could do for them in a fraction of the time. While independence is mostly related to self-efficacy and a sense of control, in certain contexts it must be challenged. If a person does not find meaning in preparing breakfast for herself, a task that may take her 45 minutes, perhaps another person could do it for her in five minutes. There are sacred assumptions, such as autonomy, that need to be questioned, with, and on behalf of rehabilitation patients. The main message for individual reactive work is to ensure that others, including professionals or family members, do not project onto the patient their unresolved issues (such as 'get over it already!' or 'pull yourself together,') or unchecked assumptions about power or independence.

Proactive interventions with individuals have to address the societal sources of smoking, drinking, binging, and sitting for too long. To begin addressing the societal causes of disease, it is important to politicize community members. We believe it can be empowering for a young woman with an eating disorder to understand and take action against the media. Feminists use anger toward societal oppression in empowering ways (Riger, 2000). So do narrative therapists and advocates of just therapy (Community Mental Health Project, 1998). There is a need to connect corporate agendas with personal suffering. In a smoking prevention programme with children and youth we discussed at length the commercial roots of addictions. Children in the programme protested in shopping malls against tobacco companies and made a presentation to the city council on the subject (Prilleltensky, Nelson, and Sanchez Valdes, 2000). These are examples of linkages between personal risk factors and their societal origins. We have to make these connections for the benefit of people who are at risk today and for the benefit of those who will be at risk tomorrow if corporations continue to infect the public with toxic products (Swift, 2001). As critical health psychologists, we have to ask ourselves whether we want to support the status quo by treating its victims, or whether we want to join with them to challenge noxious consumerism and global assaults on public health (Garrett, 2000). But, obviously, this is not easy. In class, students and I (Isaac) often discuss the role of the media in eating disorders and alcohol abuse. Both in Canada and in Australia the prevalence of these conditions is quite high. A paradox usually ensues following these discussions. We all express disgust at norms that exploit women for advertising purposes, but then nothing changes with respect to students' behaviour regarding consumerism. They continue to buy the same offending magazines, and they continue to consume the same beer and alcohol products whose advertising they decried as exploitive. I have had ten years of experience witnessing this phenomenon. It taught me that not only is information insufficient to change behaviour but also that unhealthy social norms are hard to overcome.

Interventions for group and organisational well-being

We consider possible interventions in hospital and work settings in turn. Because of the prescribed scripts that patients and doctors are expected to follow in a total institution like a hospital, we regard both of these groups as sites for action. Of course, not all patients and professionals engage in stereotypical roles of the sick and the helper, but the evidence is such that people in hospitals often do behave in hierarchical and constraining ways. Hence, at the group/organizational level we recommend interventions to improve communication between professionals and patients. Research suggests that communication between practitioners and patients is often faulty. A study by Beckman and Frankel (1984) confirms this claim. In a sample of 74 office visits, only 23 per cent of the patients had a chance to finish their explanations of concerns. Doctors were found to interrupt patients in 69 per cent of the visits. On average, doctors interrupted patients after they had spoken for only 18 seconds. In another study, West (1983) reported that patient-initiated questions were discouraged. Out of a total of 773 questions asked in 21 medical encounters, only nine per cent were initiated by patients. The use of jargon, patronizing attitudes, and patient anxiety contribute to miscommunication between doctors and patients.

While we advocate for assertiveness and communication training, we should remain sceptical of the potential for such interventions to make lasting changes. The origins of patriarchal mentality in medical settings are profound and may not be undone by workshops on communication. Lupton (1994:59) cautions that to assume that the majority of patients, given appropriate training in communication competencies, will have equal authority in the doctor–patient relationship is to ignore the structural and symbolic dimensions of this relationship. Although there is limited opportunity for patients to assert their agency, the whole nature of the doctor–patient relationship and the healing process rests on the unequal power balance and asymmetry of knowledge between patient and doctor.

It is clear that more fundamental changes in the medical establishment will have to occur to democratize the patient–doctor relationship. Work towards that goal, however, does not invalidate the need to empower patients while they are the subject of medical investigations and interventions.

The health psychologist can also intervene in work settings. Solidarity among workers is very important. It is a source of social support and even empowerment. But not all aggression in the workplace comes from the top. Horizontal violence is quite prevalent (Keashley, 1998). Programmes that address workplace bullying and that build cohesion among workers can have substantial health benefits. By linking health with solidarity we are politicizing well-being and supporting cohesion among workers.

We touched here on hospital and workplace actions. Table 8.2 mentions other possible interventions with groups and organisations. We move now to consider tasks at the community and societal levels.

Interventions for community and societal well-being

Within the reactive and indicated framework, there is much that needs to be done to ensure that minorities have adequate access to health care. 'Lack of access can have deadly consequences' (Weitz, 1996:61). Advocacy, lobbying, and solidarity partnerships are vehicles to pressure governments to act on behalf of vulnerable populations. Although the formal medical system is not the only means to health, it is a social resource that needs to be distributed equally among all. We see this type of political work as integral to the work of critical health and community psychologists. The practice of health promotion at the social and community levels is appealing, but only insofar as it includes a critique of capitalist market rules. We link health promotion to a critique of corporate ruling because, otherwise, we focus on individuals and neglect the societal and market origins of illness (Korten, 1995). As Lupton (1994:57) noted, 'although the health promotion perspective relies heavily on a critique of the biomedical model, it fails to challenge the hegemony of ideologies that deflect the responsibility of health maintenance from the state to the individual'. Therefore, we advocate a combined approach that couples health promotion to activities designed to challenge corporate ruling of health and illness. What we watch, eat, drink, and breathe have a lot to do with global capitalism, an economic structure that has proven detrimental to global health (Feuerstein, 1997; Kim et al., 2000; Korten, 1995; Marmot and Wilkinson, 1999; Swift, 2001).

Re-inventing ourselves as advocates, social critics, community leaders and psychologists at the same time is a necessity that may not sit well with health psychologists. However, to remain at the level of reactive or person-centred interventions is to deny a massive body of evidence linking social and economic structures to physical and psychological health. Critical health psychology is well positioned to break interdisciplinary barriers and address well-being in a truly ecological way.

Alternative settings dealing with HIV/AIDS prevention and treatment, women's health organizations, and health collectives helping the poor offer psychologists an opportunity to work in settings that are congruent with the values of social justice and empowerment. Inspiring work by psychologist Brinton Lykes (2000) integrates empowerment, community development, and health promotion for Mayan women in Guatemala. Her work is admirable because it combines citizen empowerment with the promotion of health and human rights. Many others in developing countries struggle to establish basic infrastructure for health. Feuerstein (1997) outlines several strategies for collaborating with the poor for improved health, including financial services and credit for the poor. It is in these places, where inequality is most prevalent, that critical health psychologists are most needed.

Conclusion

What health psychologists do mostly is not necessarily what helps the most. Whereas most health psychologists work with individuals already affected by, or at risk for, health problems, evidence suggests that the most promising ways to promote overall health is to work with entire communities in a proactive fashion (Kaplan, 2000). Critical and community psychologists used to argue that the focus on the individual is not enough. New information indicates that working with groups at risk is not good enough either. By the time groups of people develop symptoms, it is extremely difficult to revert unhealthy behavioural patterns. Furthermore, most risk conditions do not reside within the individual but within the social and physical environments. As a result, preventive efforts for people at risk have proven only minimally effective (Kaplan, 2000; Wilkinson, 1996). This was the rather disappointing result of the largest trial of behavioural change ever conducted. The Multiple Risk Factor Intervention Trial (MRFIT) 'attempted to change diet, smoking and exercise among white men identified as being in the highest 10 per cent of risk for coronary heart disease. Despite concentrated efforts over six years they only succeeded in making minimal changes' (Wilkinson, 1996:64). The implication of these findings is that risk factors are in themselves symptoms of more profound causes of disease that most behavioural interventions fail to address. In other words, these interventions do not address the causes of the causes, but only some outcomes of deeper causes.

Evidence from social determinants of health indicates that overall well-being is predicated on sufficient material resources, equality in distribution of resources, and social cohesion. These three factors are the domain of proactive universal interventions for community and societal well-being. Large international epidemiological studies demonstrate that each of these factors is a necessary but not a sufficient precursor of overall health. For optimal health to occur, they have to operate simultaneously. For critical health psychologists the implication is clear: we cannot fragment well-being into economic, social and psychosocial health; they work in synchronicity, and so should we.

9

Community Settings: Creating Capacity and Mobilizing for Change

In this chapter, we examine the ways in which critical psychologists can strive to make changes in community settings. A central thesis of the chapter is that making community change must involve partnerships between critical psychologists and oppressed groups. In organizational transformation, community development, and the creation of alternative settings, disadvantaged people should drive the change process (Nelson, Prilleltensky, and MacGillivary, 2001). Jenny Pearce has written that an authentic civil society:

> must involve the poor and the weak gaining real and meaningful rights as citizens, genuinely enfranchised and able to build organizations to defend their interests. It is about the rights of individuals to associate voluntarily. Constructing civil society cannot be essentially about building up intermediary development organizations to represent the 'poor'; it must be about empowering the poor and enabling them to fight for their own rights as citizens (Pearce, 1993:225).

While our approach to the practice of critical psychology in community settings is guided by all of the values that we have elaborated on in the first part of this book, practice in the community is particularly focused on the development of strong community infrastructures. It is through citizen participation in community settings that personal and political empowerment can be realized (Campbell and Jovchelovitch, 2000).

Community settings play a vital mediating role between individuals and larger social structures (Berger and Neuhaus, 1977). The development of strong community settings not only has an impact on individuals, but community settings can also shape society as a whole. Having a rich and diverse array of community settings is vital to the health of a civil society (Swift, 1999). The importance of community settings for personal and social change has been underscored by academic researchers and theorists, community developers, and disability groups. The development of such concepts as psychological sense of community (Sarason, 1988), community capacity (McKnight, 1995), community competence

121

(Cottrell, 1976; Iscoe, 1974), civil society (Swift, 1999), social capital (Putnam, 1993; 2000), community integration (Leighton, 1979), and inclusion (O'Brien and O'Brien, 1996; Schwartz, 1997) all reflect an emphasis on community. Having a rich array of formal and informal settings enhances people's experience of community.

As the values of many western countries have shifted toward individualism, self-interest, and the accumulation of consumer goods and personal wealth, community has been eroded (Pilisuk, McAllister, and Rothman, 1996; Putnam, 1993; Sarason, 1988). Yet this emphasis on consumption and self-gratification has left many middle-class people feeling empty and alienated. Making more money and having bigger houses, fancier cars, and more 'toys' has not made people happier (Diener *et al.*, 1999). Community has also been eroded in low-income and working-class urban communities. McKnight and Kretzmann (1984) noted that in the past, such communities often contained a number of vital settings, including churches, ethnic associations, political organizations, and labour unions. However, ethnic groups have become more geographically dispersed, with many no longer living in distinct ethnic enclaves. In addition to increased geographic mobility, identification with and participation in mainstream churches and political parties has declined. The web of natural support in many communities has weakened.

At the same time, the economy has changed such that there are fewer jobs which involve the production of goods (the industrial and manufacturing sector) and more jobs which involve providing services (McKnight, 1995). Locally-owned businesses and 'mom and pop shops' have been replaced by international chains. Frequently, the main settings that remain in low-income, urban neighbourhoods are human service organizations (for example, schools, hospitals, clinics). McKnight (1989) reported that, in one Chicago neighbourhood, for every dollar people received from welfare, 57 cents was spent on health care. McKnight argued that this is not a 'poor' neighbourhood, but a 'serviced' neighbourhood, in which low-income citizens have become commodified into 'clients'. In the past, the role of the community organizer was to develop a coalition, 'an organization or organizations', bringing together churches, ethnic groups, political parties, and labour unions (McKnight and Kretzmann, 1984). Currently, community organizers also speak of creating community coalitions (Butterfoss, Goodman, and Wandersman, 1993), but these coalitions tend to consist of professional service-providers, with limited citizen participation.

In search of meaning, purpose, community, and social justice, individuals from all social classes have pursued alternative lifestyles, have become involved in different community activities, or have created new community settings. The rise of self-help groups and grassroots organizations dealing with issues of human rights, disability, women's inequality, the natural environment, food systems, poverty, and globalization are examples of contemporary community action. In fact, Pilisuk *et al.* (1996) reported an increase in grassroots community groups over the past 25 years across the world.

We can think of community settings in at least two ways. One is the distinction between geographic and relational conceptions of community settings (Dalton, Elias, and Wandersman, 2001). A community setting can be a place (for example, a neighbourhood, a geographically-bound district or catchment area), or a community setting can be relational in nature and not defined by geographic boundaries. Relational community settings are based on mutual interests and relationships (for example, clubs, religious settings, political groups, and so on).

The second distinction that we make in this chapter about community settings is whether they are ameliorative or transformative. Ameliorative settings are those that provide support or help to improve the lives of community members, without striving to change social and community conditions. Transformative settings, on the other hand, have a more explicit focus on creating social and community change (Maton, 2000). In this chapter, we discuss how critical psychologists can contribute to three different types of community settings, which vary on a continuum from ameliorative to transformative. The three types of settings are: (a) human services, (b) voluntary associations, and (c) alternative settings. Human services are at the ameliorative end of the continuum, while alternative settings are at the transformative end of the continuum, with voluntary associations resting in between.

Describing and critiquing the status quo

Traditional practice of psychology in community settings

Psychological practice in community settings has been mostly confined to human services. Community and critical psychologists do work with voluntary associations and alternative settings, but most professional psychologists have little to do with these types of community settings. In Chapter 6, we described the traditional practices of clinical and counselling psychologists who work in these publicly funded human services. Diagnosis, referral, and therapy/treatment are the primary functions of psychologists working in such settings. As we noted in Chapter 6, the traditional practice of clinical and counselling psychology serves a social control function of people and behaviours that are seen as 'deviant' or at-odds with dominant social values and practices. Societal values are not called into question; rather the emphasis is on labelling and fixing individuals so that they can adjust to social values or on excluding and segregating citizens from the mainstream of community life. In other words, the focus of human services organizations is amelioration of individual and family problems, rather than social and community transformation. This is what 'helping' agencies have done for years with troublesome children and youth, people with disabilities, and citizens with serious mental health problems (Wineman, 1984).

Critical appraisal of psychological practice in community settings

Helping agencies often implicitly subscribe to values that maintain the status quo. First, in their emphasis on professional expertise, most human service organizations maintain considerable power imbalances between professionals and clients (Reiff, 1974), thus negating the potential for consumer empowerment (McKnight, 1989). Second, issues of diversity and oppression are seldom addressed. The stigma and exclusion of people from diverse racial and ethnic minority backgrounds, women, gays, and lesbians is not critically examined. Third, while human service organizations are located in the community, they often do not have a focus on community change, promoting community integration, or reaching out to potential helpers or supporters in natural community settings. The community is construed as the location of professional practice, rather than as a relational community which can potentially welcome, support, and integrate people who are experiencing problems in living (Nelson, Lord, and Ochocka, 2001a, b). For example, the community mental health centres in the USA have been criticized for focusing on geographic catchment areas rather than relational communities of support (Chu and Trotter, 1974). Fourth, traditional helping practices do not pay attention to the structural nature of human problems. Socio-economic inequality and poverty are causes or consequences of many problems in living, but the helping process does not typically address the vital role played by socio-economic conditions.

Shifting the paradigm in community settings
Partnerships for practice

In Table 9.1, we provide an overview of the values, assumptions, and practices for critical psychology partnerships in community settings.

Values

Community settings vary widely in the degree to which they espouse values that are ameliorative or transformative. Many human service organizations and voluntary associations emphasize the value of caring and compassion, but few emphasize collaboration or self-determination of service-users or the need for social justice for disadvantaged. A major task for critical psychologists working with people in community settings is to encourage the members of the setting to clarify the vision and values which guide the practices of the setting.

A collaborative approach which is inclusive of disadvantaged people is needed for clarification of the vision and values of the setting. Participatory processes are needed to develop, reflect on, and implement values that promote personal, relational, and collective well-being. That is, the action implications of the values need to be underscored. Otherwise, there is only a change in rhetoric with no corresponding change in practice. Later in this chapter we provide examples of how critical psychologists can work collaboratively with community settings to identify their vision and values.

Assumptions

Many community settings are not inclusive of disadvantaged people and view disadvantaged people from the lens of a 'charity' approach, rather than a social

Table 9.1   Critical psychology in community settings: Partnerships for practice

Critical psychology tenets	Qualities of the content and process
Values	*Content:* Community settings vary widely in the degree to which they espouse values that are ameliorative or transformative. A major task for critical psychologists working with people in community settings is to encourage the members of the setting to clarify the vision and values which guide the practices of the setting.
	Process: A collaborative approach which is inclusive of disadvantaged people is needed for clarification of the vision and values of the setting. Participatory processes are needed to develop, reflect on, and implement values that promote personal, relational, and collective well-being.
Assumptions	*Content:* Many community settings are not inclusive to disadvantaged people and view disadvantaged people from the lens of a 'charity' approach, rather than a social justice approach. Recognize that through participation in community settings, there is the potential for personal growth, relationship development, and social change. Encourage people in community settings to reframe the problems of disadvantaged people such that the community is seen as part of the problem and thus as a necessary part of any solution to improve the lives of disadvantaged people.
	Process: Bring together disadvantaged people with service-providers and other stakeholders to develop egalitarian partnerships. It is through such partnerships that assumptions can be challenged and alternative assumptions can be formulated. Focus on the strengths of disadvantaged people and the knowledge and skills that they bring to the partnership.
Practices	*Content:* Develop practices and programmes that are based on transformative values which promote personal, relational, and collective well-being. Focus on changing the social context, rather than changing individuals.
	Process: Disadvantaged people become active agents in the development and implementation of programmes and support networks provided by community settings. Encourage partnership processes that reflect personal, relational, and collective values which promote well-being.

justice approach. People who are 'different' in some way are often segregated in specialized settings, rather than integrated into mainstream settings. People with disabilities have experienced this segregation for many years. Marginalized people do not need or want 'pity'; they want respect, inclusion, relationships, and resources. It is through participation in community settings that the potential for personal growth, relationship development, and social change for disadvantaged people can be achieved.

Critical psychologists can encourage people in community settings to reframe the problems of disadvantaged people such that the community is seen as part of the problem and thus as a necessary part of any solution to improve the lives of disadvantaged people. Moreover, critical psychologists can strive to bring together disadvantaged people with service-providers and other stakeholders in the development of egalitarian partnerships. It is through such partnerships that assumptions about power can be critically examined and reformulated to promote power-sharing. Such a paradigm shift also involves focusing on the strengths of disadvantaged people and the knowledge and skills that they bring to the partnership.

Practices

Critical psychologists can consult with community settings to assist them in developing practices and programmes that are consistent with their vision and values. Such a focus will emphasize changing the social context, rather than changing individuals. Moreover, disadvantaged people should become active agents in the development and implementation of programmes and supports provided by community settings. Critical psychologists can encourage partnership processes that reflect personal, relational, and collective values which promote well-being of disadvantaged people.

Critical alternatives

Critical psychologists can play the roles of researcher, evaluator, participant-conceptualizer, consultant, or service-provider in partnerships with oppressed groups to create community change. In this section, we consider how these roles can be played out in different types of community settings.

Human service organizations

Human service organizations refer to those community services that are designed to help children, families, and adults cope with problems in living that they are experiencing. Such services include community mental health centres, children's mental health services, counselling agencies, alcoholism and substance-abuse treatment facilities, child welfare agencies, community-based correctional services, and services for people with disabilities. These services are typically staffed by psychologists, social workers, and a variety of other health and social service professionals. We believe that critical psychologists can play a role in transforming human service organizations using value-based approaches. Change can be created by critical psychologists working from within such organizations, by external consultants, or by some combination of internal and external change agents. Of course, human service organizations vary widely in their receptivity to innovation and change and their readiness for consultation. As Cherniss (1993) pointed out, before considering an intervention in a human service organization, it is important to consider such questions as: Whose interests will be served? Is there value congruence between the change agent and those with whom she or he will be consulting? What form will the intervention take (for example, action research, consultation, skills training)? What previous interventions have been tried and with what success?

We begin this section with an example of organizational and community trans-formation in the field of adult community mental health for people with serious mental health problems. Mental health services began to shift from institutional settings to community programmes beginning in the 1960s. It was assumed that this process of deinstitutionalization would lead to more humane and effective practices, but there has been increasing recognition that many community men-tal health programmes have retained the values and character of the institutional settings that they were designed to replace (Nelson and Walsh-Bowers, 1994; Nelson, Walsh-Bowers, and Hall, 1998). While there have been changes in language (for example, 'patients' are now 'clients') and emphasis (that is, more emphasis on rehabilitation and psychosocial deficits rather than medical treatment and psychiatric diagnoses), the underlying values of community treatment and rehabilitation are quite similar to those of institutional treatment (Nelson *et al.*, 2001b).

First, community-based programmes such as case management and Assertive Community Treatment still maintain considerable power imbalances between professional case managers and service-users (McCubbin and Cohen, 1996; Solomon, 1992). Moreover, coercive practices are part and parcel of such pro-grammes (Gomory, 1999; Spindel, 2000). Second, some community mental health services segregate people with mental health problems from the community. For example, housing in the community includes segregated, group-living settings (for example, group homes), that are based on a philosophy of a residential continuum of services (from high-support group settings to independent living) (Carling, 1995). Similarly, sheltered workshops do not provide real jobs with decent pay and they too are segregated settings, operated exclusively for people with serious mental health problems. While residents of such settings may live in the community, they are not necessarily integrated into the mainstream of community life and thus continue to be subject to stigma from the wider community. Third, community mental health programmes do not typically address the larger social and economic determinants of health, such as income, employment, housing, and education. Most people with serious mental health problems continue to live in conditions of poverty and unemployment (Nelson *et al.*, 2001b).

There have been calls for a paradigm shift in community mental health, with new approaches based on an alternative vision and values (Carling, 1995; Nelson *et al.*, 2001b). According to its proponents, the key values underlying this emerging paradigm are consumer empowerment, community integration, and social justice. Mental health consumers play an active role in this paradigm and there is an emphasis on their strengths, potential for recovery, and partnership (Carling, 1995; MacGillivary and Nelson, 1998; Nelson *et al.*, 2001b). Pockets of innova-tive practice based on this emerging paradigm include consumer-directed support (Dunst and Trivette, 1989), self-help/mutual aid (Constantino and Nelson, 1995; Nelson, Ochocka *et al.*, 1998), social network interventions (Gottlieb and Coppard, 1987), and supported housing, education, and employment, in which consumers 'choose, get, and keep' the type of housing, education, and employ-ment they want with the assistance of community support workers (Bond *et al.*, 1997; Carling, 1995; Mowbray, 1999; Parkinson, Nelson, and Horgan, 1999).

Geoff and his colleagues, John Lord and Joanna Ochocka, have participated in and documented the process and outcomes of the transformation of mainstream community mental health services in their community (Lord *et al.*, 1998; Nelson *et al.*, 2001b; Nelson, Lord, and Ochocka, 2001a; Ochocka, Nelson, and Lord, 1999). They found that organizational renewal processes which were based on developing a shared vision and values congruent with those of the emerging paradigm led to changes in organizational practices and programmes, which in turn led to positive impacts on the people served by the organizations. The organizations that were studied engaged in a conscious reversal of power in which mental health consumers were encouraged to step up and play a major role in organizational decision-making and the provision of services and supports. Finally, they also found that with the change occurring in mainstream organizations and the creation of a consumer-controlled, self-help organization, that change extended beyond the organizations to the community level. In essence, an alternative community narrative regarding people with mental health problems had been created (Rappaport, 1993).

Similarly, Isaac, Geoff, and colleagues, Leslea Peirson and Judy Gould, consulted with a children's mental health agency in a review of its mandate. A value-based approach was utilized as the foundation for organizational change (Peirson *et al.*, 1997; Prilleltensky, Peirson *et al.*, 1997). As consultants, we negotiated with the agency to have an advisory committee with representation from management, staff, board members, parent-consumers, service-providers from other agencies, and members of the community at large. The primary guiding values of the mandate review were self-determination (what stakeholders want), collaboration (participation of stakeholders), and distributive justice (how stakeholders believe the agency should allocate scarce resources). Focus groups and survey questionnaires were used to gather data regarding the agency's values and vision, needs, resources, and mission from a wide range of stakeholders, including youth involved with the agency, non-referred youth, parent-consumers, non-referred parents, agency workers and board members, school personnel, and other service-providers. This approach was designed to be highly inclusive in gaining input on stakeholders' views about what the mandate of the agency should be.

A number of interesting findings emerged from this consultation. First, when youth were asked what their service needs were, the youth stressed the importance of employment opportunities, making sure parents, teachers, and service-providers listen to and understand youth, youth support groups for different problems, and prevention programmes. In other words, the youth wanted community change and community-oriented intervention approaches, not traditional clinical interventions. These findings underscore the importance of asking youth what they want and need. A second interesting finding concerned how the agency should allocate its resources. We asked agency staff and other service-providers how they would allocate the budget of the agency to different service areas. In the preferred budget, respondents indicated that 39 per cent of the budget should be devoted to prevention and consultation programmes. While the agency did provide some prevention programmes at the time of the review, these findings suggested that the agency should increase its commitment to prevention. This was quite interesting as when we were first interviewed for the job of the mandate review, we explicitly acknowledged our bias in favour of prevention, and staff were concerned that we would push our agenda on them. We indicated that while we were biased toward prevention, that decisions about prevention vs. treatment would be made by them, not us. In the end, the staff wanted more prevention too! In our follow-up with the agency, we found that several of the final recommendations and directions were being implemented by the agency.

In this section, we have provided two examples of attempts to transform human service organizations. Incorporating value-based frameworks for service can move human service organizations along the continuum away from an exclusive focus on amelioration to more of a focus on social and community transformation. While such consultative interventions are important, there is a need to move outside the human services bubble to more normalized community settings.

Voluntary associations

Voluntary associations are those in which community members come together to address a particular issue in their community or to improve or enrich their community in some way. Neighbourhood organizations, community centres, religious settings, and ethnic associations are examples of voluntary associations. Critical psychologists can work in partnership with community members and oppressed groups using a community (or locality) development approach, which we outlined briefly in Chapter 5 (Pilisuk *et al.*, 1996). Critical psychologists can act as facilitators to the process, striving to encourage local ownership and initiative. Weick (1984) has argued for a 'small wins' approach to community change. When people set modest goals and achieve them, momentum and motivation build for further change. Over the long run, many 'small wins' can lead to substantial changes in a community.

Critical psychologists can also conduct participatory action research with citizens who are involved in community development. For example, community psychologists have examined citizen participation and the processes and outcomes of individual and community empowerment in neighbourhood associations and community centres that have been created in low-income or mixed-income neighbourhoods (for example, Eisen, 1994; Powell and Nelson, 1997; Wandersman and Florin, 2000).

Derksen and Nelson (1995) reported on two central power dynamics in neighbourhood organizations. One is the relationship between professional community developers and neighbourhood residents. They found an ongoing 'push and pull' in these relationships regarding who has power. Initially residents are quite suspicious and mistrustful of professionals who enter their community. Over time and through positive working relationships, this mistrust can be diminished. However, professionals must be willing to share power and encourage residents to take control of the intervention process. A second power dynamic is the relationship between low-income and higher-income residents participating in neighbourhood associations. They found that higher-income residents can have prejudices about 'those people' (that is, low-income residents) and are often not attuned to their unique life stressors and circumstances. They identified the importance of 'bridgers,' residents and staff who can effectively link these two groups and build common ground.

Derksen and Nelson (1995) outlined three implications of their study for the critical practice of community development in low-income neighbourhoods. First, community development must involve consciousness-raising for professionals and community members to overcome victim-blaming mythologies and to move from a charity model of intervention to a social justice model. Second, material and human resources must be reallocated to facilitate the process of community development. Low-income residents experience multiple barriers to participation. Providing honoraria, childcare, transportation, and hiring low-income residents are some tangible ways to overcome material barriers. Third, conflict is an integral part of the empowerment process. Working across differences of social class and social status (professional vs. community members) is inherently conflictual. But this conflict presents opportunities for growth and change for everyone who is involved in the community development process.

While neighbourhood associations and community centres are examples of geographically-based community interventions, ethnic organizations are an example of relationally-based communities. Immigrants, refugees, racial minorities, and aboriginal people often experience a number of obstacles to participation in community life, including poverty, racism, poor housing, unemployment, and past traumatic experiences (Beiser *et al.*, 1995; Canadian Task Force on Mental Health Issues Affecting Immigrants and Refugees, 1988; Naidoo and Edwards, 1991). Critical psychologists can work in partnership with ethnic groups to address these social problems. Our colleagues Mary Sehl (1987) and Ed Bennett used a community development approach with new Canadians to create an 80-unit housing cooperative with affordable rents for new Canadians. Sand Hills Cooperative Homes became a springboard for a variety of other community-based initiatives. For example, Isaac became involved with Latin American families in the Sand Hills project, and together they formed the Latin American Educational Group. Using a participatory action research approach, the group identified the need to promote the Spanish language skills of children and prevent smoking (Prilleltensky, 1993). Heritage language classes were created, as well as a smoking prevention programme with a community action component which addressed the role of cigarette companies in promoting youth addiction to tobacco (Prilleltensky, Nelson, and Sanchez-Valdes, 2000).

Other community development approaches with ethnic groups have addressed traumatic experiences. Danjela Seskar-Hencic (1996) and Peggy Nickels (1999) focused on refugee families that had suffered torture and other traumatic experiences. Using participatory action research, they examined the needs of this population and developed an informal organization called the Community Support Group and a subgroup called the Survivors of Torture and Trauma Working Group. This organization brought together school teachers, service-providers, immigrants, and refugees to engage in programme development, school change, and advocacy.

Similarly, Aboriginal communities have recently emphasized community healing to deal with the traumatic experience of child sexual abuse (Connors and Maidman, 2001). For example, members of the Hollow Water reserve have used an approach which involves initial disclosure and protection of the child, confrontation of the perpetrator, community support to encourage the perpetrator to take responsibility, and the use of a healing contract. This is a highly participatory community approach, which ends with a community cleansing ceremony. Positive impacts of this approach have been noted (Connors and Maidman, 2001).

Traditional cultures, such as Amish people, are also under assault by global forces, which threaten their way of life. Bennett (in press) has written about the collusion of agri-business and the state in attempting to restrict Amish people's access to land and to not allow them places to stable their horses (their means of transportation) or build new churches, cemeteries, or second residences through land-use planning regulations. Bennett described his role as a critical community psychologist in mediating between the Amish community and the state, using a variety of legal, policy, media, and community economic development activities to fight for the preservation of the traditional lifestyle of the Amish people.

Alternative settings

Alternative settings are also voluntary associations that are created and controlled by oppressed groups. Within alternative settings, there is a strong emphasis on creating a supportive community, on a holistic approach to health, on horizontal organizational structures that promote participation and power-sharing, on building on the strengths of diverse people who do not 'fit' into existing programmes, and on advocacy for social change (Reinharz, 1984; Riger, 2000). Such settings are formed as an alternative to mainstream organizations that are not based on these same values and which often blame the victims for not adjusting to existing social conditions (Cherniss and Deegan, 2000). Critical psychologists can assist in the creation of such settings, as well as with ongoing consultation (Reinharz, 1984; Sarason, 1972).

One form of alternative setting is self-help/mutual aid organizations and groups (Humphreys and Rappaport, 1994; Levy, 2000). Self-help/mutual aid groups have several characteristics. They are small groups in which people who share a common problem, experience, or concern come together to both provide and receive support. Members are equals, and the groups are voluntary and not for profit. Some of the more well-known groups are Alcoholics Anonymous (AA) and Parents Without Partners. There is a wide variety of such groups and organizations including the following: loss-transition groups (for example, bereavement groups, separation/divorce support groups), groups for people who do not have a problem themselves but who have a family member with a problem (for example, Association for Children with Learning Disabilities – parent support group, Al Anon, and Alateen – a group for children of alcoholics), stress, coping, and support groups (for example, AA, psychiatric survivor groups), and consciousness-raising and advocacy groups (for example, Mothers Against Drunk Driving, women's groups). There is a large range of different types of self-help groups available to people, and it has been estimated that in the USA., more than ten million people participate in a self-help group every year (Kessler, Mickelson, and Zhao, 1997).

How should professionals relate to self-help groups? When self-help group members are asked this question, they basically state that they want professionals to be 'on tap but not on top' (Constantino and Nelson, 1995; MacGillivary and Nelson, 1998). In other words, self-helpers want professionals to practice good partnership, emphasizing respect, collaboration, equality, and appreciation for the knowledge and experience of self-helpers. One vehicle through which professional and self-help collaboration has occurred is through self-help clearinghouses and resource centres (Madara, 1990). Self-help clearinghouses are organizations which promote the self-help concept through information and referral, education, networking, consultation, and research. Critical psychologists can assist self-helpers through research and evaluation, consultation, and advocacy (Nelson, Ochocka et al., 1998). However, it is crucial that critical psychologists act in an enabling manner rather than in a way that promotes professional dominance and consumer dependency.

In this section, we have identified human service organizations, voluntary associations, and alternative settings, both geographically-based and relationally-based, with which critical psychologists can form profitable partnerships for the advancement of disadvantaged people. We have also provided examples of some of the different roles and activities of critical psychologists in these types of community settings. While voluntary associations and alternative settings provide support to disadvantaged people, many of these settings also have a social action and advocacy emphasis.

Conclusion

In this chapter, we considered the importance of community settings for personal well-being and social change. While community has been eroded in many instances, new settings have emerged to enhance civil society. We also considered some of the ways in which critical psychologists can work with people in community settings. Traditionally, psychologists' community involvement has revolved around human services organizations. Moreover, the practice of psychology in human service organizations follows a traditional model which reinforces rather than disrupts the status quo. Alternatively, we suggested ways in which critical psychologists can work in the transformation of human services organizations in line with the values that we have proposed in this book. Furthermore, we argued that critical psychologists can and should become involved in voluntary associations and alternative settings. We provided examples of some of the transformational work that critical psychologists have done in such settings.

10
Work Settings: Working Critically within the Status Quo

Depending on country and continent, psychologists employed by organizations to improve effectiveness have been called industrial/organizational, occupational or work psychologists. Under these rubrics, psychologists have been recruited to help organizations to increase productivity and improve human relations for almost a hundred years (Hollway, 1991). Although psychologists in the fields of industrial/organizational, occupational or work psychology have been typically employed by profit-making companies, psychologists and organizational consultants have more recently been hired to help not-for-profit agencies as well. In this chapter we deal with the roles of psychologists in both types of organizations, in profit-making corporations and in human services.

The website of division 14 of the American Psychological Association, The Society for Industrial and Organizational Psychology, provides a summary of the main activities of psychologists working in this field: selection and placement of employees, training and development, organizational development, performance measurement, quality of work life, consumer and engineering psychology. In this chapter we will deal with selected aspects of most areas, with the exception of consumer and engineering psychology.

From a critical psychology perspective, opportunities to implement desired values of social justice, empowerment, and respect for diversity will depend a great deal on the setting and the contract under which the psychologist is working. Human service organizations are much more amenable to value-based interventions than profit-making corporations where the value of social justice does not feature prominently in their mission statement (Thompson, 1998). Hence, we are careful to avoid illusions that what may be accomplished in community-based organizations can be similarly achieved in insurance companies or competitive business. The terms of employment are crucial for the ability of the psychologist to enact critical psychology principles.

Describing and critiquing the status quo

The traditional practice of psychology in work settings

Organizations usually hire psychologists to provide a range of services related to satisfaction and effectiveness, team building, analysis of organizational structures and recommendations for change, introduction of new procedures, evaluation of programmes, quality of work life initiatives and the like. Organizational development entails some kind of needs assessment, a consultative process with various stakeholder groups, feedback to advisory committees on recommended changes and implementation procedures (Dimock, 1992).

The objectives of the particular project vary according to the aims of management. Some goals include better working relationships among people from various units, work restructuring deriving from budget cuts, and interventions to lift workforce morale. Community-based organizations often engage in organizational development following goal-setting exercises that may or may not involve service users. Business corporations usually pursue changes related to financial utility. To fulfil these different expectations, psychologists engage in organizational analysis, conflict resolution, group facilitation, intergroup coordination, consultation, vision setting, report writing and programme evaluation (Fallon, Pfister, and Brebbner, 1989).

Practitioners working in personnel psychology are usually required to advise on selection, placement, training, evaluation and promotion of employees. In that capacity, psychologists advise on testing and interviewing techniques to assess a worker's performance.

Critical appraisal of psychology in work settings

The argument has been made that organizational psychology is handmaiden to industry. Certainly there is a history of siding with owners to enhance productivity, often at the expense of worker well-being (Baritz, 1974; Deetz, 1992; Herman, 1995; Hollway, 1991; Ralph, 1983; Steffy and Grimes, 1992). Based on that history and on public relations campaigns by organizational psychologists, companies look for psychologists to improve communication, alleviate industrial unrest, select and train employees, foster supportive climates and evaluate programmes. A critical psychology agenda seeks to pursue personal, relational and collective well-being, promote worker empowerment and resist oppression. There will be various grades of compatibility between these two agendas. It seems likely that human, health and social services will be more amenable to the critical psychology philosophy, but we would not rule out possibilities to form partnerships with certain business organizations that may be sympathetic to forms of workplace democracy. Examples of such enterprises include co-operatives, worker-owned businesses and non-government organizations (Quarter, 1992; Quarter and Melnyk, 1989).

Companies are attuned to worker well-being more than to worker oppression. The former has a health ring to it, whereas the latter has a very political connotation. In an ideal world well-being would be enhanced by transformational and political interventions, not just by attitudinal changes and improved health habits. Improving well-being in politically restricted environments is a struggle that many of us face in our own places of employment. The particular context of the contract of the psychologists will determine the space that he or she will have to invoke structural issues.

Very little work from an explicit critical perspective has been carried out in organizational psychology. Our way of interpreting typical expectations derives from the values, assumptions and practices articulated in Chapter 2. Reminiscent of Sandra Harding's book *Whose Science? Whose Knowledge?* (1991), we ask *whose values, whose power, whose good life* and *whose interventions* is the psychologist asked to promote? In simple terms, *whose agent* is the psychologist? Although these are categorical questions that may not have categorical answers, it is still worth posing the questions in sharp terms to raise awareness of the different interests that are at stake in organizations.

Written and unwritten contracts may stipulate that the psychologist is to respond to management's requests. After all, management pays the salary. Within those parameters, we, as critical psychologists, can conduct an evaluation of what degrees of freedom we will have to advance workers' well-being. A critical formulation requires that we go beneath the surface of a rhetoric of well-being and collective empowerment. Human resources and management writings call for organizational development, a term which by itself may appear neutral or benevolent (Warwick, 1978). Once we start to ask questions about whose interests will be advanced and whose idea was it to initiate the intervention we can adopt a healthy degree of scepticism. We do not endorse scepticism for its own sake, but rather as a tool that precedes action (Sánchez Vidal, 1999).

The testing and classification of individuals, another popular task for organizational psychologists, carries many risks. The first risk is that people are categorized according to cultural norms that may benefit one group and disadvantage another. Norms of success and productivity manufactured by apologists of the capitalist system may very well narrow the meaning of a good and productive life. To some extent, buying into the testing industry is buying into norms that privilege some and disadvantage others. A second risk is that tests usually discriminate against people from other backgrounds. The third risk is that test results artificially fixate an individual at a certain level of ability, thus restricting his or her potential for change until dramatic changes in performance occur. The fourth danger is that the act of testing internalizes skills and deficits and eclipses the influence of environmental and structural factors in productivity and performance. Testing is one of the most individualizing and atomizing acts in society; success and failure are attributed to intrapsychic forces; no need to look for social explanations. 'Individuals are presented as numerical objects that can be observed, held over time, retrieved, analysed and shared by interested parties. Information not measured, often information depicting the employee as unique, dynamic and ever-changing, may be largely discounted and ignored' (Steffy and Grimes, 1992:191). Psychology has contributed enormously to this culture of individuo-centric performance. Another risk is that we venerate test results as cultural icons that define personal success, or failure, in terms of psychometric properties.

Much has been written about the discriminatory use of testing in industry, immigration, and education (Bird, 1999; Steffy and Grimes, 1992). In addition, many have noted the objectifying, stereotyping, and labelling potential of tests (Cernovsky, 1997). Insofar as tests can restrict life opportunities unfairly and represent only one narrow vision of the good life, there are reasons to reconsider automatic endorsement of testing practices.

The obvious question now is this: What is a critical psychologist to do with the expectation that she or he will have to test, evaluate, and select employees for jobs and promotions? If tests discriminate against people from non-mainstream cultures and potentially affix people to undesirable categories, what is there to be done? In the next section we explore the options.

Shifting the paradigm in psychology in work settings

Partnerships for practice

In line with the framework presented in Chapter 2, we provide in Table 10.1 an overview of values, assumptions and practices guiding critical psychology in work settings. Our ability to infuse these principles in organizations will depend on the openness of the institution to alternative perspectives. We are not sanguine about such openness but we realize that we need guidelines to push the boundaries of organizations willing to consider alternative views.

Remarkably little has been written from an explicit critical psychology perspective on organizations. Lateral discussions invoke feminist and community psychology principles in organizational settings (Bond, 1999; Lawthom, 1999), but it is hard to find writings on how to practise critical psychology in industrial settings.

Values

Table 10.1 describes how the values we espouse can inform a psychologist's job in creating partnerships in work settings. We have already established that psychologists are not, nor can they be, value-neutral. The appearance of value-neutrality would be deceiving, primarily in institutions set up to make money and influence public opinion on the merits of consumerism (Alvesson and Willmott, 1992; Baritz, 1974). We suggest making relevant to workplace managers and employees the importance of balancing values for personal, relational and collective well-being. The individual well-being of workers, largely dependent on their ability to exercise control over their environment, is just as important as giving and receiving social support and functioning in a sanitary and well-paying work place. Employers are likely to focus on personal and relational values and needs such as self-determination and social support, for they have been proven to increase satisfaction and productivity (Daniels and Harris, 2000; Sperry, 1991). They are unlikely, in many cases, to improve working conditions and remuneration because they may cut into profits. Variations in organizations' willingness to engage in processes to promote collective well-being will no doubt be found. But in any case, the psychologist with a critical orientation should be prepared for opposition when it comes to collective well-being issues, as they involve social justice and sharing of profits.

Table 10.1 Critical psychology in work settings: Partnerships for practice

Critical psychology tenets	Possibilities for action
Values	*Content:* Discuss with various stakeholders the importance of attending to personal, relational and collective well-being as the well-being of individuals within the setting depends on meeting needs at all these three levels. Supportive relationships and structures enable workers to feel good about themselves and their work. Imbalance caused by excessive expectations of structures on individuals leads to burn-out and illness.
	Process: Ask various stakeholders groups what they require to meet their own personal and relational needs and what they can do to help others within the organization to meet their own individual and collective needs. This process acknowledges that all members of an organization have personal needs and are expected to contribute to the collective well-being at the same time. Using Table 1.1, workers can identify their own needs and the needs of others towards which they can make a contribution.
Assumptions	*Content:* Draw attention to power differentials within the organization and its effects on the health of workers. Power and ability to control aspects of the job determines subjective well-being of employees. Discuss also norms within workplace regarding good life. Examine expectations for personal sacrifice for the company and/or its clients. Culture of overwork, prevalent in many places, can have oppressive effects on workers.
	Process: Engage various stakeholders groups in discussions about their vision for a healthy workplace. Compare and contrast their vision with actual state of affairs. Bring to attention of power holders within the organization the vision and needs of those with less power in the setting. Examine with stakeholders how power differentials affect their own health and position within the workplace and how they influence the well-being of colleagues in the setting.
Practices	*Content:* Include in problem definition structural issues related to work settings and power differentials. Devise interventions that address not only individual or interpersonal factors but also organizational arrangements. Consider preventive interventions that promote the well-being of workers through social support and improved working conditions.
	Process: Initiate dialogue with workers on their well-being needs. Alliances with workers or managers will determine to what extent psychologist can promote consciousness raising about oppressive conditions in the workplace. Labour will welcome consciousness-raising whereas management will oppose initiatives designed to challenge their interests and authority in the business.

Assumptions

The role of power and control in organizations is central to the well-being of workers (for example, Daniels and Guppy, 1992; Marmot *et al.*, 1999). For that reason, all kinds of organizations espouse worker empowerment. The challenge though is to distinguish between interventions that afford real versus just imagined control. Sophisticated discourses in business create the *impression* of giving more power to workers (for an example of this phenomenon see Boyett and Conn, 1991), when in fact not much changes in their ability to make decisions.

Whereas discussions about power and control may be off-limits, deliberations about mission statements may be more acceptable. Table 10.1 refers to prevalent conceptions of the good life and the good society in organizations. Many companies, for-profit and not-for-profit alike, engage in revision of mandate and mission statements. These processes may offer an opportunity to critical psychologists to introduce the importance of creating a vision for the organization that includes values of self-determination, caring and compassion, personal growth, respect for diversity, social support and social justice. Needless to say, some organizations create poetic mission statements that serve exclusively public relations purposes. However, given the few opportunities that may exist for psychologists to make changes in organizations, this may be a precious chance.

Practices

The third part of Table 10.1 deals with potential practices in work settings. Problem definition, organizational diagnosis and needs assessments are central practices in organizational work. A major thrust that the critical psychologist needs to resist is the tendency to individualize problems and locate them within the head of workers. Structural arrangements of work dictate, to a large extent, the level of well-being of the organization and its workers. Oppressive practices within managements or within units can cause burn-out or emotional abuse. The potential abuse and exploitation of workers need not necessarily occur from the top to the bottom, as workers can discriminate among themselves on the bases of race, gender and ability (Bond, 1999; Keashley, 1998).

Critical alternatives

We deal here with critical alternatives for evaluation of worker performance and organizational development. Although it may not be feasible in selection procedures for initial employment, it may be possible in performance evaluation to devise participatory means of evaluation that do not include testing or intrusive measures. Workers' input into evaluation procedures increases a sense of control. Indeed, performance evaluations are a source of anxiety for many workers. The personal and collective well-being of workers may be enhanced when they are part of the group constructing evaluation procedures. Depending on the overall working environment, it may be feasible to have a high level of worker representation on committees looking at workplace productivity and promotions.

Another strategy to de-individualize work performance is to conduct an ecological analysis of working conditions along with employees' performance. This means instituting procedures to look at the whole work environment and conduct a systemic evaluation of the entire place, including psychological atmosphere, social support, power relations, and the like. Many workers report that their productivity and well-being are highly influenced by human relations (Briner, 2000; Goleman, 1998). Therefore, individualizing performance in test scores or productivity units is to obviate the influence of the social and physical conditions of work.

Action and process management approaches advocate a constant learning model whereby the organization is always involved in reflective practice (Senge, 1990; Senge et al., 1994). This strategy, which, granted, may be currently reserved for upper management only, has the potential to incorporate learning and renewal throughout the organization.

It may not be possible for the critical psychologist to evade requests for testing altogether, in which case efforts can be made to note the limitations of tests. Promoting more participatory and systemic means of evaluating individuals and teams may gradually introduce a new culture in the workplace. In either case, the critical psychologist is in a tough position, akin to critical management practitioners who are aware of potential misuses of test results but whose jobs depend on harmony with executive officers (Nord and Jermier, 1992).

With respect to organizational development, we emphasize the need to work in partnerships. We believe in creating a partnership with the various stakeholder groups affected by the process and outcomes of change. The principles we recommend for the formation of partnerships are as follows: (a) create partnerships; (b) clarify values and vision and derive working principles; (c) accept difference but move towards common goals; (d) define the problem and intervention collaboratively; and (e) evaluate intervention collaboratively.

Step I: Create partnerships

The first step in organizational development work is to identify the groups affected by the problem or proposed change. Depending on the nature of the project the partners may include people who are internal and/or external to the organization. Deciding who will sit at the table can be a contentious issue. The person hiring the psychologist or organizational consultant may wish to exert full control over potential partners. Senior managers of a hospital or a community agency may not want consumers represented at the table. Corporate officers may fear challenges by consumers. In a sense, this is the first test for the critical psychologist wanting to empower disadvantaged groups: will he or she succeed at bringing to the table all concerned?

In our view, it is imperative that everyone affected by institutional practices be represented in decision-making processes. Particular emphasis should be placed on bringing workers and consumers to the table, as they tend to be under-represented in partnerships. The critical psychologist can use a variety of methods to attain this aim. We try to argue for the value of self-determination of partners and for the need for representation and collaborative and democratic participation. But we do not delude ourselves that everyone will listen to the plea for democratic dialogue. Artful persuasion and negotiation skills are required to explain that all partners should be present at the decision-making table.

Once everyone who needs to join the partnership has been invited, efforts should be made to ensure that all participants feel welcome and are not threatened. Consumers and workers who feel relatively powerless when they sit with professionals, owners, or high-ranking professionals should be given an opportunity to speak up their mind. Power dynamics in meetings must be attended to in order to prevent the silencing of those with less perceived or actual power. As a group facilitator, the psychologist is to enable all parties to feel comfortable. Giving participants an opportunity to express their needs and wishes for the organizational development process is a good place to start.

Step II: Clarify values and vision and derive working principles

Presenting values and vision for the organizational development allows partners to have a say in the direction of the process. This step requires a consultation with various stakeholder groups on their desired outcomes and mechanisms. A certain amount of conflict and differences of opinions is expected. The psychologist enables clarification of divergent positions and tries to find common ground; a position that is acceptable by all concerned. This phase may be quick or very slow, depending on the distance between different partners at the outset. We advise against skipping this step because if consensus is not reached a heavy price will be paid later. Striving for consensus means that partners are satisfied that their concerns have been addressed, and that if they gave up something about their vision, they know why and feel at ease with that decision. This is really an exercise in unearthing hidden agendas as much as possible. The psychologist will have to be able to contain tension and live with tension for a while. He or she will decide when common ground has been found regarding the vision and values to guide the process. Decisions will have to be made as to who will benefit from the process, who may be negatively affected by new working conditions, who will oversee the process, and most importantly, what values will guide the project.

In our experience, it is productive to ask people what values they wish to have upheld in the process. People may suggest empowerment, respect, honesty, or other values. Once these values have been articulated, the next challenge is to derive working principles for these moral values. In other words, how do we translate respect? How do we implement empowerment? What criteria do we use to ensure that these principles are being enacted in practice? The development of such criteria is part of this phase. We recommend being explicit about criteria and circulating to all partners the agreement reached concerning values, working principles, and criteria for evaluating the implementation of working principles. Working principles for empowerment and democratic participation may determine that major decisions affecting the process will be taken in consultation with the entire group, or that consumers will have a majority representation in certain committees dealing with service users and service delivery.

Step III: Accept difference but move towards common goals

Throughout the preceding tasks psychologists are encouraged to build on the strengths of different perspectives. This is really an exercise in recognition of different partners' positions. The point is not to eliminate differences, which may remain well after the organizational development process, but to reach a point whereby dialogue can be pursued and different players appreciate diverse needs and interests. What happens in partnerships is a microcosm of the larger society where differences must be negotiated for co-existence.

Instead of pointing to people's defences we suggest building on people's perceived needs. We believe that expression of personal and collective needs is a good place to start the dialogue. Accusations, instead, lead to defensive postures that block dialogue. While efforts should be directed at finding common ground, it is possible that such ground will not be found, and that open conflict may be the best option left to workers to attain improvement in working conditions. Confrontation may also be the only solution for consumers wishing to draw attention to their grievances against the medical or psychiatric system. In other words, although we favour conflict resolution and mediation, we are aware that these methods may not always lead to better conditions for the oppressed. Hence, we are not unconditionally in favour of partnerships when these do not result in empowerment of the disadvantaged.

Step IV: Define the problem and intervention collaboratively

Assuming the process so far has rendered a common understanding of goals, the psychologist would guide the partners to define the main problems and devise the intervention collaboratively. The critical psychologist is to be always alert to potential hijacking of the agenda by powerful players. We hasten to point out though that powerful players are not necessarily those with more money or organizational prestige behind them. Isaac was part of a mutual-help group for immigrants and refugees where a woman from the group injected fear in others. On the surface she was not unlike others in many characteristics, but she wielded a lot of power by her aggressive interpersonal style.

Throughout negotiations with partners, we see the role of the critical psychologist as ensuring that the values of democratic participation, respect for diversity, collaboration and social justice are carefully considered. This is what differentiates a critical psychologist perhaps from other organizational consultants. Whereas others may be satisfied with getting results and getting the job done, the critical psychologist insists on practising from a value-based perspective that seeks to overcome oppression in the workplace.

Step V: Evaluate intervention collaboratively

Organizational development may take the form of changed work routines, improved physical conditions, different communication and reporting patterns, interdisciplinary collaboration, consumer representation, working groups, or others. In all cases, the changes will affect the stakeholders in different ways. Change that may have been conceived as positive may turn out to be detrimental. This is why it is important to evaluate collaboratively the effects of interventions. In some quarters, a process evaluation is suggested so that members of the partnerships get feedback on their work as they go along. Others prefer a summative evaluation. We recommend both, for it is dangerous to wait until the end of the project to find out that something was not right from the start.

Listening and influencing skills, negotiating ability, group facilitation, leadership, empathy, and conflict resolution are basic competencies for organizational development. The critical psychologist will benefit from being a good listener, a skilled negotiator and a seasoned group leader. These skills have been documented by organizational consultants as essential for success (Dimock, 1992; Goleman, 1998). But to these skills the critical psychologist needs to add a few more competencies. The ability to recognize power dynamics, to enact values of empowerment and social justice, and to reflect critically on her or his role in perpetuating oppressive conditions, are all vital. These are not the type of skills that are usually taught in graduate school: empathy, listening, yes; power and politics, no. Critical psychology brings to practice a self-reflective stance that is missing in most industrial/organizational approaches. Most texts and training materials, for instance, erase power relations from their curriculum (Barling, 1988; Steffy and Grimes, 1992).

This self-reflective stance is difficult to attain in isolation, just as it is difficult to be an activist in isolation. Psychologists with a critical orientation are expected to practise in unconventional ways that require them to examine their own role in perpetuating oppression. This is not something we are trained to do, or can easily do on our own. Hence, peer support is crucial for the pursuit of alternative practices. The pull to be in line with accepted 'best practice'–practice that rarely includes scrutiny of the role of our discipline in exploiting workers–is very strong.

Conclusion

We end the chapter where we started: with caveats and hopes. First, caveats: In 1974, Baritz claimed that industrial organizational psychologists act as 'servants of power'. In 1978, Warwick noted that effective organizational development interventions 'almost always change or reinforce the balance of power, influence and authority in a system. Some individuals and groups will gain in the ability to pursue their interests and intentions, while others will lose' (149). In 1987, Wells wrote that quality of working life projects are 'simply a softer, subtler management-control strategy, yet one that is more ambitious and all-embracing than anything seen before. Management is no longer satisfied with making workers obey: it now wants them to *want* to obey' (5–6). In 1992, Steffy and Grimes argued that personnel psychology ignores 'structural constraints, collective actions and issues endemic to the analysis of collectives such as conflict, class, politics and power' (189). Maintaining clarity with respect to one's values in such an environment is a challenging, but not impossible task. This brings us to hope. We believe that critical psychologists supporting each other can make a difference in work settings. We proposed the development of partnerships in organizational development as well as worker and consumer input in leadership. We advocated for participatory means of evaluating work performance and for leader accountability. Furthermore, we offered means of disentangling issues of power, values, and interests. These are, we hope, entry points for critical psychologists working in organizations.

In the past, unions have been reluctant to engage with psychologists because of the perception that psychologists are in league with managers (Huszczo, Wiggins, and Currie, 1984). Unions, however, represent just another group with whom critical psychologists can form meaningful partnerships. The principles presented in Chapter 9 dealing with community groups apply all the same to unions and labour organizations. As critical psychologists, we have expertise in the deconstruction of power discourses and in the establishment of partnerships for solidarity, an excellent combination for collaboration with labour.

Part IV

Change

You are a psychologist, you've heard of critical psychology, you agree with its tenets. Still, you have a hard time translating its ideas into practice. As a clinician, you enact the values of self-determination and respect for diversity within the therapeutic session. You show caring and compassion and even talk with your clients about the negative effects of oppressive social structures and dominant discourses. Question: Is this enough to call your practice critical psychology?

Many people struggle with that question. Psychologists tell me they enact critical psychology values in the micro-setting of therapy but don't know how to extend the work beyond these boundaries. That's a valid point. To get stuck in the micro-setting is to obviate the need for change in the very structures that employ us. Indeed, throughout the book we have emphasized the need to work across levels of intervention. We can be very empathic and empowering within the confines of therapy, but what about those who don't come to see us for therapy? What about the pressures to do reactive work when we can be preventing stress in disadvantaged populations in the first place? How do we overcome expectations to do individual work when changes in the social environment may be more effective in the long run? Facing dilemmas of this kind on your own can be difficult and disheartening. Getting together with others who share your concerns is a first step in making a change.

Critical psychology is not a specific technique but a position with respect to values, assumptions and practices. It does not invalidate useful therapeutic methods or community interventions. Rather, it compels us to examine all these tools with a critical eye. Furthermore, it makes us think about our own work practices. Different settings require more or less changes to become empowering places for workers and clients alike. On your own, these changes are hard to make. With support from partners the process of change is easier.

Just as we want our clients to be strategic about their lives, we should be strategic about critical psychology as well. Through the lenses of critical and feminist psychology many people have come to question existing practices. To generate change, many psychologists have come together to vent their discontent and conceive of positive alternatives. Dennis Fox and I convened a meeting of psychologists with radical impulses at a meeting of the American Psychological Association in Toronto in 1993. About two dozen people attended. We shared aggravations about mainstream psychology. We came from different fields of psychology – social, community, clinical, developmental – but we had a similar aim: to create alternatives to the constraining way of doing psychology that we were all taught. Since that meeting many projects have taken place. With the help of some people, Dennis Fox led the establishment of the *Radical Psychology Network (RadPsyNet, see http://www.radpsynet.org)*, an informal network of support for psychologists across the world. For many psychologists, *RadPsyNet* provides a source of support. For many students, it provides a source of hope. Many practitioners cannot find the support they need within their own places of employment. As with *RadPsyNet*, we need to create alternative or parallel structures where we can address the radical impulses that our own jobs suppress. Through *RadPsyNet*, people have established an electronic journal, members have exchanged reading lists, Dennis and I co-edited *Critical Psychology: An Introduction*, and Sandra Pacheco and her students in California organized in 2001 a critical psychology conference.

In the late eighties, soon after I started working for the Child Guidance Clinic of Winnipeg, Canada, I began to realize that not all was right with the way the educational system treated children who were categorized as troubled or troubling. Although my discomfort evolved rather quickly, my power to change things within the school system evolved rather slowly. As in many service organizations, the well-being of the service recipient is not always at the forefront of the people in charge. School principals would want to get rid of trouble-makers, parents would blame the kids, teachers would blame the parents, kids would blame the teachers, clinicians would blame them all. For the most part, adults were invested in fixing the problem in ways that involved minimal or no amount of change on their part. Solutions were welcome for as long as they did not disturb the status quo. Veiled threats were insidious. Teachers were afraid of being incompetent, clinicians were afraid of not being helpful, parents were afraid of being blamed for the child's problems, kids were afraid to be thrown out of school. As a worker, I formed certain opinions as to how things should change for children, but it was not until I felt secure enough that I could act on my convictions without feeling at risk for rocking the boat. With time, I resisted the pressure to diagnose children, I was able to push for prevention and not just reactive therapies, and was able to afford children and parents a more prominent place at the negotiating table.

Five years after I left the clinic I returned to do some research and consulting. I was no longer an employee but an outsider with inside connections. With some colleagues I explored ethical dilemmas of mental health workers practising in the school system. As an outsider who was offering to do research for free (we had a federal grant to pay for expenses), I had a certain degree of latitude. Our research team followed a partnership model and the project evolved from research on ethical dilemmas to organizational development. I regard the project as fairly successful in that the organization was willing to reconsider some of its ways to meet the needs of children. The key to the positive outcomes was the care that was taken in forming a partnership with the organization through extensive and inclusive consulting with the various units and disciplines in the clinic.

We describe in this section some strategies for critical psychology praxis that may help you consolidate your own pathway towards critical work. It may require initiative and calling a few meetings where only a few people show up. But you don't really need a lot of people to start a process of change. It's a misconception to think that lots of bodies are needed to generate alternatives. My friend Dennis

Fox says that 'one loud individual can always be dismissed as a crackpot. Two as some bizarre pair. But three critics are the beginning of a social movement, with a mailing list, and a future' (Fox, 2000:32).

Isaac Prilleltensky

Introduction

More than anything else, critical psychology practice and action is about creating transformative change. In the first section, we outlined the foundations of a critical psychology that is concerned with change. We described a journey of personal and political change that occurs at multiple levels of analysis (self, relationships, community, and society) and that is guided by the core concepts of values (personal, relational, and collective), oppression, empowerment, and well-being. The overarching goal of critical psychology is for psychologists to form partnerships with disadvantaged groups to overcome oppression and to promote well-being. This involves a process of empowerment, in which power imbalances are identified and in which steps are taken to reverse such imbalances.

In the second section, we provided directions for training in critical psychology in teaching, research, and applied work. Critical psychology teaching is not about students getting filled up with psychological facts and theories; it is about consciousness-raising and helping students in their journey as social-change agents. Critical psychology research is not about knowledge for knowledge's sake, with the psychologist as *the* knower of truth; it is learning with disadvantaged people and using the knowledge that is gained for social change. Critical psychology practice/action is not about a professionalized and decontextualized application of psychological techniques to human problems; it is about entering into the social world of oppressed individuals, groups, and communities and working in partnership with them to create change. In the third section, we focused on applying critical psychology concepts and approaches in diverse settings, including clinical, counselling, school, health, community, and work environments. For each setting, we described and critiqued the status quo of traditional psychological practice, and we outlined the values, assumptions, and practices needed to shift the paradigm in such settings towards an agenda that is consistent with the values of critical psychology.

In this final section, we focus in more depth on transformative change. How can critical psychology shift the paradigm in training and practice? What are the obstacles that are encountered in the process? In Chapter 11, we focus on critical psychologists as agents of social change. We describe potential roles that critical psychologists can play in creating change and the challenges that they face. The focus of Chapter 12 is on the process of change. In this chapter, we outline a model of critical psychology praxis that links needs, context, vision, and action. Moreover, we discuss the importance of partnerships for the change process. In the final chapter, we argue that a critical object of change is that of social policy. We review perspectives on social policy and consider strategies for affecting policy change. In our discussion of policy change, we describe the current socio-political context and the challenges that the current context poses for creating radical changes in social policy.

Throughout this section on change, we relate personal dilemmas and changes that we have experienced in our work as critical psychologists. Change is very much a reflective process, in which the agent, the process, and the object of change are in a fluid state. The metaphor of 'a work in progress' aptly sums up our thoughts and experiences regarding critical psychology and the issue of change.

11

Psychologists as Agents of Change: Getting Ready to Make a Difference

Whereas in the previous section we discussed the role of psychologists as helpers in specific settings, in this section we consider the role of psychologists as change agents in their own workplace, in voluntary organizations and other community settings. The focus here is not so much on the professional role of psychologists, but rather on their role as citizens who wish to promote change. The critical psychologist cannot promote change on his or her own – support from peers and partners is crucial. Therefore, we need to concentrate on what can be done in different settings to bring them more in line with the philosophy of critical psychology. We offer here some suggestions for assuming the role of internal-change agent. In the next two chapters, we discuss strategies for acting on larger societal structures.

Critical psychologists can exert considerable influence on the culture of a setting. This influence is exercized through their own personal agency. The book edited by Tod Sloan, *Critical Psychology: Voices for Change* (Sloan, 2000), documents struggles and successful actions by critical psychologists around the globe. Our formulation of agency postulates that agents of change have to mediate differences and propose visions of justice and empowerment.

Our formulation of agency for critical psychology is based on a model of value-based leadership (Prilleltensky, 2000). The model is based on tensions among values, interests, and power; tensions that take place within and among workers, organizational leaders, and community groups. The model is premised on the assumption that people experience internal conflicts related to values, interests, and power; and external conflicts related to disagreements with the public, co-workers, or managers. Critical practice is predicated on the ability to alleviate these tensions in order to move the agenda of critical psychology forward.

Conflicts related to values, interests and power

Critical agency fosters emancipation and collectivism in consideration of personal interests and degrees of power. This type of practice is based on the understanding

149

that vested interests and social power can, and do, interfere with the promotion of values. Critical psychologists need to monitor how subjective, interpersonal and political processes facilitate or inhibit service for people who experience oppression; oppression that is often exacerbated by service providers themselves.

Critical agency concerns partnerships and conflicts among various groups; principally among psychologists themselves, other workers within a setting, and the citizens served by the organization. Each group contends with a triangle of concerns formed by values, interests and power. Not only are groups vested in promoting certain values, but also in protecting their interests and using their power to do so. But power is not used only to advance personal or group interests, for it can also be used to advance collective values. In the light of the model presented in Chapter 1, we do not see power as necessarily or exclusively negative.

Action for Children was a coalition that Isaac helped to establish in the Waterloo region in Ontario, Canada. The group started with personal invitations to about 30 community members interested in children's rights. About half that number attended the first session, and a core of ten people sustained the coalition. Membership was diverse and people represented diverse interests indeed. There were physicians, journalists, psychologists, social workers, mothers who worked at home, workers from social services and from child welfare agencies. Some were volunteers, some saw this as part of their job. As chair of the coalition, Isaac had to negotiate differences of opinion and interpersonal conflicts. While pronounced, conflicts had to do with strategy and not with principle. Together, we advanced a common vision of eliminating child abuse in the region. As a group, we used our power to promote children's rights and advocate for better services and policies. We had ads in newspapers, launched petitions for child-friendly policies, convinced the major charity in the region to increase funding for child abuse prevention and challenged government officials to do the same. Our collective power was put to good use.

Agents of change need to understand the dynamic interaction among values, interests and power in each of the various groups forming a partnership. Conflicts may arise within individuals, who struggle to harmonize their interests with their values, as well as within and across groups. Members of a group may differ with respect to their values and interests, and may use their differential power to get their way (Bradshaw, 1998; DiTomaso and Hooijberg, 1996). Similarly, groups may disagree about preferred values and may have conflicting interests. Whereas values promote the welfare of others in society, interests represent an investment in our own well-being. Workers, leaders, and community members have their own economic, material, social and psychological interests to protect.

For as long as personal interests are not threatened, and vision and values are clear, individuals are likely to engage in value-based actions. But once their interests are at risk, violated, or in conflict with a common mission, their commitment to values will likely diminish (Brumback, 1991; DiTomaso and Hooijberg, 1996). In *Action for Children*, we had a common vision, people came out of their own volition, and nobody felt threatened. A climate of respect and camaraderie quickly developed.

Positive examples notwithstanding, we should not assume that we will pursue justice and empowerment because they have been clearly articulated; we should be mindful of the ways in which interests may interfere with critical practice. It is not possible for colleagues to suppress their subjectivity in the name of altruistic causes, primarily when doing so may jeopardize their occupational standing, emotional well-being, or perceived status.

As noted in Chapter 1, power can be defined as the ability and possibility to influence the course of events in one's life. The ability to promote personal well-being depends on one's economic, social and psychological power. If a person commands sufficient power to fulfil and protect his or her personal interests, the chances are that he or she would be more inclined to pursue value-based actions. But while the power to protect personal interests may be a necessary condition, it is not a sufficient condition for the promotion of values. Instead of using power to share resources with others, some people use power to achieve more personal power (Bradshaw, 1998; DiTomaso and Hooijberg, 1996).

In every setting, power suffuses every aspect of the collective endeavour. As Bradshaw (1998) clearly indicated, the power of those in authority can be exercized through overt or covert means. While some democratic gestures may be explicit, hidden dynamics of system-maintenance may operate at deeper levels. There is the risk of pretending to be democratic and sharing power with employees on minor issues but retaining a tight control on major issues. The pretence of democracy and power equalization at the surface is undermined by subtle mechanisms that reproduce the status quo.

Within-group tensions are very prevalent. Co-workers argue about how to serve the public best and how to allocate burdens and resources within the organization. Conflicts can be strictly of values – how to promote the well-being of a client population; or related to power – how to distribute the workload among professionals. When power differentials are introduced, conflicts within groups are very pronounced. Physicians order nurses, psychiatrists tell social workers what to do, supervisors control interns, and the like. Interdisciplinary teams are known for power struggles related to values and interests (Chambliss, 1996).

From a critical psychology perspective, the role of the change agent is to facilitate in him or herself, in the group, and in the community it serves, congruence among values, interests, and power. The objective should be to enhance the zone of congruence among the various groups and members within them. Expanding zones of congruence among diverse people is a difficult task. In the next section we provide some directions.

Roles for the change agent

Critical psychologists strive to promote values for personal, relational, and collective well-being. Table 11.1 provides some suggestions for enacting the three sets of values within organizations and communities. But for these guidelines to work we need to be careful of potential subversions that might occur along the way. To guard against distortions of good intentions, we describe below roles and tasks for the change agent, as well as factors that facilitate or threaten the job. We explain below four central tasks for the agent of change.

Table 11.1   Partnerships for balancing personal, relational, and collective well-being in diverse settings

Values for	Guidelines
Personal well-being	
Self-determination	Promote the ability of colleagues and disadvantaged community members to pursue their chosen goals in life *in consideration* of other people's needs.
Health	Promote the physical and emotional well-being of colleagues and disadvantaged community members through acquisition of skills and behavioral change *in consideration* of structural and economic factors impinging on the health of the population at large.
Personal growth	Promote the personal growth of colleagues and disadvantaged community members *in consideration* of vital community structures needed to advance individual health and self-actualization.
Relational well-being	
Respect for diversity	Promote respect and appreciation for diverse social identities *in consideration* of need for solidarity and risk of social fragmentation.
Collaboration and democratic participation	Promote peaceful, respectful, and equitable processes of dialogue whereby citizens have meaningful input into decisions affecting their lives, *in consideration* of need to act and not just avoid conflicts.
Collective well-being	
Social justice	Promote fair allocation of bargaining powers, resources, and obligations in community and settings *in consideration* of people's differential power, needs and abilities.
Support for community	Promote vital structures that meet the needs of workers and disadvantaged communities *in consideration* of the risks of curtailing individual freedoms and fostering conformity and uniformity.

Clarify position of organization with respect to values

Values for personal, relational, and collective well-being should exist in a state of balance. The needs of the individual have to be in harmony with the needs of the collective. To achieve balance between individual and collective values we require relational principles to mediate between conflicting interests. The role of the change agent is to help the organization clarify its values and reach a balance between the well-being of its members and the welfare of service recipients. In *Action for Children*, we worked together to advocate for abused children, and rallied behind a clear and common goal: The elimination of child abuse by the year 2020.

The task of value clarification requires the engagement of three stakeholder groups: citizens, workers, and organizational leaders. The change agent is to facilitate a participatory process whereby representatives from these groups debate their vision and values for the setting. A participatory process of value articulation encourages collective ownership over the mission of the groups or organization (Maton and Salem, 1995; Racino, 1991; Senge, 1990). An open forum for the community of workers and clients is a good place to start the process of value clarification. This process is similar to the formation of partnerships discussed in Chapter 10.

Although we value what partners have to offer, we have to remember that it is possible for a group to choose values in a biased way. The group may privilege values for personal well-being at the expense of collective welfare. The group may unwittingly and unknowingly foster individualism instead of collaboration between citizens and communities. Given the dominance of individualism in our culture, this is a likely scenario. In the case of skewed preferences for either personal or collective well-being, or in the case of neglect of relational well-being, it is the role of the critical psychologist to suggest a more balanced approach.

While change agents may be sincere in their desire to formulate a cogent set of values, their good intentions are threatened by a number of risks. The first risk is to remain at a level of abstraction that makes for an internally coherent set of values but that is of little use in practice. How often have we seen mission state-ments that bear absolutely no resemblance to what happens on the ground? One of our favourites is a school district whose mission statement is 'empowering life-long learners who strive for excellence in a changing world'. Values have to be articulated in such a way that they can be translated into concrete policies and guidelines, not in a way that makes mission statements completely unattainable.

Another risk inherent in the process of value clarification is confusing personal preferences with morally legitimate principles (Becker, 1998). Some management books outline a process of value clarification that relies primarily on what workers prefer, but not necessarily on what is legitimate (Senge *et al.*, 1994). Values derive their legitimacy from grounded input by people, but also from moral philosophy. Values proposed by citizens have to be scrutinized for their ability to promote personal, relational, and collective well-being. Unless they are morally defensible, statements of values amount to no more than preferences (Becker, 1998); prefer-ences that may be reprehensible. Citizens are known to have wished upon others horrible things, like ethnic cleansing.

Prevent personal power and self-interests of some from undermining the well-being of others

This role entails the development of awareness of how personal power and vested interests suffuse all aspects of our work. This is an awareness that should be spread throughout the organization. Workers and leaders need to reflect on how their personal lives and subjective experiences influence what they deem ethical or valu-able for the organization, for themselves, and for the public they serve. Awareness, however, is only the first step in buffering vested interests. The satisfaction of personal needs is another important requisite. Workers are more likely to abide by collective values and norms when they feel that their personal needs are being met. Lack of satisfaction can result in disengagement from the mission of helping. When workers or peers feel disenfranchised they harbour resentment and choose to withdraw. Wounded and withdrawn peers help neither themselves nor others.

Research consistently points to the need for a safe space where workers can disclose their ethical dilemmas without feeling judged (Goleman, 1998; Prilleltensky, Walsh-Bowers, and Rossiter, 1999; Rossiter, Prilleltensky, and Walsh-Bowers, 2000). Professionals yearn for a space where they can talk with peers about their conflicts. An organizational climate of openness and acceptance can foster disclosure of problems and paths towards resolution.

The process of balancing interests with values can be subverted in various directions. One possible subversion is the development of a discourse on values that legitimizes self-interests. For example, the notion of a 'self-made person', which is quite prevalent in western countries, can lead to justification of privilege (Prilleltensky, 1994). The value of personal merit can be distorted into a pretext for not sharing power or resources. Self-determination, skills and perseverance may be good qualities, but when they come to justify privilege they lose their legitimacy.

Another potential subversion is the creation of a safe space that does not challenge but rather soothes a guilty conscience. A safe space for the discussion of value dilemmas should not turn into a confessional for absolution. Rather, these spaces should foster dialogue from which different practices can emerge. The object of safe spaces is not to repent, or merely complain, but to initiate new practices.

It is not easy to moderate personal power or vested interests. Serving others' needs is an admirable goal that is forever plagued by personal interests. In order to enhance our own accountability, our efforts should be scrutinized by partners. This requires that we put on the table our own personal interests. This recommendation demands serious commitment to values, a commitment that goes beyond adherence to mission statements. Geoff and his research colleagues faced many challenges by consumer/survivors in the community. The research team was asked to be accountable to the group and to share resources from a research grant. When you choose to be open and upfront about your values, there is no place to hide.

But walking the talk in one setting is not a guarantee for walking the talk in all settings. The two of us are aware that personal blinders may get in the way. We may wish to operate from a value-based perspective and to share power, but we may use covert strategies to maintain unjust practices that benefit us personally. There are many ways to support the status quo. Ironically, sharing power is one of them. When power is shared on minor issues, there are less chances that partners will demand equality on major issues (Bradshaw, 1998). Our own hidden interests can distort our declared values.

Enhance zone of congruence among disadvantaged communities, workers, and organizational leaders

The model of agency we propose is based on expanding zones of congruence. First, agents of change try to establish concordance among their own personal values, interests, and power. Then, they spread this process throughout the organization to ask peers to do the same. The next step is to enhance the zone of congruence among communities and workers in a particular setting. Agents of change need to create partnerships among the various groups to achieve concordance of values and objectives. *Action for Children* started with value congruence among a few organizations but later expanded to include others who embraced similar positions.

As noted in earlier discussions, the primary task in the creation of partnerships is the establishment of trust. This is achieved by meaningful and collaborative participation of workers and communities in decision-making processes. Democratic and participatory processes among multiple stakeholders require a prolonged involvement of change agents in the community. Token consultative processes subvert the intent of partnerships. When consumers realize that their voice is minimally respected but maximally exploited for public relations aims they are understandably upset.

Partnerships can flounder because of two primary reasons: lack of honesty or lack of skills. If agents of change wish to form partnerships merely for strategic purposes and do not really endorse a collaborative philosophy, consumers and workers are bound to find out and withdraw. But partnerships can also falter because of lack of skills. Sensitivity to group dynamics is crucial, as is the ability to move the process forward (Nelson, Amio et al., 2000).

Isaac struggled with moving a process forward. This time in the university. Geoff, who would have typically supported Isaac, was on sabbatical, and Isaac was facilitating a process of curriculum reform in the MA programme in community psychology. We had a participatory approach whereby students and staff could offer input into the new curriculum. Unfortunately, progress came to a stand still. We could not make a decision. The group struggled with respecting diversity of opinions and moving forward at the same time. Valuing diverse perspectives was important, but it meant that many meetings were spent discussing options and not reaching closure. Eventually, people started to drop out of the process because there was a lot of talk and not a lot of action. As programme director, Isaac was cautious not to impose his ideas on the rest of the team but ultimately took action and shared with the group his concerns. This helped to get us unstuck and to heal a process that was nearly fatally wounded. I, Isaac, took responsibility for not acting more assertively at an earlier stage.

A measure of accountability can be achieved by creating horizontal forms of collective leadership and by ensuring representation from various stakeholders (Racino, 1991). Equal and meaningful representation in advisory committees is not easy to achieve because many community members lack the skills or the confidence to make their views known. To make sure that consumers' voices are heard, leaders have to facilitate an empowering process whereby people are made to feel comfortable and receive training in expressing their needs (Nelson, Prilleltensky, and MacGillivary, 2001).

Confront people and groups subverting values, abusing power, or allowing self-interests to undermine the well-being of others in the organization or community

Efforts by change agents to promote value-based practice notwithstanding, it is likely that some people will behave in ways that contradict the vision and values of the setting. This is when change agents need to engage in conflict resolution with the person or group undermining the values.

A culture of openness and critique facilitates the resolution of conflict. In a climate of respectful debate, opposing parties can come to an agreement that is in line with the vision of the setting. But there are occasions when a healthy climate will not prevent serious conflict. If the conflict is about ideas and differing interpretations of values, the chances are that a resolution may be easily reached. That was the case in *Action for Children*. But if the conflict is about personal interests or power, differences may be hard to bridge. Isaac experienced conflict with a member of the Latin American Educational Group. Isaac felt that the personal interests of a member were undermining the mission of the group. The member was interested in deriving personal benefit, in the form of part-time jobs and access to resources, at the expense of group cohesion. This person spread rumours about other members of the group and tried to create divisions. By the time the person left the group, a lot of damage had been caused. In retrospect, the group, Isaac included, should have acted earlier to prevent damage.

Confrontation may be used for the good of the setting and the public, but it may also be used to suppress legitimate voices of discontent. In the latter case, agents of change can exercise their power to simply silence opposing views. This is an example of how conflict resolution can be subverted in the interest of enhancing the power of leaders or change agents. But confrontations can also be used by workers and clients to undermine legitimate leadership. When peers or consumers have unreasonable demands they may launch a complaint that is not necessarily justified.

Change agents can sweep under the carpet unethical behaviour of colleagues. They may do so to avoid unpleasant conflict. Therefore, it is important for us to be cautious about hyper- or hypo-confrontational styles. Whereas the former may be an expression of anger, the latter may be a manifestation of fear.

The model presented here may be more appealing to organizations committed to equality than to organizations committed to dollars. Although the latter may proclaim adherence to democracy and power-sharing, one should question their motives. Is their commitment to these principles based on a sincere adoption of values or a sincere motive to appease workers? (Bradshaw, 1998). Organizations fall somewhere between the two poles of unquestioned hierarchy and commitment to equality. Our job is to find room for value-based work in all types of organizations.

Conclusion

Critical agency is a big balancing act. It is a balance between promoting justice and empowerment on one hand, and attending to subjective barriers on the other. Another balancing act is between the values and interests of the public on one hand, and the needs of workers and volunteers on the other. Harmony between these groups is fostered in meaningful partnerships. The change agent faces a major task in trying to bridge across diverse groups. Opposition to partnerships comes from many corners and it requires a lot of skill to bring people from the corner to the centre. We are not interested in ideological or intellectual purity that achieve nothing. On the contrary, we are keen to make changes and to include partners along the way.

In this chapter our focus was on the challenges of agency faced by the critical psychologist. In the next chapter we concentrate on the process of change and on praxis. Along with the last chapter on the object of social change, these three chapters focus on the who, how, and what of social change.

12

Psychologists and the Process of Change: Making a Difference in Diverse Settings

The overall aim of critical psychology is to understand the relationship between psychology and power to improve the well-being of those who are marginalised by dominant practices. However, the seeds of critical psychology are difficult to grow in arid settings. Multiple players and institutional regulations have the power to either facilitate or inhibit critical work. In this chapter, we concern ourselves with the process of making a difference in diverse settings. In the previous chapter we concentrated on the agent of change and his or her responsibilities. Here we focus on praxis, or the process of change. We propose a cycle of praxis through which partners can critique existing practices and offer empowering alternatives.

Praxis for change

For us, critical psychology praxis is a cycle of constant and fluid reflection across vision, theory, research and practice. Figure 12.1 portrays a cycle of research and action that links needs, cultural context, vision and action. Action is at the centre of the circle because the other dimensions should converge, in our view, in social practices for change (Goodley and Parker, 2000; Prilleltensky, 1999). Critical praxis follows from attending to these four dimensions of inquiry and action. Praxis is what lies between what is desirable and what is achievable. The double headed arrows in the figure represent the reciprocal determinism in the connections among the various components of praxis.

Table 12.1 expands on the schematic representation of Figure 12.1 by outlining the questions, resources, and methods we need to use in critical work. We suggest a cycle of inquiry whereby we portray a vision, understand the social and cultural context, explore the needs of the population, and engage in action. The table shows the questions we ask under each one of the four domains: the state of affairs we study, the subject of inquiry, and the outcome. As noted in Figure 12.1, these four dimensions are interactive and reciprocal, but a measure of independence among them is required for critical inquiry. It is important to distinguish between

Table 12.1   Cycle of praxis in critical psychology

Dimensions	State of affairs	Subject of study	Outcome
Vision and values	What should be ideal vision? What values should guide our vision?	Social organizations that promote a balance among values for personal, relational, and collective well-being	Vision of justice, well-being and empowerment for disadvantaged communities
Cultural and social context	What is actual state of affairs?	Psychology of individual and collective as well as economy, history, society and culture	Identification of prevailing norms and social conditions oppressing minorities
Needs	How is state of affairs perceived and experienced?	Grounded theory and lived experience	Identification of needs of disadvantaged groups
Action	What can be done to change undesirable state of affairs?	Theories of personal and social change	Personal and social change strategies

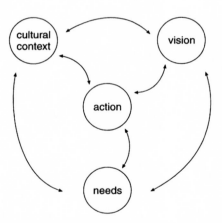

Figure 12.1   Cycle of praxis in critical psychology

what is desirable and what is achievable. We have to have a plan for reaching the ideal, for reaching a vision. At the same time, it is crucial to understand what is attainable under what circumstances. If we push for unattainable aims, people will dismiss us as dreamers. On the other hand, if we don't have visions for a better state of affairs we will always be stuck with the status quo. Praxis is the art of moving us closer to the ideal.

We have heard critics say that visions exist just in the heads of philosophers or idealistic critical psychologists. Furthermore, some claim that a vision may be appealing to one group but not to others, thereby stripping it of its legitimacy.

Our argument is that without a vision, however partial and temporal, we don't have a map to guide us. To have a vision at one point in time is not to hold on to it forever, or to exclude other points of view. Furthermore, the process of formulating a vision is as important as the vision itself. If we collaborate with others in a democratic fashion to construct a vision, and people have sufficient time and appropriate conditions to offer input, then we can claim that the process contributes to the legitimacy of the vision.

Visions are not constructed out of context. There are specific visions for specific people and groups. We study a specific context to understand what is impeding the attainment of a better state of affairs for them. What is blocking the way towards a more meaningful life? The next step in our model is to engage in action to bridge the gap between the ideal and the actual state of affairs.

The way to apply this model is quite simple. Assume we want to advance the well-being of a specific population. They can be working-class women, survivors of the mental health system, or kids who are bullied at school. First, we envision a state of affairs that meets their needs and affords them fulfilling lives. That's our point of departure. We have an idea where we want to go and what we want to achieve. Next, we study their context and expressed needs. After that, we are in a position to launch interventions for change. We could not launch interventions before we know what our vision is, or what is the current context we want to change. This simple model can be applied to any situation in which we pursue change. We start with the ideal vision, we proceed with a study of the context, and we conclude by suggesting actions.

Although visions of a good society will be influenced by the needs of the people, the needs themselves are subjected to personal and group interests. Therefore, we do not assume that we can accept what people express as needs without critical scrutiny. A group of people may express a need to live in a racially segregated society where people of colour do not mix with white people. Needs may reflect biases against marginalised groups. This is why we subject needs to close scrutiny. To do this we require a set of values or criteria to assess the legitimacy of expressed needs. The framework presented in the first part of the book can be of help. We have to reach a balance between values for personal, relational, and collective well-being, and we have to be very sensitive to the role of power in the process. For power can be used to promote well-being and empowerment, but also to oppress and dominate.

Naturalistic studies on the effects of injustice and oppression are very germane to critical psychology praxis. They can help in designing a vision, understanding context, and recommending actions. Valerie Walkerdine (1997) explored the internalization of oppression in working-class women in Britain, whereas Pilar Quintero (1992) studied the reproduction of oppressive messages in educational practice in South America. Geoff and his colleagues studied practices of empowerment in the community mental health field (Nelson, Lord, and Ochocka, 2001b), while Sprague and Hayes (2000) explored self-determination and empowerment in the context of disability. Estrada and Botero (2000), in turn, documented the context of the lives of poor Colombian women in a project of economic solidarity. These are examples of studies that can help us at different stages of the cycle of praxis, either with vision, context, needs or action.

The praxis framework for critical work is very interdisciplinary. It relies on the skills and knowledge of various groups, including of course the knowledge of community members themselves. As can be seen, the framework culminates in action. In other words, vision, context, and needs inform action for personal and social change. This praxis framework is about politically-committed, action-oriented, interdisciplinary work. Studies of needs that are detached from the social and cultural context are useful but very limited. Similarly, portrayals of visions that are not grounded in community needs can be interesting but inapplicable. Contextual analyses can also be fascinating, but if they are not followed by action they fall short. This is why we see critical practice as having to involve itself with the four dimensions of the praxis cycle. Otherwise, work can be interesting, but not transformative.

Partnerships for change

We have established that critical psychology involves the active participation of colleagues, students, potential allies, and community members. We invite community members and other partners as full collaborators in the process of change. We partner to fight oppression and further justice and equality. Specifically, we form partnerships to accomplish two things: Critique and visioning. In the Freirian tradition of education (Freire, 1970, 1975, 1999), critique is the act of recognizing and naming injustice, whereas visioning is the practice of hope, desire, and social change (Freire, 1994, 1999).

Partnerships for critique

As practitioners we are always caught in a web of values, interests and power. We have critical postulates to advance, but we have our own interests to protect. Depending on the circumstances of our workplace, we may or may not have sufficient power to defend our convictions and guard our interests at the same time. Conviviality may be at stake. It may not be in our interest to push for a radical agenda too forcefully in our settings.

We have to come to terms with external impositions we may have internalized or assimilated into our work, impositions that may obstruct a critical agenda. The subjectivity we ascribe to others is very much present in ourselves. What we do with conflicts among radical social values and vested personal interests is an open question and a source of struggle. Our subjectivity is suffused with agency and cultural influences at the same time. We are neither autonomous agents nor controlled automatons; we are always struggling to establish an identity that reflects our moral posture but that is constrained by messages of conformity at the same time. Conformity leads to unquestioning attitudes. To break the silence of conformity, practitioners need to find a place where it is safe to express discontent. Without a climate of safety and support, transformational practice is inhibited. Under threat, workers are unlikely to share their dreams, hopes, passions and fears. Hence, we suggest the formation of partnerships where a climate of acceptance is conducive to meaningful critique. We are not just political actors, we are also, and always, psychological actors as well. Tending the psychological land cultivates the political terrain as well. Hence, we suggest getting together with people who share similar concerns. In a climate of tolerance and acceptance, partners come together to denounce and to build. Once a positive climate has been established, it is safer to share critiques of work or societal practices, whatever the focus of the partnership might be.

Denunciation is making explicit the dynamics implicated in oppression and injustice, either at work or in the community. We concentrate here on three targets for critique: hegemonic definitions of problems in living, illegitimate authority, and group pressure (Prilleltensky, 1994). In each case we focus on the *said* and the *unsaid*.

Hegemonic definitions of norms and human problems preclude considerations of alternative visions. Dominant political discourses are built around what Canadian author, Linda McQuaig (1998), calls the 'cult of impotence'. 'There is nothing that can be done', 'market forces dictate economic policy', 'such is human nature', 'it hasn't worked before', 'these problems are too big for us', 'people have tried it in the past without success' – such are the defeatist messages that we are faced with. Challenging and deconstructing these messages is a productive exercise in critique. The *said* in these discourses needs to be scrutinized as much as the *unsaid*. Who coined these defeatist messages? Whose interests do they serve?

Paulo Freire and Donaldo Macedo distinguish between reading the *word* and reading the *world* (Macedo, 1994). While the former refers to traditional literacy, the latter refers to critical literacy that incorporates the political context within which learning takes place. The world is largely the *unsaid* part in psychological discourses. The historical circumstances surrounding the definition of a subject matter are hidden from view; they are *unsaid*. Critical psychology practice favours a reading of the said as well as the unsaid. Macedo claimed that:

> Almost without exception, traditional approaches to literacy do not escape the fragmentation of knowledge and are deeply ingrained in a positivistic method of inquiry...In general, this approach abstracts methodological issues from their ideological contexts and consequently ignores the interrelationship between the sociopolitical structures of a society and the act of reading and learning. In part, the exclusion of social, cultural, and political dimensions from literacy practices gives rise to an ideology of cultural reproduction that produces semiliterates (Macedo, 1994:21).

We question not only hegemonic definitions of human predicaments and social values, but also the very authority of those who author such definitions. Social power, managerial positions or academic expertise are not necessarily a source of moral legitimacy. Hence, we invite partners to study the context in which certain theories are created, the interests they serve, and the allegiances they represent. In brief, we do not take for granted what we read in psychological texts or manuals of operations. We critique what is *said* in what we study, and we invoke what is *unsaid* and absent from the text. We interrogate the legitimacy of the messages we get about what is proper psychology and proper practice (Willig, 1999). In work settings we don't take it for granted that diagnosing and labelling are helpful, nor that clients or their families should follow professional advice without scrutiny. We challenge the received wisdom and question its legitimacy.

The third target of critique is group and social pressure. In fact, great pressure can be exerted on colleagues and others to accept received wisdom without scrutiny. Subtle coercion is exercized all the time. We are asked to comply with institutional, disciplinary and professional regulations. The conformity achieved by group pressure 'can be preserved only so long as the individual is incapable of questioning the legitimacy of norms from an independent ethical perspective' (Schneiderman, 1988:70). Critical psychology needs to denounce these sources of pressure and offer alternatives. In the Child Guidance Clinic where I (Isaac) worked there was a perennial request for psychometric assessments. The preoccupation with assessments was such that other means of helping could hardly be conceived. Gradually, I persuaded a few schools that the best assessment was a meeting of all people involved in the situation. In effect, I suggested forming a partnership around the particular child experiencing problems. As opposed to labelling the child, I redirected the intervention and responsibility onto the group. In my view, the partnerships were much more helpful than most psychometric assessments – most people already knew what were the strengths and weaknesses of the child.

In this section we discussed targets and methods of critique. Partnerships for interrogating hegemony, illegitimate authority and social pressure were suggested. We highlighted the importance of deconstructing the *said* as well as the *unsaid*. In the next part we deal with visioning and transformation.

Partnerships for visioning and transformation

In a climate of respect and solidarity, debates can progress from critique to action. Visioning and transformation can take place within the class, the clinic, or the community at large. We suggest fostering values of personal, relational, and collective well-being as explicit objectives of the partnership. We think of how we can improve our situation as workers, how we can help service recipients, and how we can contribute to social change.

Oppression has political and psychological sources and representations. Affording partners an opportunity to examine those dynamics can be very liberating. Helping partners to take action, however minimal, to overcome familial or systemic repressive messages can be very empowering. But we reject viewing our partners, or anybody for that matter, merely as victims of oppression, for we all engage in oppressive acts ourselves. The partnership should allow for the exploration of how we, as psychologists, dominate or control others in our lives. What is it about our lives, our friends, our family and our culture that hurts us, that makes us feel diminished? What is it that makes us dominate others in our personal and working lives?

In narrative therapeutic practices there is a method called 'outside witnessing group' (White, 2000). In this procedure a person tells a story about his or her life without interruption by the audience. This phase is called the telling. In the second stage members of the audience reflect on their personal experience of hearing the story by the first person. This is called the retelling. In the third phase the person who told the story reflects on the reflections of the audience. This is the retelling of the retelling. Experience shows that this method is very powerful in creating bonds of solidarity and support among members of a group. At times we have used similar techniques in class and group situations to provide support and affirmation to members in our partnerships.

At a later stage we encourage students and partners to contemplate how they may inadvertently act as oppressors of others, near to them and removed from them. Previously we invoked the idea of the said and the unsaid, now we introduce the notion of *visible* and *invisible*. It is easier to identify how we might hurt others near to us, but it is quite difficult to realize how our actions may have repercussions on *invisible* others who live in poor areas of town, or altogether in other countries. Buying certain products perpetuates child labour and exploitation, buying certain magazines helps to perpetuate sexism. Remaining silent in the face of racist jokes or acquiescing to discriminatory practices at work may hurt *invisible* people. Invisible not because they don't count, but because they remain outside of our consciousness. Considering the repercussions of our actions on the seemingly invisible is an act of transformation. It opens up possibilities for changing practices as small as boycotting certain products or as big as joining international campaigns to eliminate child exploitation.

As faculty members teaching in community psychology programmes, first together in Canada, later also in Australia in Isaac's case, we have worked with students in joining communities of refugees, of psychiatric consumer/survivors, and of poor people in solidarity projects (Nelson, Prilleltensky, and MacGillivary, 2001). Many of our students learn from joining marginalised people in struggles for social justice. We identify strongly with the legacy of Paulo Freire. Like him, we believe that:

> We have an ethical responsibility to struggle to unveil situations of oppression. I believe we have a responsibility to create ways of understanding political and historical realities that will create possibilities for change...We must endeavour to create the context for people to challenge fatalistic perceptions of their circumstances so that we can all play our part in making history (Freire, 1999:37).

Joining grass roots organizations, self-help groups, advocacy bodies and labour unions are all legitimate and exciting grounds for visioning and transformation. Although much can and should be learned from working in clinical agencies and human service organizations, these represent only a fraction of settings where psychologists can witness and challenge injustice.

Visioning is about taking the learning into the outside world. It is about deriving action implications from discussions and debates in a climate that is conducive to personal and social transformation. An example of a partnership for transformation in community mental health comes from the Dulwich Centre Community Mental Health Project in Adelaide (Community Mental Health Project, 1998). This was a project to support community members with psychiatric diagnoses.

The Community Mental Health Project takes the approach that the stories through which we understand and live our lives are profoundly influenced by the dominant stories of our culture. In western culture there is a dominant belief or 'story' about what it means to be a person of moral worth. This belief system emphasises self-possession, self-containment, self-actualisation, and so on. It stresses individuality at the expense of community, and independence at the expense of connection. These are culturally specific values which are presented as universal, 'healthy', 'human' attributes to be striven for. Many of these ideas of health and well-being are often imposed by mainstream services. The attempt to live up to these dominant ideas of what it means to be a human being can have profoundly negative consequences for people's lives (Community Mental Health Project, 1998:13).

This challenging attitude enables workers and community members alike to engage in visioning of hitherto unthinkable ways of being. As a project team member pointed out,

The project provides an opportunity for project team members and community members to challenge together a lot of taken-for-granted ideas about what it means to be a real person or a whole person... Thinking through these ideas frees workers from any of these goals for other people's lives... It makes it more possible for workers to relate to the purposes that community members have for their own lives that might not have anything to do with reproducing venerated notions of personhood in our culture (Community Mental Health Project, 1998:13).

This is an example of workers in the field of mental health collaborating with service recipients in the creation of empowering alternatives. What we propose is using the cycle of praxis in devising action plans. In the case of the Dulwich Centre team, service recipients and providers formed a partnership, studied the plight of the consumers, and together devised actions. Judging from the quotes, participants found the process meaningful and empowering.

Vision, context, needs and action. These are the four phases we cycle through in critical praxis. We can apply this cycle in work with people who are marginalised and in work with colleagues in our own settings. We have power we can use to denounce injustice but also to envision new practices.

As mentioned in Chapter 5, Geoff was part of a coalition to improve housing for people who were consumers/survivors of the mental health system (Nelson, 1994). The coalition lobbied to increase funding for affordable housing. The group had a vision, an understanding of the context and the needs of the people, and, crucially, a plan. Success was tangible in that funding for housing was increased and more people with psychological problems could afford decent accommodation.

Action for Children was interested in the prevention of child abuse. We formed a partnership with the local United Way (a major social services charity in Canada) and devised a plan to increase funding for prevention programmes and for shifting priorities in social agencies from reactive to proactive approaches. We were a diverse group from various organizations. We came together to fight a common cause. Our vision was to eliminate child abuse in the region by the year 2020.

In fact, our vision was called vision 2020. Our plan entailed forming partnerships with various sectors – health, education, housing, business, welfare – to
contribute towards the eradication of the causes of abuse. A first step in reaching
the vision was convincing the local board of the United Way to increase funding
for prevention. After we obtained their support, we developed a plan of action
that included studying the local context, the needs of disadvantaged families, and
considering the most effective actions. We cycled through the phases of vision,
context, needs, and action.

Conclusion

'As progressive educators, one of our greatest tasks seems to be how to generate
in the people political dreams, political wishes, political desires' (Freire, 1999:38).
We see critical psychologists as involved in the task so clearly articulated by Freire.
This entails two main steps: critique and visioning. Much needs to be done to
expose oppressive discursive practices, and even more needs to happen to change
them. Education, research and action offer us opportunities to advance social
change towards those aims. We repeat, praxis is what lies between what is
desirable and what is achievable.

Critical psychology examines the silent issues, those issues that are either too
controversial or too complicated for positivist psychology. Critical psychology
delves into the complicated relations between values, interests and power. In each
and every one of our interactions with students, service recipients, or community
members our values intersect with our own interests and the interests of others.
To complicate matters, our behaviour is determined in large part by our own
power and the power of our partners in psychology. In the end, the way we
behave towards others is the result of a struggle between our own values, interest,
and power; and the values, interests and power of others. These are difficult
connections to disentangle, but worth exploring nevertheless. By ourselves, the
task can be overwhelming. With others, it is more palatable. We don't believe in
heroes who change practices and dominant discourses by themselves. We believe
in coalitions of people who come together to share the burden and the joy of
change.

13

Psychologists and the Object of Social Change: Transforming Social Policy

Throughout this book, we have emphasized the value of social justice for the practice of critical psychology in diverse settings. But often the social justice work that we are espousing is practised at the micro and meso levels. Moreover, what disadvantaged people and critical psychologists are able to achieve within micro and meso level settings is constrained by macro-level social structures, processes, and policies. For critical psychologists working in solidarity with disadvantaged people to achieve more fully an agenda of social justice, there must be a focus on macro-level change (Prilleltensky and Nelson, 1997).

In this final chapter, we focus on the object of social change for critical psychology: social policies that promote the collective values of strong community infrastructures and social justice. While there are specific policies for the different types of settings in which critical psychologists practice (for example, educational policy, health policy), there are also policies that cut across these specific areas (for example, employment, income distribution, housing, and family support). These cross-cutting policies address the macro-level determinants of well-being. We begin this chapter with a discussion of different perspectives on social policy and the current context of social policy. We then consider roles for critical psychologists working in partnership with disadvantaged people to influence the policy-making process.

Social policy

> Social policy is all about social purposes and the choices between them. These choices and the conflicts between them have continuously to be made at the governmental level, the community level and the individual level (Titmus, 1974:131).

Titmus' definition of social policy points out that policy has to do with setting priorities and that policy decisions occur at multiple levels of analysis. While there are many different models of policy-making (Wharf and McKenzie, 1998), these approaches can be subsumed under two broad perspectives. In this section, we consider these two different perspectives, along with their implications for the roles that psychologists can play in influencing social policy.

The rational-technical perspective

One perspective on social policy is a rational-technical approach (Wharf and McKenzie, 1998). This perspective is based on a problem-solving approach and involves defining the problem, formulating and prioritizing goals, developing policy options, and evaluating those policy options in terms of their costs and effectiveness. This perspective assumes that when a social problem occurs, that the policy-making process is initiated by planners to address the problem. Planning and policy are presumed to proceed in a logical way to address the problem based on the best available scientific evidence, with policy experts formulating policy solutions. The problem-solving approach is rational and empirical in nature. Progress in addressing the issue is gradual and incremental as the knowledge base for action grows.

Mainstream scientific psychology has allied itself with this rational-technical perspective of social policy. As M.B. Smith (1990:534) has argued, scientific psychologists:

> have argued that the APA, and its members when they speak as psychologists, should only present the conclusions of our scientific research, only on the basis of data. Only when we have solid data have we a right to speak as psychologists, they insist, and our advocacy should be restricted to summarizing and interpreting the data 'objectively'.

From a critical perspective, this social policy framework is problematic (Taylor, 1996). First, there are often widely different opinions about what constitutes a social problem and what role, if any, government should play in addressing the problem. Second, this perspective typically ignores the voices of different stake-holder groups, particularly those disadvantaged people who are most affected by the issue. Policy-making is the domain of experts. Third, the rational-technical approach also presumes to be 'objective' and value-neutral. However, if we ask how the problem is framed, whose interests are served by the policy choices, and by what criteria effectiveness is judged, we find that this perspective on social policy typically supports the societal status quo. In their review, Caplan and Nelson (1973) found that psychological research on social problems was characterized by a narrow, person-centred focus which blamed individuals for their problems.

The resource mobilization perspective

In contrast, an alternative approach to social policy focuses on values, politics, and power at multiple levels of analysis (Phillips, 2000; Taylor, 1996; Wharf and McKenzie, 1998). Psychologist Seymour Sarason (1978) recognized the importance of these dimensions in his analysis of the nature of problem-solving in social action. He argued that in the real world of social policy-making (376):

> the choice of formulation has less to do with data than with the traditions, value, world outlooks, and the spirit of the times; that the goal of social action is not once-and-for-all solutions in the scientific sense but to stir the waters of change, hoping and sometimes praying that more good than harm will follow; that the very process of formulating a problem, setting goals, and starting to act not only begins to change your perception of problems, goals, and actions but, no less fateful, the perceptions of others related to or affected by the process in some way.

In other words, policy-making is not a rational and technical response to problem identification, but rather an intensely political, value-saturated process involving the different stakeholders who are affected by the policy issue.

Resource mobilization theory provides an alternative perspective on how social policy is made (Jenkins, 1983; Morris and Mueller, 1992). According to this perspective, the definition of a social problem is a claims-making activity (Humphreys and Rappaport, 1993; Spector and Kitsuse, 1987). Different stakeholders make a claim as to what constitutes a social problem and the nature of the problem. To create social change, resource mobilization theory asserts that there must be organized stakeholders that make claims from the bottom-up and press for change to address the social issue (Jenkins, 1983; Mintrom and Vergari, 1996; Morris and Mueller, 1992). Thus, resource mobilization theory emphasizes a grounded, grassroots, participatory approach to policy-making.

The resource mobilization perspective also acknowledges that social problems are deeply embedded in a socio-historical context and are very difficult to change. Moreover, there are often competing narratives about a social problem. In their analysis of helping services for children, Levine and Levine (1992) found that during conservative times, social policies for children are based on the view that children's problems are caused by intrapsychic factors, whereas in more progressive times, policies are based on a belief in environmental causation of children's problems. Jenkins (1983) has argued that when the electorate is closely divided politicians become more likely to work with claims-makers to earn their support, thus favouring one narrative over the other. In summary, the resource mobilization perspective underscores the importance of context for policy change.

In our opinion, values provide the moral foundation for social policy (Prilleltensky, 1999). Values capture how people view the good life and the good society. We agree with Fisher (1994) and McCubbin and Cohen (1999) who have argued that policy reform must pay close attention to values. While we believe that social policy needs to emphasize collective values, we also recognize that collective values are currently in jeopardy throughout the world due to the growing power of global capitalism.

The current policy context: global capitalism

Social policies that are designed to reduce social and economic inequality and provide universal health, education, and social services are under assault by transnational corporations (Barlow and Campbell, 1995; Clarke, 1997). Whereas capital used to be centred around nation states, capital has increasingly gone global. More than half of the world's largest economic powers are now transnational corporations; corporate mergers and acquisitions are at record levels; symbols of corporate advertising (for example, McDonald's golden arches, the Coca Cola logo) are recognized throughout the world; corporations have moved jobs from developed nations to developing nations where there is a cheap pool of labour, few or no unions, and weak environmental and labour laws; trade agreements – for example, FTAA (Free Trade Area of the America) – are being forged in relative secrecy with no democratic input into the process; and these trade agreements give broad powers to transnational corporations, including the right to sue governments for having unfair trade advantages (including providing government funding for health, education, social services, the environment).

The corporate sector has become well organized in pursuing its agenda of creating a more 'business friendly' climate across the world. In Canada, for example, the Business Council on National Issues (BCNI) formed in 1977 is a coalition of 140 of the largest corporations and banks in Canada. The BCNI has played a major role in controlling the direction of federal and provincial policies. The BCNI supports parties that support their agenda and helps to get them elected. The corporate sector has created conservative 'think tanks' and owns many of the media outlets to promote its propaganda and manufacture the consent of the public (Herman and Chomsky, 1988). Again, in Canada, the majority of daily newspapers are owned by two of the country's wealthiest men, one of whom has created his own national newspaper. Moreover, in many governments, social policy has taken a back seat to fiscal policy. It is now the finance ministers, no longer the ministers of health, education, and social welfare, who hold the power in government cabinets.

Transnational corporations have become so powerful that they are striving to hold governments hostage to their demands. The basic message that they give to governments is 'if you make us pay taxes, we will move elsewhere'. 'Tax relief' has become the new mantra of the corporate sector. When large corporations and wealthy individuals pay lower rates of tax, that means that there is considerably less money in the public coffers for social programmes. In recent and current history, neo-conservative and neo-liberal governments in the USA, Canada, Australia, the UK, and New Zealand have all strived to reduce taxes; they have cut funding to the public sector; they have begun to privatize what were formerly public services; they have weakened environmental and labour laws and standards for health, education, and social services; and they have targeted and blamed poor people and public service workers for social problems. It is the most disadvantaged members of societies who have been the hardest hit by these shifts in policy. In Canada, for example, child poverty rates have increased over the past two decades (Canadian Council on Social Development, 2001).

Every hour, about 1140 young children die; most of them from malnutrition and preventable diseases. Annually, this is about ten million lives. In sub-Saharan Africa, the rate of under-five mortality is 172 per 1000 live births. In industrialized countries, the rate is six per 1000. While many in the west worry about obesity in children, 149 million children in developing countries experience malnourishment. Some people drink bottled water, others drink only filtered water; 1.1 billion people around the globe have no access to safe water at all (UNICEF, 2001).

But poverty is not something that happens only in remote places to different people. It happens in industrialized countries as well. One in every six children in OECD (Organisation for Economic Cooperation and Development) nations lives in poverty. This is about 47 million children. 'Despite a doubling and redoubling of national income in most (OECD) nations, a significant percentage of their children are still living in families so materially poor that normal health and growth are at risk' (UNICEF Innocenti Research Centre, 2000:5). 'Relative' poverty is a common definition used in industrialized countries. It refers to families with incomes below 50 per cent of the national median. According to that formula, child poverty in OECD countries ranges from 2.8 per cent of all children in Sweden, to 7.9 per cent in France, 12.6 per cent in Australia, 15.5 per cent in Canada and 22.4 per cent in the USA.

Another way to appreciate the toll of poverty is in life expectancy. In 1986, life expectancy for males in Russia at age 15 was 52 years. In 1994, after the collapse of the economy, males at age 15 could be expected to live only to age 45 (Marmot, 1999). For males, probability of death between ages 15 and 60 in the year 2020 is 32 per cent for former socialist economies of Europe and sub-Saharan countries, 18 per cent for Latin America, and 12 per cent for most OECD countries (Marmot, 1999). In Britain, life expectancy at age 15 varies considerably among social classes. Data for the period 1987–91 show that women in the bottom two social classes are expected to live 3.4 years less (62.4 years) than those in the top two classes (65.8). For men, the disparity is greater: those in the lower classes will live 4.7 years less (55.8) than those in the upper classes (60.5 years) (Shaw, Dorling, and Smith, 1999).

The values of rugged individualism, competition, and self-interest that are being promoted by transnational corporations and the governments that support them stand in direct opposition to the values underlying critical psychology practice that we have articulated throughout this book. What is most disturbing is the anti-democratic nature of global capitalism. Wealth and power are increasingly being concentrated in the hands of a very small group (of rich, white men), who cannot be held accountable for their actions in the same way that publicly elected officials can. If we are serious in wanting to pursue an agenda of social justice at the macro level, then we must name, confront, and resist the current trends of global capitalism. In the next section, we consider strategies that critical psychologists can use to influence social policy.

Social policy change: Strategies and roles for critical psychologists

Within psychology, various authors have written about the values, goals, and strategies of social intervention aimed at transformative change (Bennett, 1987; Goldenberg, 1978; Seidman, 1983). A common theme in these writings is the importance of reframing social problems (Seidman and Rappaport, 1986). The initial problem definition shapes how the problem will be addressed. In this regard, critical psychologists who practise social intervention emphasize clarifying the underlying values and assumptions about social interventions, so as to disrupt rather than reinforce the societal status quo. Because social interventionists assume that many social problems are due to inequalities in power, social intervention involves advocacy and conflict-oriented strategies, as well as research and education strategies (Pilisuk *et al.*, 1996).

In this section, we consider three different roles and strategies that critical psychologists can use to create social policy change: (a) social policy research and dissemination, (b) coalitions and partnerships with social movement organizations, and (c) fighting global capitalism through research, education, and resistance.

Social policy research and dissemination

As we noted earlier in this chapter, many psychologists seem to be most comfortable in influencing social policy through the dissemination of social science research. While this strategy has traditionally been conservative in nature, we believe that conducting and disseminating social policy research which is based on the values of participatory action research (discussed in Chapter 4) has transformative potential. While it has been noted that community psychologists have not taken their role in influencing social policy seriously enough (Phillips, 2000; Sarason, 1984), social policy research and dissemination is one strategy that has been pursued by community psychology.

Community psychologist George Fairweather (1972) developed an approach to social change that he called 'experimental social innovation'. He argued for the creation of innovative programmes, rigorous experimental evaluation of such programmes to demonstrate their effectiveness, and then active dissemination of the empirically-validated innovation. As an example, Fairweather and colleagues developed a community alternative to institutionalization for people with serious mental health problems called the 'lodge society'. The lodge was a residential setting that emphasized what we would now recognize as self-help principles. Former patients lived cooperatively and operated small businesses. A randomized controlled trial showed that the lodge residents were less likely to be rehospitalized and more likely to work than patients with typical discharge services. An experimental approach to dissemination was also used, but few sites fully adopted the lodge model. Mayer and Davidson (2000) have reviewed this area of research and intervention and have reported that innovations in education and the criminal justice system have been successfully disseminated.

One issue with existing work on dissemination of innovations is that it has been dominated by experimental research methods. While experimental methods provide valuable information, we argue that other research strategies, particularly qualitative and participatory methods would be useful in documenting innovative services and supports. The voice of the consumer has been absent in much of this work, and we need to ask consumers what they believe is innovative and helpful and work with them to spread such innovations. There are some exciting stories of innovation, such as mental health consumer/survivor-run businesses (Trainor and Tremblay, 1992), that have not been experimentally tested, but which are worthy of emulation and further research.

To influence policy-makers and practitioners, critical psychologists need to carefully consider their dissemination strategies. The most active dissemination strategies appear most likely to lead to adoption (Mayer and Davidson, 2000). Consultation and workshops can be offered in this regard. Another under-utilized strategy is that of videotape productions. In our work, we have found the use of videos to be a very important dissemination tool in catching the eyes and the interests of potential users. Different types of print media are also needed. Many policy-makers and practitioners are not likely to read books or journal articles. We have found that newsletters, short progress reports, and summary bulletins are alternative print sources that people find useful. Those who are interested can always access lengthier documents for more technical detail. For our Family Well-being project, we distributed across Canada thousands of summary bulletins in English and French on different facets of how to promote family well-being and prevent child maltreatment (Prilleltensky, Nelson, and Peirson, 2001).

Critical psychologists can also work as insiders in conducting and disseminating research that is pertinent to social policy. Some psychologists work as policy analysts within government; and some public officials have policy advisors who are psychologists; and in a few cases, psychologists have successfully run for public positions (see Lorion *et al.*, 1996). More training opportunities, like those provided at the pre-doctoral internship training programme at the Florida Mental Health Institute, are needed to prepare psychologists to work on social policy issues (Weinberg, 2001).

Coalitions and partnerships with social movement organizations

Critical psychologists can collaborate with community settings and social movement organizations as organizers, consultants, researchers, and as citizens exercizing their democratic rights to have a voice on social issues that concern them (Maton, 2000). There are civic associations and alternative settings, described in Chapter 9, that have a social change focus and that have strived to influence public policy.

Some neighbourhood organizations have included political consciousness-raising and advocacy for social justice as a part of their agenda, particularly with municipal governments (Powell and Nelson, 1997). Ethnic organizations have also challenged the status quo. In Isaac's work with the Latin American community (Prilleltensky, Nelson and Sánchez Valdes, 2000), parents and youth were involved in advocacy activities against cigarette companies. The Community Support Group organized by Danjela Seskar-Hencic (1996) and Peggy Nickels (1999) vigorously lobbied the public school board against cutting English as Second Language teachers. Aboriginal groups have pursued land rights and self-governance (Richardson, 1989). Bennett (in press) described educational and advocacy activities with different levels of government on behalf of the Amish community to ensure their right to pursue their traditional lifestyle.

Many alternative settings also have a social justice agenda. Some psychiatric-survivor self-help organizations have been vocal in protesting against psychiatry and for the civil and social rights of people who have experienced mental health problems (Burstow and Weitz, 1988; Chamberlin, 1990). Similarly, self-help organizations for people with disabilities have actively lobbied for resources and for the rights of citizens with disabilities (Balcazar *et al.*, 1994). The Independent Living Centres (ILCs) movement is a good example of advocacy by people with disabilities. ILCs are cross-disability, consumer-driven, and community-based self-help organizations that have a socio-political analysis of disability (Hutchison and Pedlar, 1999). ILC advocates have pushed for a new paradigm approach to disability policy and practice, emphasizing consumer control, housing, employment, mutual support, and civil rights. Finally, rape crisis centres have been a focal point for feminist organizing for social change (Campbell, Baker, and Mazurek, 1998). Examples of feminist social action include organizing public demonstrations to raise awareness about violence against women (for example, Take Back the Night marches in many Canadian and US cities), lobbying different levels of government to influence legislation regarding violence against women, and the development of programmes to prevent violence against women (Campbell *et al.*, 1998).

While the language of social change often focuses on empowerment of disenfranchised groups, psychologist Ingrid Huygens (1997) has argued that what is needed is the 'depowerment' of privileged groups in society. Moreover, she asserts that social change can be facilitated when members of the dominant culture take responsibility for educating themselves and making changes that benefit disadvantaged groups. She has provided examples of partnerships between dominant groups and disenfranchised groups to eliminate racism (Huygens, 1996a) and violence against women (Huygens, 1996b).

As we have argued elsewhere (Prilleltensky and Nelson, 1997), there are a number of other social movement organizations with which critical psychologists could ally themselves. These include feminist movement organizations, labour unions, university-based Public Interest Research Groups, social justice and anti-poverty organizations, peace organizations, and environmental organizations. These organizations are often coalitions of groups and individuals who view themselves as a part of broader movements for social change. The guiding vision is one of a society free of racism, sexism, heterosexism, poverty, violence, and environmental degradation, a society which celebrates diversity, shares wealth, and practises equality, peace, sustainability, and preservation of the natural environment.

While social justice coalitions offer power in numbers, they can also be problematic. Sometimes coalition members can have different views, emphases, and preferred strategies. This creates strain, tension, and sometimes splintering within such coalitions. In our experience, it is not important that coalition members agree on everything. What is important is that members strive to find common ground and to advocate on those issues on which there is agreement.

Nevertheless, maintaining group solidarity is an ongoing challenge for people who work with coalitions.

Fighting global capitalism: Research, education, and resistance

As we indicated earlier in this chapter, critical psychologists must work in partnership with disadvantaged groups and other allies to confront global capitalism. One successful example of fighting global capitalism is the international boycott of the Nestlé corporation over the distribution of infant formula in developing countries. Psychologist David Hallman (1987) described his role working for the United Church of Canada on the boycott of the Nestlé corporation. Nestlé was the major marketer of infant formula, developed in the 1800s by Henri Nestlé, to women in developing nations. Advertising in hospitals and free samples were provided to new mothers with infant formula as a symbol of western affluence and progress. By the time the free samples were exhausted, mothers' breast milk had dried up and they were forced to use formula. This resulted in increased rates of infant malnutrition and mortality because of poor conditions for the use of formula in developing countries, including lack of clean water, lack of refrigeration, mothers' diluting formula because it is quite expensive for them, and difficulty sterilizing bottles and nipples. All of these conditions can increase infants' exposure to sources of infection.

As these problems became evident to healthcare workers, a coalition of community groups across the world was formed in 1977 to oppose the promotion of formula. The Infant Formula Action Coalition (INFACT), which consisted of religious organizations, healthcare organizations, women's groups, nurses, the La Lèche league, and others, decided to conduct an international boycott of Nestlé products. The United Church of Canada donated David Hallman's time to work with INFACT and the boycott committee. In 1984, three years after the boycott started, Nestlé met with INFACT representatives and resolved all issues, thus ending the boycott. This social intervention speaks to the importance of coalitions for social change. What is remarkable about this intervention is that there was an organized worldwide outcry and opposition to a major international corporation which had a successful impact that has benefited babies throughout developing countries.

Targeting one issue and one transnational corporation as INFACT did is a useful strategy for creating social change. However, there is also a need for a broader-based social movement to fight global capitalism at a more global level. In Canada, social activists Maude Barlow and Tony Clarke (Barlow and Campbell, 1995; Clarke, 1997; Clarke and Barlow, 2001) have worked with labour unions, social justice organizations, environmental activist organizations, students, and churches to organize a citizen's movement against the business agenda of transnational corporations.

Research, education, and organizing are the main strategies that they have used to confront the increasingly powerful role of transnational corporations and governments which support them. National and international protests have been organized against international trade agreements, which serve the interests of corporations at the expense of poor people, labour unions, health, education, social services, and the environment. Recent protests of trade summits in the

USA, France, Germany, and Canada have shown worldwide opposition to the corporate agenda. The defeat of the Multilateral Agreement on Investment is one indicator of the kinds of success that are possible when citizens organize into broad-based coalitions for social justice.

In this section, we have touched on the importance of critical psychologists becoming actively involved in social movement organizations in their communities. In fact, we consider it a moral imperative for critical psychologists to engage in action with social movement organizations.

Conclusion

We consider social justice and social policy change to be the next frontier for critical psychology. Individuals come to critical psychology from many different perspectives and with many different agendas. But in the face of the rising trend of global capitalism, coalitions must be formed to fight this trend and to maintain and enhance social policies that promote social justice. Critical work at the micro and meso levels is increasingly being impacted by the dismantling of social policies that protect health, education, social services, labour, and the environment. We have argued for a number of different strategies aimed at creating policy change, with critical psychologists working inside or outside government in research, education, advocacy, and organizing roles.

As we bring this book to a conclusion, we reflect on the essence of critical psychology: standing with disadvantaged people, speaking out against social injustice, and acting for social change. Psychology needs to get more political. In closing, we are reminded of the following passage by Pastor Niemoller, who died in the Holocaust.

> First they came for the Jews
> and I did not speak out
> because I was not a Jew.
> Then they came for communists
> and I did not speak out
> because I was not a communist.
> Then they came for trade unionists
> and I did not speak out
> because I was not a trade unionist.
> Then they came for me
> and there was no one left
> to speak out for me.

REFERENCES

Aisenberg, N. and Harrington, M. (1988). *Women of Academe: Outsiders in the Sacred Grove*. Amherst: University of Massachusetts Press.

Albee, G.W. (1996). 'Revolutions and counterrevolutions in prevention', *American Psychologist*, **51**, 1130–3.

Albee, G.W. (1990). 'The futility of psychotherapy'. *Journal of Mind and Behavior*, **11**, 369–84.

Alcalde, J. and Walsh-Bowers, R. (1996). 'Community psychology values and the culture of graduate training: A self-study'. *American Journal of Community Psychology*, **24**, 389–411.

Allwood, R. (1996). 'I have depression, don't I?: Discourses of help and self-help books'. In E. Burman, G. Aitken, R. Allwood, T. Billington, B. Goldberg, A.G. Lopez, C. Heenan, D. Marks, and S. Warner (eds). *Psychology Discourse Practice: From Regulation to Resistance* (17–36). London: Taylor and Francis.

Alpert, J.L. and Meyers, J. (eds). (1983). *Training in Consultation: Perspectives from Mental Health, Behavioral, and Organizational Consultation*. Springfield, IL: C. C. Thomas.

Alvesson, M. and Willmott, H. (eds). (1992). *Critical Management Studies*. London: Sage.

Anthony, W.A. (1993). 'Recovery from mental illness: The guiding vision of the mental health service system in the 1990s'. *Psychosocial Rehabilitation Journal*, **16**, 11–23.

Apple, M.W. (1982). *Education and Power*. London: Routledge and Kegan Paul.

Aristide, J.B. (2000). *Eyes of the Heart: Seeking a Path for the Poor in the Age of Globalization*. Monroe, ME: Common Courage Press.

Arnold, R., Burke, B., James, C., Martin, D. and Thomas, B. (1991). *Educating for Change*. Toronto: Between the Lines.

Aronowitz, S. (2000). *The Knowledge Factory: Dismantling the Corporate University and Creating True Higher Learning*. Boston: Beacon Press.

Austin, S. and Prilleltensky, I. (2001). 'Contemporary debates in critical psychology: Dialectics and syntheses'. *Australian Psychologist*, **36**, 75–80.

Bagley, C. and Thurston, W.E. (1998). 'Decreasing child sexual abuse'. In *Canada Health Action: Building on the Legacy—Determinants of Health, Vol. I—Children and Youth* (133–73). Sainte Foy, PQ: Éditions Multimondes Inc.

Baird, B. N. (1999). *The Internship, Practicum, and Field Placement Handbook: A Guide for the Helping Professions* (2nd edn). Upper Saddle River, NJ: Prentice-Hall.

Balcazar, F.E., Keys, C.B., Kaplan, D.L. and Suarez-Balcazar, Y. (1998). 'Participatory action research and people with disabilities: Principles and challenges'. *Canadian Journal of Rehabilitation*, **12**, 105–12.

Balcazar, F., Mathews, R.M., Francisco, T., Fawcett, S.B. and Seekins, T. (1994). 'The empowerment process in four advocacy organizations of people with disabilities'. *Rehabilitation Psychology*, **39**, 189–203.

Bannerji, H., Carty, L., Delhi, K., Heald, S. and McKenna, K. (1991). *Unsettling Relations: The University as a Site of Feminist Struggle*. Toronto: Women's Press.

Baritz, L. (1974). *The Servants of Power: A History of the Use of Social Science in American Industry*. Westport, CT: Greenwood.

Barling, J. (1988). 'Industrial relations: A "blind" spot in the teaching, research, and practice of I/O psychology'. *Canadian Psychology*, **29**(1), 103–8.

Barlow, M. and Campbell, B. (1995). *Straight through the Heart: How the Liberals Abandoned the Just Society*. Toronto: Harper Collins Publishers Ltd.

Barrera, M., Jr. and Prelow, H. (2000). 'Interventions to promote social support in children and adolescents'. In Cicchetti, D., Rappaport, J., Sandler, I. and Weissberg, R.P. (eds). *The Promotion of Wellness in Children and Adolescents* (309–39). Washington, DC: Child Welfare League of America Press.

Bartky, S.L. (1990). *Femininity and Domination: Studies in the Phenomenology of Domination*. New York: Routledge.

Bartunek, J. M. and Keys, C.B. (1982). 'Power equalization in schools through organization development'. *Journal of Applied Behavioral Science*, **18**, 171–83.

Basic Behavioral Science Task Force of the National Advisory Mental Health Council (1996). 'Basic behavioral science research for mental health: Family processes and social networks'. *American Psychologist*, **51**, 622–30.

Bayer, R. (1981). *Homosexuality and American Psychiatry: The Politics of Diagnosis*. New York: Basic Books.

Becker, T.E. (1998). 'Integrity in organizations: Beyond honesty and conscientiousness'. *Academy of Management Review*, **23**, 154–61.

Beckman, H. and Frankel, R.M. (1984). 'The effects of physician's behaviour on the collection of data'. *Annals of Internal Medicine*, **101**, 692–6.

Beiser, M., Dion, R., Gowiec, A., Hyman, I. and Vu, N. (1995). 'Immigrant and refugee children in Canada'. *Canadian Journal of Psychiatry*, **40**, 67–72.

Belar, C. and Deardorff, W. (1996). *Clinical Health Psychology in Medical Settings*. Washington DC: APA Books.

Belenky, M., Clinchy, B., Goldberger, N. and Tarule, J. (1986). *Women's Ways of Knowing: The Development of Self, Voice, and Mind*. New York: Basic Books.

Bell, B., Gaventa, J. and Peters, J. (ed.). (1990). *We Make the Road by Walking: Conversations on Education and Social Change – Myles Horton and Paulo Freire*. Philadelphia: Temple University Press.

Bennett, E.M. (in press). 'Emancipatory responses to oppression: The template of land use planning and the Old Order Amish of Ontario'. *American Journal of Community Psychology*.

Bennett, E.M. (ed.). (1987). *Social Intervention: Theory and Practice*. Lewiston, NY: The Edwin Mellen Press.

Bennett, E.M. and Hallman, D. (1987). 'The centrality of field experience in training for social intervention'. In E. M. Bennett (ed.), *Social Intervention: Theory and Practice* (93–123). Lewiston, NY: The Edwin Mellen Press.

Bennett, P. (2000). *Introduction to Health Psychology*. Philadelphia: Open University Press.

Bennett, P. and Murphy, S. (1997). *Psychology and Health Promotion*. Philadelphia: Open University Press.

Berger, P. and Neuhaus, R. (1977). *To Empower People*. Washington, DC: American Enterprise Institute.

Bird, L. (1999). 'Towards a more critical educational psychology'. *Annual Review of Critical Psychology*, **1**, 21–33.

Boggs, C. (1976). *Gramsci's Marxism*. London: Pluto Press.

Bond, G.R., Drake, R.E., Mueser, K.T. and Becker, D.R. (1997). 'An update on supported employment for people with severe mental illness'. *Psychiatric Services*, **48**, 335–46.

Bond, L., Belenky, M. and Weinstock, J. (2000). 'The listening partners program: An initiative toward feminist community psychology in action'. *American Journal of Community Psychology*, **28**, 697–730.

Bond, M.A. (1999). 'Gender, race, and class in organizational contexts'. *American Journal of Community Psychology*, 27, 327–55.

Bond, M.A. (1995). 'Prevention and the ecology of sexual harassment: Creating empowering climates'. *Prevention in Human Services*, 12(2), 147–73.

Bond, M.A. and Keys, C.B. (1993). 'Empowerment, diversity, and collaboration: Promoting synergy on community boards'. *American Journal of Community Psychology*, 21, 37–57.

Bond, M.A., Hill, J., Mulvey, A. and Terenzio, M. (2000). 'Weaving feminism and community psychology: An introduction to a special issue'. *American Journal of Community Psychology*, 28, 585–97.

Botvin, G.J., Baker, E., Dusenbury, L., Tortu, S. and Botvin, E. M. (1990). 'Preventing adolescent drug abuse through a multimodal cognitive-behavioral approach: Results of a three-year study'. *Journal of Consulting and Clinical Psychology*, 58, 437–46.

Botvin, G., Schinke, S. and Orlandi, M. (1995). 'School-based health promotion: Substance abuse and sexual behavior'. *Applied and Preventive Psychology*, 4, 167–84.

Boyett, J. and Conn, H. (1991). *Workplace 2000: The Revolution Shaping American Business*. New York: Penguin.

Bradshaw, P. (1998). 'Power as dynamic tension and its implications for radical organizational change'. *European Journal of Work and Organizational Psychology*, 7, 121–43.

Brickman, P., Rabinowitz, V.C., Karuza, J., Coates, D., Cohn, E. and Kidder, L. (1982). 'Models of helping and coping'. *American Psychologist*, 37, 368–84.

Briner R.B. (2000). 'Relationships between work environments, psychological environments and psychological well-being'. *Occupational Medicine*, 50, 299–303.

Brooks-Gunn, J., Duncan, G.J. and Britto, P.R. (1999). 'Are socioeconomic gradients for children similar to those for adults? Achievement and health of children in the United States'. In D. P. Keating and C. Hertzman (eds), *Developmental Health and the Wealth of Nations: Social, Biological, and Educational Dynamics* (94–124). New York: The Guilford Press.

Broverman, I.K., Broverman, D.M., Clarkson, F.E., Rosenkrantz, P. and Vogel, S.R. (1970). 'Sex role stereotypes and clinical judgments of mental health'. *Journal of Consulting Psychology*, 34, 1–7.

Brown, L.S. (1994). *Subversive Dialogues: Theory in Feminist Therapy*. New York: Basic Books.

Brown, L.D. and Tandon, R. (1983). 'Ideology and political economy in inquiry: Action research and participatory research'. *Journal of Applied Behavioral Science*, 19, 277–94.

Browne, A. (1993). 'Violence against women by male partners: Prevalence, outcomes, and policy implications'. *American Psychologist*, 48, 1077–87.

Brumback, G.B. (1991). 'Institutionalizing ethics in government'. *Public Personnel Management*, 20, 353–64.

Brydon-Miller, M. (1997). 'Participatory action research: Psychology and social change'. *Journal of Social Issues*, 53, 657–66.

Bulhan, H.A. (1985). *Franz Fanon and the Psychology of Oppression*. New York: Plenum Press.

Bunch, C. (1987). *Passionate Politics*. New York: St. Martin's Press.

Burman, E., Atiken, G., Alldred, P., Allwood, R., Billington, T., Goldberg, B., Gordo Lopez, A.J., Heenan, C., Marks, D. and Warner, S. (eds). (1996). *Psychology, Discourse, Practice: From Regulation to Resistance*. London: Taylor and Francis.

Burston, D. (1991). *The Legacy of Erich Fromm*. Cambridge, MA: Harvard University Press.

Burstow, B. and Weitz, D. (eds).(1988). *Shrink Resistant: The Struggle against Psychiatry in Canada*. Vancouver, B.C.: New Star Books.

Butterfoss, F.D., Goodman, R. M. and Wandersman, A. (1993). 'Community coalitions for prevention and health promotion'. *Health Education Research*, **8**, 315–30.

Campbell, R., Baker, C.K. and Mazurek, T. L. (1998). 'Remaining radical? Organizational predictors of rape crisis centers' social change initiatives'. *American Journal of Community Psychology*, **26**, 457–83.

Campbell, C. and Jovchelovitch, S. (2000). 'Health, community and development: Towards a social psychology of participation'. *Journal of Community and Applied Social Psychology*, **10**, 255–70.

Canadian Council on Social Development (2001). *The Progress of Canada's Children 2001*. Ottawa: Canadian Council on Social Development.

Canadian Task Force on Mental Health Issues Affecting Immigrants and Refugees. (1988). *Review of the Literature on Immigrant Mental Health*. Ottawa: Ministry of Supply and Services.

Caplan, N. and Nelson, S.D. (1973). 'On being useful: The nature and consequences of psychological research on social problems'. *American Psychologist*, **28**, 199–211.

Caplan, P. (1991). 'How do they decide who is normal? The bizarre but true tale of the DSM process'. *Canadian Psychology*, **32**, 162–70.

Carling, P.J. (1995). *Return to Community: Building Support Systems for People with Psychiatric Disabilities*. New York: The Guilford Press.

Cauce, A.M., Comer, J.P. and Schwartz, D. (1987). 'Long term effects of a systems-oriented school prevention program'. *American Journal of Orthopsychiatry*, **57**, 127–31.

Cernovsky, Z. (1997). 'A critical look at intelligence research'. In D. Fox and I. Prilleltensky (eds), *Critical Psychology: An Introduction* (121–33). London: Sage.

Chamberlin, J. (1990). 'The ex-psychiatric patients' movement: Where we've been and where we're going'. *The Journal of Mind and Behavior*, **11**, 323–36.

Chambliss, D. (1996). *Beyond Caring*. Chicago: University of Chicago Press.

Chapman, J.G. (1999). 'Educating students to make-a-difference: Community-based service learning' [Special issue]. *Journal of Prevention and Intervention in the Community*, **18**(1/2).

Cherniss, C. (1993). 'Pre-entry issues revisited'. In R.T. Golembiewski (ed.), *Handbook of Organizational Consultation* (113–18). New York: Marcel Dekker.

Cherniss, C. and Deegan, G. (2000). 'The creation of alternative settings'. In J. Rappaport and E. Seidman (eds), *Handbook of Community Psychology* (359–77). New York: Kluwer Academic/Plenum Publishers.

Cherniss, C., Trickett, E.J., D'Antonio, M. and Tracy, K. (1982). 'Involving students in organizational change in a high school'. In J. L. Alpert (ed.), *Psychological Consultation in Educational Settings* (108–42). San Francisco: Jossey-Bass.

Chesler, P. (1990). 'Twenty years since *Women and Madness*: Toward a feminist institute of mental health and healing'. *Journal of Mind and Behavior*, **11**(3/4), 313–22.

Chesler, P. (1989). *Women and Madness*. New York, NY.: Harcourt Brace Jovanovich.

Chu, F. and Trotter, S. (1974). *The Madness Establishment: Ralph Nader's Study Group Report on the National Institute of Mental Health*. New York: Grossman.

Cicchetti, D., Rappaport, J., Sandler, I. and Weissberg, R.P. (eds). (2000). *The Promotion of Wellness in Children and Adolescents*. Washington, D.C.: Child Welfare League of America Press.

Clarke, T. (1997). *Silent Coup: Confronting the Big Business Takeover of Canada*. Toronto: Canadian Centre for Policy Alternatives and James Lorimer and Company Ltd.

Clarke, T. and Barlow, M. (2001). *Global Showdown: Citizen Politics and the WTO.* North York, Ontario: Stoddart Publishing.

Comer, J. (1985). 'The Yale-New Haven primary prevention project: A follow-up study'. *Journal of the American Academy of Child Psychiatry,* 15, 535–45.

Community Mental Health Project. (1998). 'Companions on a journey: The work of the Dulwich Centre Community Mental Health Project'. In C. White and D. Denborough (eds). *Introducing Narrative Therapy.* Adelaide: Dulwich Centre Publications.

Community Education Team. (1999). 'Fostering relationality when implementing and evaluating a collective-drama approach to preventing violence against women'. *Psychology of Women Quarterly,* 23, 95–109.

Connors, E. and Maidman, F. (2001). 'A circle of healing: Family wellness in aboriginal communities'. In I. Prilleltensky, G. Nelson and L. Peirson (eds), *Promoting Family Wellness and Preventing Child Maltreatment.* University of Toronto Press.

Constantino, V. and Nelson, G. (1995). 'Changing relationships between self-help groups and mental health professionals: Shifting ideology and power'. *Canadian Journal of Community Mental Health,* 14(2), 55–73.

Cottrell, L.S. (1976). 'The competent community'. In B. H. Kaplan, R. N. Wilson and A. H. Leighton (eds), *Further Explorations in Social Psychiatry* (195–209). New York: Basic Books.

Cowen, E.L. (2000). 'Community psychology and routes to psychological wellness'. In J. Rappaport and E. Seidman (eds), *Handbook of Community Psychology* (79–99). New York: Kluwer Academic/Plenum Publishers.

Cowen, E.L. (1996) 'The ontogenesis of primary prevention: Lengthy strides and stubbed toes', *American Journal of Community Psychology,* 24, 235–49.

Crossley, M. (2000). *Introducing Narrative Psychology: Self, Trauma and the Construction of Meaning.* Philadelphia. Open University Press.

Curtis, A. (2000). *Health Psychology.* London: Routledge.

Curtis L.C. and Hodge, M. (1994). 'Old standards, new dilemmas: Ethics and boundaries in community support services'. *Psychosocial Rehabilitation Journal,* 18(2), 13–33.

Cushman, P. and Gilford, P. (2000). 'Will managed care change our way of being?' *American Psychologist,* 55, 985–96.

Dallaire, B., McCubbin, M., Morin, P. and Cohen, D. (2000). 'Civil commitment due to mental illness and dangerousness: The union of law and psychiatry within a treatment-control system'. *Sociology of Health and Illness,* 22, 679–99.

Dalton, J.H., Elias, M.J. and Wandersman, A. (2001). *Community Psychology: Linking Individuals and Communities.* Stamford, CT: Wadsworth Thomson Learning.

Daniels, K. and Harris, C. (2000). 'Work, psychological well-being and performance'. *Occupational Medicine,* 50, 304–9.

Daniels, K. and Guppy, A. (1992). 'Control, information seeking preferences, occupational stressors and psychological well-being'. *Work and Stress,* 6, 347–53.

Danziger, K. (1990). *Constructing the Subject: Historical Origins of Psychological Research.* New York: Cambridge University Press.

Deetz, S. (1992). 'Disciplinary power in the modern corporation'. In M. Alvesson and H. Willmott (eds), *Critical Management Studies* (21–45). London: Sage.

Denzin, N.K. (1994). 'The art and politics of interpretation'. In N. K. Denzin and Y. S. Lincoln (eds), *Handbook of Qualitative Research* (500–15). Thousand Oaks, CA: Sage.

Denzin, N.K. and Lincoln, Y.S. (eds). (1994). *Handbook of Qualitative Research.* Thousand Oaks, CA: Sage.

Derksen, B. and Nelson, G. (1995) 'Partnerships between community residents and professionals: Issues of power and social class across the lifespan of neighbourhood organizations'. *Canadian Journal of Community Mental Health*, **14(1)**, 61–77.

DeRubeis, R.J. and Crits-Christoph, P. (1998). 'Empirically supported individual and group psychological treatments for adult mental disorders'. *Journal of Consulting and Clinical Psychology*, **66**, 37–52.

Diener, E., Suh, E.M., Lucas, R.E. and Smith, H.L. (1999). 'Subjective well-being: Three decades of progress'. *Psychological Bulletin*, **125**, 276–302.

Dimock, H. (1992). *Intervention and Empowerment: Helping Organizations to Change*. North York, Ontario: Captus Press.

DiTomaso, N. and Hooijberg, R. (1996). 'Diversity and the demands of leadership'. *Leadership Quarterly*, **7**, 163–87.

Doherty, W.J. (1995). *Soul Searching: Why Psychotherapy must Promote Moral Responsibility*. New York: Basic Books.

Dryfoos, J.G. (1994). *Full-service Schools: A Revolution in Health and Social Services for Children, Youth, and Families*. San Francisco: Jossey-Bass.

Dryfoos, J.G. (1990). *Adolescents at Risk: Prevalence and Prevention*. New York: Oxford University Press.

Dudgeon, P., Garvey, D. and Pickett, H. (2000). *Working with Indigenous Australians: A Handbook for Psychologists*. Perth, WA, Australia: Gunada Press.

Dunst, C.J. and Trivette, C.M. (1989). 'An enablement and empowerment perspective of case management'. *Topics in Early Childhood Special Education*, **8**, 87–102.

Dunst, C.J., Trivette, C.M. and Deal, G. (1988). *Enabling and Empowering Families: Principles and Guidelines for Practice*. Cambridge, MA: Brookline Books.

Eckersley, R., (2000). 'The mixed blessing of material progress: Diminishing returns in the pursuit of progress'. *Journal of Happiness Studies*, **1**, 267–92.

Eglin, P. (1996). *Globalization, Economic Restructuring, Partnerships and Academic Freedom in the Corporate University: The Case of Wilfrid Laurier University*. Paper presented at the First Annual Laurier Conference on Business and Professional Ethics, 'Ethics and Restructuring in Business, Health, and Education,' Wilfrid Laurier University, Waterloo, October 24–26, 1996.

Eimer, B. and Freeman, A. (1998). *Pain Management Psychotherapy*. New York: John Wiley and Sons.

Eisen, A. (1994). 'Survey of neighborhood-based, comprehensive community empowerment initiatives'. *Health Education Quarterly*, 21, 235–52.

Elias, M.J. (1995). 'Primary prevention as health and social competence promotion'. *Journal of Primary Prevention*, **16**, 5–24.

Elias, M.J. (1987). 'Improving the continuity between undergraduate psychology and graduate community psychology: Analysis and case study'. *Journal of Community Psychology*, **15**, 376–86.

Elias, M.J. and Tobias, S.E. (1996). *Social Problems-solving Interventions in the Schools*. New York: Guilford.

Ellsworth, E. (1989). 'Why doesn't this feel empowering? Working through the repressive myths of critical pedagogy'. *Harvard Educational Review*, 59, 297–324.

Estrada, M.A. and Botero, M.I. (2000). 'Gender and cultural resistance: psycho-social transformations of gender identity'. *Annual Review of Critical Psychology*, **2**, 19–34.

Eysenck, H.J. (1952). 'The effects of psychotherapy: An evaluation'. *Journal of Consulting Psychology*, **16**, 319–24.

Fairweather, G.W. (1972). *Social Change: The Challenge to Survival*. Secaucus, NJ: General Learning Press.

Fallon, B., Pfister, H. and Brebner, J. (1989). *Advances in Organizational Psychology*. New York: Elsevier.

Fanon, F. (1963). *The Wretched of the Earth*. New York: Grove Press Inc.

Felner, R. and Adan, A. (1988). 'The School Transition Environment Project: An ecological intervention and evaluation'. In R. Price, E.L. Cowen, R.P. Lorion and J. Ramos-McKay (eds.), *Fourteen Ounces of Prevention: A Casebook for Practitioners* (111–22). Washington, DC: American Psychological Association.

Feuerstein, M. (1997). *Poverty and Health*. London: Macmillan – now Palgrave Macmillan.

Fine, M. (1994). 'Working the hyphens: Reinventing self and other in qualitative research'. In N.K. Denzin and Y.S. Lincoln (eds), *Handbook of Qualitative Research* (70–82). London: Sage.

Fisher, D.B. (1994). 'Health care reform based on an empowerment model of recovery by people with psychiatric disabilities'. *Hospital and Community Psychiatry*, **45**, 913–15.

Fook, J. (1993). *Radical Casework: A Theory of Practice*. St. Leonards, Australia: Allen and Unwin.

Forrest, L. and Rosenberg, F. (1997). 'A Review of the Feminist Pedagogy Literature: The Neglected Child of Feminist Psychology'. *Applied and Preventive Psychology*, **6**, 179–92.

Foucault, M. (1997). 'The ethics of the concern of the self as a practice of freedom'. In P. Rabinow (ed.), *Michel Foucault: Ethics, Subjectivity and Truth* (281–301). New York: The New Press.

Foucault, M. (1984). 'Truth and power'. In P. Rabinow (ed.), *The Foucault Reader* (51–75). New York: Penguin.

Foucault, M. (1980). *Power/Knowledge*. New York: Pantheon.

Foucault, M. (1980). *Historia de la sexualidad* [The History of Sexuality]. Madrid: Siglo Veintiuno.

Foucault, M. (1979). *Discipline and Punish*. Harmondsworth, England: Penguin.

Fox, D., (2000). 'The critical psychology project: Transforming society and transforming psychology'. In T. Sloan (ed.). *Critical Psychology: Voices for Change* (21–33). London: Macmillan – now Palgrave Macmillan.

Fox, D. and Prilleltensky, I. (eds). (1997). *Critical Psychology: An Introduction*. London: Sage.

Freedman, J. and Combs, G. (1996). *Narrative Therapy: The Social Construction of Preferred Realities*. New York: W. W. Norton & Co.

Freire, P. (1999). 'Making history and unveiling oppression'. *Dulwich Centre Journal*, **3**, 37–9.

Freire, P. (1994). *Pedagogy of Hope*. New York: Continuum.

Freire, P. (1975). 'Cultural action for freedom'. *Harvard Educational Review Monograph*, **1**.

Freire, P. (1970). *Pedagogy of the Oppressed*. New York: Continuum.

Freund, P. and McGuire, M. (1999). *Health, Illness, and the Social Body: A Critical Sociology*. Upper Saddle River, NJ: Prentice Hall.

Fromm, E. (1965). *Escape from Freedom*. New York, NY: Avon Books.

Fryer, D. (Guest Editor). (1998). 'Mental health consequences of economic insecurity, relative poverty, and social exclusion: Community psychological perspectives on recession' [Special Issue]. *Journal of Community and Applied Social Psychology*, **8, 2**, 75–180.

Fullan, M. and Stiegelbauer, S. (1991). *The New Meaning of Educational Change*. New York: Teachers College Press, Columbia University.

Gammell, D.J. and Stoppard, J.M. (1999). 'Women's experiences of depression: Medicalization or empowerment?' *Canadian Psychology*, **40**, 112–28.

Garbarino, J. (1992) *Children and Families in the Social Environment*, (2nd edn). New York: Aldine de Gruyter.

Garrett, L. (2000). *Betrayal of Trust: The Collapse of Global Public Health*. New York: Hyperion.

Garnets, L. and D'Augelli, A. (1994). 'Empowering lesbian and gay communities: A call for collaboration with community psychology'. *American Journal of Community Psychology*, **22**, 447–70.

Gensheimer, L.K. and Diebold, C.T. (1997). 'Free-standing doctoral programs in community psychology: Educational philosophies and academic models'. *Journal of Prevention and Intervention in the Community*, **15**(1), 45–64.

Gil, D. (1996). 'Preventing violence in a structurally violent society: Mission impossible'. *American Journal of Orthopsychiatry*, **66**, 77–84.

Giroux, H.A. (1988). 'Border pedagogy in the age of postmodernism'. *Journal of Education*, **170**(3), 162–81.

Giroux, H. A. and McLaren, P. (1986). 'Teacher education and the politics of engagement: The case for democratic schooling'. *Harvard Educational Review*, **56**(3), 213–38.

Glidewell, J. C. (1984). 'Training for the role of advocate'. *American Journal of Community Psychology*, **12**, 193–8.

Goldenberg, I. I. (1978). *Oppression and Social Intervention*. Chicago: Nelson-Hall.

Goldenberg, I. and Goldenberg, H. (1983). 'Historical roots of contemporary family therapy'. In B. J. Wolman and G. Stricker (eds), *Handbook of Family and Marital Therapy* (77–89). New York: Plenum.

Goleman, D. (1998). *Working with Emotional Intelligence*. New York: Bantam.

Gomory, T. (1999). 'Programs of Assertive Community Treatment (PACT): A critical review'. *Ethical Human Sciences and Services*, **1**, 147–63.

Goodley, D. (1996). 'Tales of hidden lives: A critical examination of life history research with people who have learning difficulties'. *Disability and Society*, **11**, 333–48.

Goodley, D. and Parker, I. (2000). 'Critical psychology and action research'. *Annual Review of Critical Psychology*, **2**, 3–18.

Gottlieb, B.H. and Coppard, A. E. (1987). 'Using social network therapy to create support systems for the chronically mentally disabled'. *Canadian Journal of Community Mental Health*, **6**(2), 117–31.

Graczyk, P.A., Matjasko, J.L., Weissberg, R.P., Greenberg, M.T., Elias, M.J. and Zins, J.E. (2000). 'The role of the Collaborative to Advance Social and Emotional Learning (CASEL) in supporting implementation of quality school-based prevention programs'. *Journal of Educational and Psychological Consultation*, **11**, 3–6.

Gramsci, A. (1971). *Selections from the Prison Notebooks*. London: Lawrence and Wishart.

Griffin Cohen, M. (1997). 'From the welfare state to vampire capitalism'. In P. M. Evans and G.R. Wekerle (eds), *Women and the Canadian Welfare State* (28–67). Toronto, Ontario: University of Toronto Press.

Gruber, J. and Trickett, E.J. (1987). 'Can we empower others? The paradox of empowerment in the governing of an alternative public school'. *American Journal of Community Psychology*, **15**, 353–71.

Guba, E.G. and Lincoln, Y.S. (1994). 'Competing paradigms in qualitative research'. In N.K. Denzin and Y.S. Lincoln (eds), *Handbook of Qualitative Research* (105–17). Thousand Oaks, CA: Sage.

Hall, B. (1993). 'Introduction'. In P. Park, M. Brydon-Miller, B. Hall and T. Jackson (eds), *Voices of Change: Participatory Research in the United States and Canada* (xiv-xii). Westport, CT: Bergen and Garvey.

Hallman, D. (1987). 'The Nestlé boycott: The success of a citizen's coalition in social intervention'. In E.M. Bennett (ed.), *Social Intervention: Theory and Practice* (187–229). Lewiston, N.Y.: The Edwin Mellen Press.

Hardey, M. (1998). *The Social Context of Health*. Philadelphia: Open University Press.

Harding, S. (1991). *Whose Science? Whose Knowledge?*. Ithaca, NY: Cornell University Press.

Hare-Mustin, R.T. and Maracek, J. (1997). 'Abnormal and clinical psychology: The politics of madness'. In D. Fox and I. Prilleltensky (eds), *Critical Psychology: An Introduction* (104–120). London: Sage.

Harris, G.T., Hilton, N.Z. and Rice, M.E. (1993). 'Patients admitted to psychiatric hospital: Presenting problems and resolution at discharge'. *Canadian Journal of Behavioural Science*, **25**, 267–85.

Hawkins, J.D., Catalano, R.F. and Associates. (1992). *Communities that Care: Action for Drug Abuse Prevention*. San Francisco: Jossey-Bass.

Heller, K. Price, R.H., Reinharz, S., Riger, S. and Wandersman, A. (1984). *Psychology and Community Change: Challenges of the Future*. Homewood, IL: Dorsey Press.

Henriques, J., Hollway, W., Urwin, C., Venn, C. and Walkerdine, V. (eds). (1984). *Changing the Subject: Psychology, Social Regulation and Subjectivity*. London: Methuen.

Herbert, E. and McCannell, K. (1997). 'Talking back: Six First Nations women's stories on recovery from childhood sexual abuse and addictions'. *Canadian Journal of Community Mental Health*, **16(2)**, 51–68.

Herman, E. (1995). *The Romance of American Psychology: Political Culture in the Age of Experts*. Berkeley, CA: University of California Press.

Herman, E.S. and Chomsky, N. (1988). *Manufacturing Consent: The Political Economy of the Mass Media*. New York: Random House.

Hertzman C. (1999). 'Population health and human development'. In D. Keating, C. Hertzman (eds), *Developmental Health and the Wealth of Nations* (21–40). New York: Guilford.

Hollingshead, A.B. and Redlich, F.C. (1958). *Social Class and Mental Illness*. New York: Wiley.

Hollway, W. (1991). *Work Psychology and Organizational Behaviour*. London: Sage.

Holtzworth-Munroe, A., Markman, H., O'Leary, K.D., Neidig, P., Leber, D., Heyman, R.E., Hulbert, D. and Smutzler, N. (1995). 'The need for marital violence prevention efforts: A behavioral-cognitive secondary prevention program for engaged and newly married couples'. *Applied and Preventive Psychology*, **4**, 77–88.

hooks, b. (1994). *Teaching to Transgress: Education as the Practice of Freedom*. New York: Routledge.

Horvath, A. O. (1994). 'Research on the alliance'. In A.O. Horvath and L.S. Greenberg (eds), *The Working Alliance: Theory, Research, and Practice* (259–86). New York: Wiley.

Horvath, A.O. and Symonds, B.D. (1991). 'Relation between working alliance and outcome in psychotherapy: A meta-analysis'. *Journal of Counseling Psychology*, **38**, 139–49.

Humphreys, K. (1996). 'Clinical psychologists as psychotherapists: History, future, and alternatives'. *American Psychologist*, **51**, 190–7.

Humphreys, K. and Rappaport, J. (1993). 'From the community mental health movement to the war on drugs: a study in the definition of social problems'. *American Psychologist*, **48**, 892–901.

Humphreys, K. and Rappaport, J. (1994). 'Researching self-help/mutual aid groups and organizations: Many roads, one journey'. *Applied and Preventive Psychology*, **3**, 217–31.

Hurst, S.A. and Genest, M. (1995). 'Cognitive-behavioural therapy with a feminist orientation: A perspective for therapy with depressed women'. *Canadian Psychology*, **36**, 236–57.

Huszczo, G.E., Wiggins, J.G. and Currie, J.S. (1984). 'The relationship between psychology and organized labor'. *American Psychologist*, **39**, 432–40.

Hutchison, P. and Pedlar, A. (1999). 'Independent Living Centres: An innovation with mental health implications?' *Canadian Journal of Community Mental Health*, **18(2)**, 21–32.

Huygens, I. (2001, June). *Journeys Away from Dominance: Dissonance, Struggle and Right Relationships–the Journey to Accepting Indigenous Authority.* Paper presented at the 8th Biennial Conference of the Society for Community Research and Action, Atlanta, Georgia.

Huygens, I. (1997, May). *Towards Social Change Partnerships: Responding to Empowerment of Oppressed Groups with Voluntary Depowerment of Dominant Groups.* Paper presented at the 6th Biennial Conference of the Society for Community Research and Action, Columbia, South Carolina.

Huygens, I. (1996a, September). *Anti-racism Education: Example of a Partnership Protocol.* Project Waitangi, Aotearoa, New Zealand.

Huygens, I. (1996b, September). *Gender Safety: Example of a Partnership Protocol.* Men's Action, Hamilton and Women's Refuges, Aotearoa, New Zealand.

Institute of Medicine (IOM). (1994) *Reducing Risks for Mental Disorders: Frontiers for Preventive Intervention Research.* Washington, DC.: National Academy Press.

Iscoe, I. (1984). 'Austin–A decade later: Preparing community psychology students for work in social policy areas'. *American Journal of Community Psychology*, **12**, 175–84.

Iscoe, I. (1974). 'Community psychology and the competent community'. *American Psychologist*, **29**, 607–13.

Ivey, A., Ivey, M. and Simek-Morgan, L. (1997). *Counseling and Psychotherapy: A Multicultural Perspective* (4th edn). Needham Heights, MA: Allyn and Bacon.

James, S. and Prilleltensky, I. (in press). 'Cultural diversity and mental health: Towards integrative practice'. *Clinical Psychology Review.*

Jenkins, J.C. (1983). 'Resource mobilization theory and the study of social movements'. *Annual Review of Sociology*, **9**, 527–53.

Jones, B. and Silva, J. (1991). 'Problem solving, community building, and systems interaction: An integrated practice model for community development'. *Journal of the Community Development Society*, **22(2)**, 1–21.

Journal of Health Psychology. (2000). 'Reconstructing health psychology'. *Journal of Health Psychology*, Special Issue, **5,3**.

Julnes, G., Pang, D., Takemoto-Chock, N., Speidel, G.E. and Tharp, R.G. (1987). 'The process of training in processes'. *Journal of Community Psychology*, **15**, 387–96.

Kaplan, M.S. and Kaplan, H.E. (1985). 'School psychology: Its educational and societal connections'. *Journal of School Psychology*, **23**, 319–25.

Kaplan, R. (2000). 'Two pathways to prevention'. *American Psychologist*, **55**, 382–96.

Kaschak, E. (1992). *Engendered Lives: A New Psychology of Women's Experience.* New York: Basic Books.

Kazdin, A.E. and Weisz, J.R. (1998). 'Identifying and developing empirically supported child and adolescent treatments'. *Journal of Consulting and Clinical Psychology*, **66**, 19–36.

Keashley, L. (1998). 'Emotional abuse in the workplace: Conceptual and empirical issues'. *Journal of Emotional Abuse*, **1**, 85–117.

Keating, D. and Hertzman, C. (eds). (1999a). *Developmental Health and the Wealth of Nations.* New York: Guilford.

Keating D. and Hertzman, C. (1999b). 'Modernity's paradox'. In D. Keating, C. Hertzman (eds), *Developmental Health and the Wealth of Nations*. (1–17). Guilford: New York.

Kelly, J.G. (1979). "Tain't what you do, it's the way you do it." *American Journal of Community Psychology*, 7, 244–58.

Kenway, J. and Modra, H. (1992). 'Feminist pedagogy and emancipatory possibilities'. In C. Luke and J. Gore (eds), *Feminisms and Critical Pedagogy* (138–66). New York: Routledge.

Kessler, R.C., Mickelson, K.D. and Zhao, S. (1997). 'Patterns and correlates of self-help group membership in the United States'. *Social Policy*, 27(3), 27–46.

Kidder, L.H. and Fine, M. (1997). 'Qualitative inquiry in psychology: A radical tradition'. In D. Fox and I. Prilleltensky (eds), *Critical Psychology: An introduction* (34–50) London: Sage.

Kieffer, C. (1984). 'Citizen empowerment: A developmental perspective'. *Prevention in Human Services*, 3, 9–35.

Kim, J., Millen, J., Irwin and Gersham, J. (eds). (2000). *Dying for Growth: Global Inequality and the Health of the Poor*. Monroe, ME: Common Courage Press.

Kincheloe, J.L. and McLaren, P.L. (1994). 'Rethinking critical theory and qualitative research'. In N.K. Denzin and Y.S. Lincoln (eds), *Handbook of Qualitative Research* (138–57). Thousand Oaks, CA: Sage.

Kingry-Westergaard, C. and Kelly, J.G. (1990). 'A contextualist epistemology for ecological researchers'. In P. Tolan, C. Keys, F. Chertok and L. Jason (eds), *Researching Community Psychology* (23–32). Washington, D. C.: American Psychological Association.

Kirby, S.L. and McKenna, K. (1989). *Experience, Research, Social change: Methods from the Margins*. Toronto: Garamond Press.

Kitzinger, C. (1997). 'Lesbian and gay psychology: A critical analysis'. In D. Fox and I. Prilleltensky (eds), *Critical Psychology: An Introduction* (202–16). London: Sage.

Knudson-Martin, C. and Mahoney, A.R. (1996). 'Gender dilemmas and myth in the construction of marital bargains: Issues for marital therapy'. *Family Process*, 35, 137–53.

Korten, D.C. (1995). *When Corporations Rule the World*. San Francisco: Berret-Koehler.

Koss, M.P. (1993). 'Rape: Scope, impact, intervention, and public policy responses'. *American Psychologist*, 48, 1062–9.

Kramer, M. (1992). 'Barriers to the primary prevention of mental, neurological, and psychosocial disorders of children: A global perspective'. In G. W. Albee, L. A. Bond and T.V. Cook Monsey (eds), *Improving Children's Lives: Global Perspectives on Prevention*. London: Sage.

Kravetz, D. (1987). 'Benefits of consciousness-raising groups'. In C.M. Brody (ed.), *Women's Therapy Groups: Paradigms of Feminist Treatment* (55–60). New York: Springer.

Krogh, K.S. (1998). 'A conceptual framework of community partnerships: Perspectives of people with disabilities on power, beliefs and values'. *Canadian Journal of Rehabilitation*, 12, 123–34.

Larner, G. (2001). 'The critical-practitioner model in therapy'. *Australian Psychologist*, 36, 36–43.

Lather, P. (1988). 'Feminist perspectives on empowering research methodologies'. *Women's Studies International Forum*, 11, 569–81.

Lawthom, R. (1999). 'Using the "F" word in organizational psychology: Foundations for critical feminist research'. *Annual Review of Critical Psychology*, 1, 67–82.

Lecovin, K.E. and Penfold, P.S. (1996). 'The emotionally abused woman: An existential-phenomenological exploration'. *Canadian Journal of Community Mental Health*, **15**(1), 39–48.

Leighton, D.C. (1979). 'Community integration and mental health: Documenting social change through longitudinal research'. In R.F. Muñoz, L.R. Snowden, J.G. Kelly and associates (eds), *Social and Psychological Research in Community Settings: Designing and Conducting Programs for Social and Personal Well-being* (275–304). San Francisco: Jossey-Bass.

Lerman, H. (1994). 'The practice of ethics within feminist therapy'. *Women and Therapy*, **15**, 85–92.

Levine, M. and Levine, A. (1992). *Helping Children: A Social History*. Oxford: Oxford University Press.

Levy, L.H. (2000). 'Self-help groups'. In J. Rappaport and E. Seidman (eds), *Handbook of Community Psychology* (591–613). New York: Kluwer Academic/Plenum Publishers.

Lewin, K. (1951). *Field Theory in Social Science*. New York: Harper and Row.

Lewin, K. (1946). 'Action research and minority problems'. *Journal of Social Issues*, **2**, 34–46.

Lewis, J.A., Lewis, M.D., Daniels, J.A. and D'Andrea, M.J. (1998). *Community Counseling: Empowerment Strategies for a Diverse Society* (2nd edn). Pacific Grove, CA: Brooks/Cole Publishing Company.

Lewis, M. (1992). 'Interrupting patriarchy: Politics, resistance, and transformation in the feminist classroom'. In C. Luke and J. Gore (eds), *Feminisms and Critical Pedagogy* (167–91). New York: Routledge.

Lincoln, Y.S. and Guba, E. (1985). *Naturalistic Inquiry*. Beverly Hills, CA: Sage.

Lord, J. and Church, K. (1998). 'Beyond "partnership shock": Getting to "yes," living with "no."' *Canadian Journal of Rehabilitation*, **12**, 113–21.

Lord, J. and Hutchison, P. (1993). 'The process of empowerment: Implications for theory and practice'. *Canadian Journal of Community Mental Health*, **12**(1), 5–22.

Lord, J., Ochocka, J., Czarny, W. and MacGillivary, H. (1998). 'Analysis of change within a mental health organization: A participatory process'. *Psychiatric Rehabilitation Journal*, **21**, 327–39.

Lorion, R.P., Iscoe, I., DeLeon, P.H. and VandenBos, G.R. (eds). (1996). *Psychology and Public Policy: Balancing Public Service and Professional Need*. Washington, DC: American Psychological Association.

Luke, C. and Gore, J. (1992). 'Women in the academy: Strategy, struggle, survival'. In C. Luke and J. Gore (eds), *Feminisms and Critical Pedagogy* (192–210). New York: Routledge.

Lupton, D. (1994). 'Toward the development of critical health communication praxis'. *Health Communication*, **61**, 55–67.

Lustig, N. (2001). 'Introduction'. In N. Lustig (ed.), *Shielding the Poor: Social Protection in the Developing World* (1–20). Washington, D.C.: Brookings Institution Press/Inter-American Development Bank.

Lykes, M.B. (2000). 'Possible contributions of a psychology of liberation: Whither health and human rights?' *Journal of Health Psychology*, **5**, 383–97.

Lykes, M.B. (1997). 'Activist participatory research among the Maya of Guatemala: Constructing meanings from situated knowledge'. *Journal of Social Issues*, **53**, 725–46.

Lykes, M.B. and Hellstedt, J.C. (1987). 'Field training in community-social psychology: A competency-based, self-directed learning model'. *Journal of Community Psychology*, **15**, 417–28.

Lynch, J. (1992). *Education for Citizenship in a Multicultural Society*. London: Cassell.

Macedo, D. (1994). *Literacies of Power: What Americans are Not Allowed to Know*. Boulder, CO: Westview Press.

MacGillivary, H. and Nelson, G. (1998). 'Partnership in mental health; What it is and how to do it'. *Canadian Journal of Rehabilitation*, 12(2), 71–83.

MacLeod, J. and Nelson, G. (2000). 'Programs for the promotion of family wellness and the prevention of child maltreatment: A meta-analytic review'. *Child Abuse and Neglect*, 24, 1127–49.

Madara, E.J. (1990). 'Maximizing the potential for community self-help through clearinghouse approaches'. *Prevention in Human Services*, 7, 109–38.

Maher, F.A. and Tetreault, M.K.T. (1994). *The Feminist Classroom*. New York: Basic Books.

Mar'i, S.K. (1988). 'Challenges to minority counselling: Arabs in Israel'. *International Journal of the Advancement of Counselling*, 11, 5–21.

Marmot, M. (1999). 'Introduction'. In M. Marmot and R. Wilkinson (eds), *Social Determinants of Health* (1–16). New York: Oxford.

Marmot, M., Siegrist, J., Theorell, T. and Feeney, A. (1999). 'Health and the psychosocial environment at work'. In M. Marmot and R. Wilkinson (eds). *Social Determinants of Health* (105–31). New York: Oxford.

Marmot, M. and Wilkinson, R. (eds). (1999). *Social Determinants of Health. New York:* Oxford University Press.

Martin, J. and Sugarman, J., (2000). 'Between the modern and the postmodern: The possibility of self and progressive understanding in psychology'. *American Psychologist*, 55, 397–406.

Martín Baró, I. (1995). 'Procesos psiquicos y poder' [Psychological processes and power]. In O. D'Adamo, V.Garcia Beaudoux, and M. Montero (eds), Psicologia de la Accion Politica [Psychology of Political Action] (205–33). Buenos Aires: Paidos.

Martín Baró, I. (1994). *Writings for a Liberation Psychology*. Cambridge, MA: Harvard University Press.

Masson, J.M. (1988). *Against Therapy: Emotional Tyranny and the Myth of Psychological Healing*. New York: Macmillan.

Maton, K.I. (2000). 'Making a difference: The social ecology of social transformation'. *American Journal of Community Psychology*, 28, 25–57.

Maton, K.I. and Salem, D.A. (1995). 'Organizational characteristics of empowering community settings'. *American Journal of Community Psychology*, 23, 631–56.

Maxwell. S. and Kenway, P. (November, 2000). 'New thinking on poverty in the UK: Any lessons for the South? *Overseas Development Institute Poverty Briefings*. 9, 1–3.

Mayer, J.P. and Davidson, W.S. II. (2000). 'Dissemination of innovation as social change'. In J. Rappaport and E. Seidman (eds), *Handbook of Community Psychology* (421–38). New York: Kluwer Academic/Plenum Publishers.

McCannell, K. (1986). 'Family politics, family policy, and family practice: A feminist perspective'. *Canadian Journal of Community Mental Health*, 5(2), 61–71.

McCubbin, M. and Cohen, D. (1999). 'A systemic and valued-based approach to strategic reform of the mental health system'. *Health Care Analysis*, 7, 1–21.

McCubbin, M. and Cohen, D. (1996). 'Extremely unbalanced: Interest divergence and power disparities between clients and psychiatry'. *International Journal of Law and Psychiatry*, 19, 1–25.

McGregor, D.M. (1960). *The Human Side of Enterprise*. New York: McGraw-Hill.

McKnight, J. (1995). *The Careless Society: Community and its Counterfeits*. New York: Basic Books.

McKnight, J. (1989). 'Do no harm: Policy options that meet human needs'. *Social Policy*, **20**, 5–15.

McKnight, J. and Kretzmann, J.P. (1984). 'Community organizing in the 80s: Toward a post-Alinsky agenda'. *Social Policy*, **14**, 15–17.

McLaren, P. (1995). *Critical Pedagogy and Predatory Culture: Oppositional Politics in a Postmodern Era*. New York: Routledge.

McLoyd, V.C. (1998). 'Children in poverty: Development, public policy, and practice'. In W. Damon (ed.-in-chief), I.E. Siegel and K.A. Renninger (vol. eds), *Handbook of Child Psychology* (5th edn) (135–208). New York: John Wiley and Sons.

McQuaig, L. (1998). *The Cult of Impotence: Selling the Myth of Powerlessness in the Global Economy*. Toronto: Viking.

McWhirter, E.H. (1994). *Counseling for Empowerment*. Alexandria, Virginia: American Counseling Association.

Memmi, A. (1968). *Dominated Man: Notes towards a Portrait*. New York: Orion Press.

Mintrom, M. and Vergari, S. (1996). 'Advocacy coalitions, policy entrepreneurs, and policy change'. *Policy Studies Journal*, **24**, 420–34.

Moane, G. (1999). *Gender and Colonialism: A Psychological Analysis of Oppression and Liberation*. London: Macmillan – now Palgrave Macmillan.

Montero, M. (2000). 'Participation in participatory action research'. *Annual Review of Critical Psychology*, **2**, 131–43.

Montero, M. (1993). 'De-ideologization, conversion, and consciousness raising'. *Journal of Community Psychology*, **22**, 3–11.

Morawski, J. (1997). 'The science behind feminist research methods'. *Journal of Social Issues*, **53**, 667–81.

Morgan, A. (2000). *'What is Narrative Therapy? An Easy-to-read Introduction'*. Adelaide, South Australia: Dulwich Publications.

Morgan, R.F. (ed.). (1983). *The Iatrogenics Handbook: A Critical Look at Research and Practice in the Helping Professions*. Toronto: IPI Publishing Limited.

Morris, A.D. and Mueller, C. (eds). (1992) *Frontiers in Social Movement Theory*. New Haven, CT: Yale University Press.

Morris, J. (1992). 'Personal and political: A feminist perspective on researching physical disability'. *Disability, Handicap and Society*, **7**, 157–66.

Mowbray, C.T. (1999). 'The benefits and challenges of supported education: A personal perspective'. *Psychiatric Rehabilitation Journal*, **22**, 248–54.

Mukherjee, A. (1992). 'Education and race relations: The education of South Asian youth'. In R. Ghosh and R. Kanungo (eds), *South Asian Canadians: Current Issues in the Politics of Culture*. Montréal: Shastri Indo-Canadian Institute.

Murray, M. (2000). 'Levels of narrative analysis in health psychology'. *Journal of Health Psychology*, **5**, 337–47.

Murray, M. and Chamberlain, K. (eds). (1999). *Qualitative Health Psychology: Theory and Methods*. Thousand Oaks, CA: Sage.

Naidoo, J.C. and Edwards, R. G. (1991). 'Combatting racism involving visible minorities: A review of relevant research and policy development'. *Canadian Social Work Review*, **8**, 211–35.

Narayan, D., Chambers, R., Kaul Shah, M. and Petesch, P. (2000). *Voices of the Poor: Crying out for Change*. New York, NY: Oxford University Press.

Narayan, D., Patel, R., Schafft, K., Rademacher, A., Koch-Schulte, S. (2000). *Voices of the Poor: Can Anyone Hear Us?* New York, N.Y.: Oxford University Press.

Nelson, G. (1994). 'The development of a mental health coalition: A case study'. *American Journal of Community Psychology*, **22**, 229–55.

Nelson, G. (1983). 'Community psychology and the schools: From iatrogenic illness to prevention'. In R.F. Morgan (ed.), *The Iatrogenics Handbook: A Critical Look at Research and Practice in the Helping Professions* (385–436). Toronto: IPI Press.

Nelson, G., Amio, J.L., Prilleltensky, I. and Nickels, P. (2000). 'Partnerships for implementing school and community prevention programs'. *Journal of Educational and Psychological Consultation*, 11, 121–45.

Nelson, G., Lord, J. and Ochocka, J. (2001a). 'Empowerment and mental health in community: Narratives of psychiatric consumer/survivors'. *Journal of Community and Applied Social Psychology*, 11, 125–42.

Nelson, G., Lord, J. and Ochocka, J. (2001b). *Shifting the Paradigm in Community Mental Health: Towards Empowerment and Community*. Toronto: University of Toronto Press.

Nelson, G., Ochocka, J., Griffin, K. and Lord, J. (1998). '"Nothing about me without me": Participatory action research with self-help/mutual aid groups for psychiatric consumers/survivors'. *American Journal of Community Psychology*, 26, 881–912.

Nelson, G., Pancer, S.M., Hayward, K. and Kelly, R. (under review). 'Prevention programs and partnerships with community residents: Experiences of the Highfield Community Enrichment project' (Better Beginnings, Better Futures).

Nelson, G., Prilleltensky, I. and MacGillivary. (2001). 'Value-based partnerships: Toward solidarity with oppressed groups'. *American Journal of Community Psychology*, 29, 649–78.

Nelson, G., Prilleltensky, I. and Peters, R.D. (1999). 'Prevention and mental health promotion in the community'. In W.L. Marshall and P. Firestone (eds), *Abnormal Psychology: Perspectives* (461–78). Scarborough, Ontario: Prentice Hall Allyn and Bacon Canada.

Nelson, G. and Walsh-Bowers, R. (1994). 'Psychology and psychiatric survivors'. *American Psychologist*, 49, 895–6.

Nelson, G., Walsh-Bowers, R. and Hall, G.B. (1998). 'Housing for psychiatric survivors: Values, policy, and research'. *Administration and Policy in Mental Health*, 25, 55–62.

Ng, R., Staton, P. and Scane, J. (eds). (1995). *Anti-racism, Feminism, and Critical Approaches to Education*. Westport, Connecticut: Begin and Garvey.

Nicholas, M., Molloy, A., Tonkin, L. and Beeston, L. (2000). *Manage your Pain*. Sydney: ABC Books.

Nickels, P. (1999). *Planning and Developing School-based Community Supports for Refugee Children*. Unpublished Master's Thesis, Wilfrid Laurier University, Waterloo, ON.

Nietzel, M.,T., Bernstein, D.A. and Milich, R. (1998). *Introduction to clinical psychology* (4th edn). Englewood Cliffs, N. J.: Prentice Hall.

Nord, W.R. and Jermier, J.M. (1992). 'Critical social science for managers? Promising and perverse possibilities'. In M. Alvesson and H. Willmott (eds), *Critical Management Studies* (202–22). London: Sage.

O'Brien, J. and O'Brien, C.L. (1996). *Members of Each Other: Building Community in Company with People with Developmental Disabilities*. Toronto: Inclusion Press.

O'Nell, T.D. (1998). 'Cultural formulation of psychiatric diagnosis: Psychotic depression and alcoholism in an American Indian man'. *Culture, Medicine, and Psychiatry*, 22, 123–36.

O'Sullivan, E. (1999). *Transformative Learning: Educational Vision for the 21st Century*. New York: Zed Books.

O'Sullivan, E. (1990). *Critical Psychology and Critical Pedagogy*. New York: Begin and Garvey.

O'Sullivan, M.J. (1997). 'Undergraduate courses in community psychology: Issues, paradigms, and experiences'. *Journal of Prevention and Intervention in the Community*, **15**(1), 5–16.

Oakley, A. (1981). 'Interviewing women: A contradiction in terms'. In H. Roberts (ed.), *Doing Feminist Research* (30–61). London: Routledge and Kegan Paul.

Ochocka, J., Janzen, R. and Nelson, G. (in press). 'Sharing power and knowledge: Professional and mental health consumer/survivor researchers working together in a participatory action research project'. *Psychiatric Rehabilitation Journal*.

Ochocka, J., Nelson, G. and Lord, J. (1999). 'Organizational change towards the empowerment-community integration paradigm in community mental health'. *Canadian Journal of Community Mental Health*, **18**(2), 59–72.

Offord, D. (1995). 'Child psychiatric epidemiology: Current status and future prospects'. *Canadian Journal of Psychiatry*, **40**, 284–8.

Offord, D., Boyle, M., Campbell, D., Cochrane, J., Goering, P., Lin, E., Rhodes, A. and Wong, M. (1994). *Mental Health in Ontario: Selected Findings from the Mental Health Supplement to the Ontario Health Survey*. Toronto: Ontario Ministry of Health.

Offord, D.R., Boyle, M.H. and Szatmari, P. (1987). 'Ontario Child Health Study, II: Six month prevalence of disorder and rates of service utilization'. *Archives of General Psychiatry*, **44**, 832–36.

Olesen, V. (1994). 'Feminisms and models of qualitative research'. In N.K. Denzin and Y. S. Lincoln (eds), *Handbook of Qualitative Research* (158–74). Thousand Oaks, CA: Sage.

Oliver, M. (1992). 'Changing the social relations of research production?' *Disability, Handicap and Society*, **7**, 101–14.

Osher, D. and Goldenberg, I. (1987). 'The School of Human Services: A case study in social intervention and the creation of alternative settings'. In E. M. Bennett (ed.), *Social Intervention: Theory and Practice* (57–91). Lewiston, NY: The Edwin Mellen Press.

Oxley, D. (2000). 'The school reform movement: Opportunities for community psychology'. In J. Rappaport and E. Seidman (eds), *Handbook of Community Psychology* (565–90). New York: Kluwer Academic/Plenum Publishers.

Page, S. and Day, D. (1990). 'Acceptance of the "mentally ill" in Canadian society: Reality and illusion'. *Canadian Journal of Community Mental Health*, **9**(1), 51–61.

Pancer, S.M. (1994). 'Resident participation in the Better Beginnings, Better Futures prevention project: Part I – The impacts of involvement'. *Canadian Journal of Community Mental Health*, **13**(2), 197–211.

Pancer, S.M. and Pratt, M. (1999). 'Social and family determinants of community and political involvement in Canadian youth'. In M. Yates and J. Youniss (eds), *Community Service and Civic Engagement in Youth: International Perspectives* (32–55). Cambridge, UK: Cambridge University Press.

Paproski, D.L. (1997). 'Healing experiences of British Columbia First Nations women: Moving beyond suicidal ideation and intention'. *Canadian Journal of Community Mental Health*, **16**(2), 69–89.

Pare, D. and Larner, G. (eds). (in process), *Critical Practice in Psychology and Therapy*. Binghampton, NY: Haworth Press.

Parker, I. (1999). 'Critical Psychology: Critical Links'. *Annual Review of Critical Psychology*, **1**, 3–20.

Parker, I., Georgaca, E., Harper, D., McLaughlin, T. and Stowell-Smith, M. (1995). *Deconstructing Psychopathology*. London: Sage.

Parkinson, S., Nelson, G. and Horgan, S. (1999). 'From housing to homes: A review of the literature on housing approaches for psychiatric consumer/survivors'. *Canadian Journal of Community Mental Health*, **18**(2), 145–64.

Parsons, R.D. and Meyers, J. (1984). *Developing Consultation Skills.* San Francisco: Jossey-Bass.

Paul, G. (1967). 'Outcome research in psychotherapy'. *Journal of Consulting Psychology,* **31**, 109–18.

Pearce, J. (1993). 'NGOs and social change: Agents or facilitators?' *Development in Practice,* **3(3)**.

Peirson, L. and Prilleltensky, I. (1994). 'Understanding school change to facilitate prevention: A study of change in a secondary school'. *Canadian Journal of Community Mental Health,* **13(2)**, 127–44.

Peirson, L., Prilleltensky, I., Nelson, G. and Gould, J. (1997). 'Planning mental health services for children and youth: Part II: Findings of a value-based community consultation project'. *Evaluation and Program Planning,* **20**, 173–83.

Penfold, P.S. (1992). 'Sexual abuse by therapists: Maintaining the conspiracy of silence'. *Canadian Journal of Community Mental Health,* **11(1)**, 5–15.

Pepler, D., King, D., Craig, W., Byrd and Bream, L. (1995). 'The development and evaluation of a multisystem social skills group training program for aggressive children'. *Child and Youth Care Forum,* **24**, 297–313.

Perez, R.M., DeBord, K.A. and Bieschke, K.J. (2000). *Handbook of Counseling and Psychotherapy with Lesbian, Gay, and Bisexual clients.* Washington, DC: American Psychological Association.

Peters, R.D. (1994). 'Better Beginnings, Better Futures: A community-based approach to primary prevention'. *Canadian Journal of Community Mental Health,* **13(2)**, 183–8.

Peters, R.D. (1990). 'Adolescent mental health promotion: Policy and practice'. In R. J. McMahon and R.D. Peters (eds). *Behavior Disorders of Adolescence* (207–23). New York: Plenum Press.

Petersen, A. (1994). *In a Critical Condition: Health and Power Relations in Australia.* St. Leonards, NSW: Australia.

Pheterson, G. (1986). 'Alliances between women: Overcoming internalized oppression and internalized domination'. *Signs: Journal of Women in Culture and Society,* **12(1)**, 146–60.

Phillips, D.A. (2000). 'Social policy and community psychology'. In J. Rappaport and E. Seidman (eds), *Handbook of Community Psychology* (397–419). New York: Kluwer Academic/Plenum Publishers.

Pilar Quintero, M. Del. (1992). 'Los programas educativos y los textos escolares como medio de transmisión de una ideología colonizadora: Base de una autoimagen negativa del venezolano?' *Boletín de la Asociación Venezolana de Psicología Social,* **15(1–3)**, 87–97.

Pilgrim, D. (1992). 'Psychotherapy and political evasions'. In W. Dryden and C. Feltham (eds), *Psychotherapy and its Discontents* (225–42). Bristol, PA: Open University Press.

Pilisuk, M. and McAllister, J. and Rothman, J. (1996). 'Coming together for action: The challenge of grassroots community organizing'. *Journal of Social Issues,* **52**, 15–37.

Pitman, A-L., Wolfe, D.A., Wekerle, C. (1998). 'Prevention during adolescence: The Youth Relationships Project'. In J.R. Lutzker (ed.), *Handbook on Research and Treatment in Child Abuse and Neglect* (341–56). New York: The Guilford Press.

Powell, B. and Nelson, G. (1997). 'The cultivation of neighbourhood centers: A life-cycle model'. *Journal of the Community Development Society,* **28(1)**, 25–42.

Pressman, B. (1989). 'Treatment of wife abuse: The case for feminist therapy'. In B. Pressman, G. Cameron and M. Rothery (eds), *Intervening with Assaulted Women: Current Theory, Research, and Practice* (21–45). Hillsdale, NJ: Erlbaum.

Prilleltensky, I. (in press). 'Understanding, resisting, and overcoming oppression: Towards psychopolitical validity'. *American Journal of Community Psychology.*

Prilleltensky, I. (2001). 'Value-based praxis in community psychology: Moving towards social justice and social action'. *American Journal of Community Psychology*, 29, 747–78.

Prilleltensky, I. (2000). 'Value-based leadership in organizations: Balancing values, interests, and power among citizens, workers, and leaders'. *Ethics and Behavior*, 10, 139–58.

Prilleltensky, I. (1999). 'Critical psychology foundations for the promotion of mental health'. *Annual Review of Critical Psychology*, 1, 95–112.

Prilleltensky, I. (1997). 'Values, assumptions, and practices: Assessing the moral implications of psychological discourse and action'. *American Psychologist*, 47, 517–35.

Prilleltensky, I. (1994). *The Morals and Politics of Psychology: Psychological Discourse and the Status Quo.* Albany, New York: State University of New York Press.

Prilleltensky, I. (1993). 'The immigration experience of Latin American families: Research and action on perceived risk and protective factors'. *Canadian Journal of Community Mental Health*, 12(2), 101–16.

Prilleltensky, I. (1990). 'Enhancing the social ethics of psychology: Toward a psychology at the service of social change'. *Canadian Psychology*, 31, 310–19.

Prilleltensky, I. and Gonick, L. (1996). 'Polities change, oppression remains: On the psychology and politics of oppression'. *Political Psychology*, 17, 127–47.

Prilleltensky, I. and Gonick, L. (1994). 'The discourse of oppression in the social sciences: Past, present, and future'. In E.J. Trickett, R.J. Watts and D. Birman (eds), *Human Diversity: Perspectives on People in Context* (145–77). San Francisco: Jossey-Bass.

Prilleltensky, I. and Nelson, G. (2000). 'Promoting child and family wellness: Priorities for psychological and social interventions'. *Journal of Community and Applied Social Psychology*, 10, 85–105.

Prilleltensky, I. and Nelson, G. (1997). 'Community Psychology: Reclaiming social justice'. In D. Fox and I. Prilleltensky (eds), *Critical Psychology: An Introduction* (166–84) London: Sage.

Prilleltensky, I., Nelson, G. and Peirson, L. (eds). (2001). *Promoting Family Wellness and Preventing Child Maltreatment: Fundamentals for Thinking and Action.* Toronto: University of Toronto Press.

Prilleltensky, I., Nelson, G. and Sánchez Valdes, L. (2000). 'A value-based approach to smoking prevention with immigrants from Latin America: Program evaluation'. *Journal of Ethnic and Cultural Diversity in Social Work*, 9(1–2), 97–117.

Prilleltensky, I., Peirson, L., Gould, J. and Nelson, G. (1997). 'Planning mental health services for children and youth: Part I–A value-based approach'. *Evaluation and Program Planning*, 20, 163–72.

Prilleltensky, I., Peirson, L. and Nelson, G. (1997). 'The application of community psychology values and guiding concepts to school consultation'. *Journal of Educational and Psychological Consultation*, 8, 153–73.

Prilleltensky, I., Rossiter, A. and Walsh-Bowers, R. (1996). 'Preventing harm and promoting ethical discourse in the helping professions: Conceptual, research, analytical, and action frameworks'. *Ethics and Behavior*, 6, 287–306.

Prilleltensky, I., Walsh-Bowers, R. and Rossiter, A. (1999). 'Clinicians lived experience of ethics: Values and challenges in helping children'. *Journal of Educational and Psychological Consultation*, 10, 315–42.

Prilleltensky, O. (1996). 'Women with disabilities and feminist therapy'. *Women and Therapy*, 18, 87–97.

Pusey, M. (in press). 'Globalisation and the impacts of economic rationalism on quality of life in "Advanced Societies"'. In D Lamberton (ed.), *Globalization, Employment, and the Quality of Life*. Toda Institute: Tokyo.

Putnam, R. (2000). *Bowling Alone*. New York: Touchstone.

Putnam, R. (1993). *Making Democracy Work*. Princeton, NJ: Princeton University Press.

Pyke, S.W. (1997). 'Education and the "woman question"'. *Canadian Psychology*, **38**, 154–63.

Pyke, S.W. (1991). *Gender issues in Graduate Education*. Trevor N.S. Lennam Memorial Lecture, University of Calgary, March 17, 1991.

Quarter, J. (1992). *Canada's Social Economy: Co-operatives, Non-profits, and Other Community Enterprises*. Toronto: Lorimer.

Quarter, J. and Melnyk, G. (eds). (1989). *Partners in Enterprise: The Worker Ownership Phenomenon*. Montreal: Black Rose.

Rabin, C. (1994). 'The egalitarian alternative: A feminist model for couples and group interventions'. *Journal of Applied Social Sciences*, **18**, 109–22.

Racino, J.A. (1991). 'Organizations in community living: Supporting people with disabilities'. *The Journal of Mental Health Administration*, **18**, 51–9.

Ralph, D. (1983). *Work and Madness*. Montreal: Black Rose Press.

Rappaport, J. (1993). 'Narrative studies, personal stories, and identity transformation in the mutual help context'. *Journal of Applied Behavioral Science*, **29**, 237–54.

Rappaport, J. (1990). 'Research methods and the empowerment social agenda'. In P. Tolan, C. Keys, F. Chertok and L. Jason (eds), *Researching Community Psychology* (51–63). Washington, DC: American Psychological Association.

Rappaport, J. (1977). *Community Psychology: Values, Research, and Action*. New York: Holt, Rinehart, and Winston.

Rappaport, J. and Stewart, E. (1997). 'A critical look at critical psychology: Elaborating the questions'. In D. Fox and I. Prilleltensky (eds), *Critical Psychology: An Introduction* (301–17). London: Sage.

Raue, P.J., Goldfried, M.R. and Barkham, M. (1997). 'The therapeutic alliance in psychodynamic-interpersonal and cognitive-behavioral therapy'. *Journal of Consulting and Clinical Psychology*, **65**, 582–7.

Regier, D.A., Myers, J.K., Kramer, M., Robins, L. N., Blazer, D.G., Hough, R.L., Eaton, W.W. and Locke, B.Z. (1984). 'The NIMH epidemiologic catchment area program'. *Archives of General Psychiatry*, **41**, 934–41.

Reicher, S. (1997). 'Laying the ground for a common critical psychology'. In T. Ibáñez and L. Íñiguez (eds), *Critical Social Psychology* (83–94). London: Sage.

Reiff, R. (1974). 'The control of knowledge: The power of the helping professions'. *Journal of Applied Behavioral Science*, **10**, 451–61.

Reinharz, S. (1992). *Feminist Methods in Social Research*. Oxford: Oxford University Press.

Reinharz, S. (1984). 'Alternative settings and social change'. In K. Heller, R. H. Price, S.Reinharz, S. Riger and A. Wandersman, *Psychology and Community Change: Challenges of the Future* (2nd edn, 286–336). Homewood, IL: The Dorsey Press.

Rich, A. (1980). 'Taking women students seriously'. In A. Rich (ed.), *On Lies, Secrets and Silence* (237–45). London Virago.

Richardson, B. (ed.). (1989). *Drumbeat: Anger and Renewal in Indian country*. Toronto: Summerhill Press, the Assembly of First Nations.

Riger, S. (2000). *Transforming Psychology*. New York: Oxford University Press.

Riger, S. (1992). 'Epistemological debates, feminist voices: Science, social values, and the study of women'. *American Psychologist*, **47**, 730–40.

Rogers, C.R. (1961). *On Becoming a Person: A Therapist's View of Psychotherapy*. Boston: Houghton Mifflin.

Rogers, E.S., Chamberlin, J., Ellison, M.L. and Crean, T. (1997). 'A consumer-constructed scale to measure empowerment of users of mental health services'. *Psychiatric Services*, **48**, 914–18.

Rose, N. (2000). *Power and Subjectivity: Critical History and Psychology*. Available from Internet site *http://www.academyanalyticarts.org/rose1.html*

Rose, N. (1999). *Powers of Freedom: Reframing Political Thought*. New York: Cambridge University Press.

Rose, N. (1985). *The Psychological Complex: Psychology, Politics and Society in England 1869–1939*. London: Routledge and Kegan Paul.

Rosenhan, D.L. (1973). 'On being sane in insane places'. *Science*, **179**, 250–8.

Rossiter, A. (1995). 'Entering the intersection of identity, form, and knowledge: Reflections on curriculum transformation'. *Canadian Social Work Review*, **10**(1), 76–90.

Rossiter, A. (1993). 'Teaching from a critical perspective: Towards empowerment in social work education'. *Canadian Journal of Community Mental Health*, **14**(1), 5–14.

Rossiter, A., Prilleltensky, I. and Walsh-Bowers, R. (2000). 'Postmodern professional ethics'. In B. Fawcett, B. Featherstone, J. Fook, and A. Rossiter (eds). *Practice and Research in Social Work: Postmodern Feminist Perspectives* (83–103). London: Routledge.

Rossiter, A., Walsh-Bowers, R. and Prilleltensky, I. (1996). 'Learning from broken rules: Individualism, bureaucracy, and ethics'. *Ethics and Behavior*, **6**, 307–20.

Rothman, J. and Tropman, J.E. (1987). 'Models of community organization and macro practice perspectives: Their mixing and phases'. In F.M. Cox, J.L. Erlich, J. Rothman and J.E. Tropman (eds), *Strategies of Community Organization: Macro Practice* (3–26). Itasca, IL: Peacock.

Seidman, E. and Rappaport, J. (eds). (1986). *Redefining Social Problems*. New York: Plenum.

Saleebey, D. (ed) (1992). *The Strengths Perspective in Social Work Practice*. New York: Longman.

Sampson, E. (2001). 'To think differently: the acting ensemble – a new unit of psychological inquiry'. *International Journal of Critical Psychology*, **1**, 47–61.

Samson, C. (1999). 'The physician and the patient'. In C. Samson (ed.). *Health Studies: A Critical and Cross Cultural Reader* (179–96). Oxford: Blackwell.

Sánchez Vidal, A. (1999). *Ética de la intervención social (Ethics of Social Intervention)*. Mexico: Paidós.

Sarason, S.B. (1996). *Barometers of Change: Individual, Educational, and Social Transformation*. San Francisco: Jossey-Bass Publishers.

Sarason, S.B. (1990). *The Predictable Failure of Educational Reform: Can we Change Course before It's too Late?* San Francisco: Jossey-Bass Publishers.

Sarason, S.B. (1988). *The Psychological Sense of Community: Prospects for a Community Psychology* (rev. edn). Cambridge, MA: Brookline.

Sarason, S.B. (1984). 'Community psychology and public policy: Missed opportunity'. *American Journal of Community Psychology*, **12**, 199–207.

Sarason, S.B. (1982). *The Culture of the School and the Problem of Change* (2nd edn). Boston: Allyn and Bacon.

Sarason, S.B. (1981). *Psychology Misdirected*. New York: Free Press.

Sarason, S.B. (1978). 'The nature of problem solving in social action'. *American Psychologist*, **33**, 370–81.

Sarason, S. (1972). *The Creation of Settings and the Future Societies*. San Francisco: Jossey-Bass.

Schmuck, R.A., Runkel, P.J. and Langmeyer, D. (1969). 'Improving organizational problem-solving in a school faculty'. *Journal of Applied Behavioral Science*, 5, 455–82.

Schneider, M. (1991). 'Developing services for lesbian and gay adolescents'. *Canadian Journal of Community Mental Health*, 10(1), 133–51.

Schneiderman, L. (1988). *The Psychology of Social Change*. New York: Human Sciences Press

Schwartz, D. (1997). *Who Cares: Rediscovering Community*. Boulder, CO: Westview Press.

Schweinhart, L. J. and Weikhart, D. P. (1989). 'The High/Scope Perry Preschool study: Implications for early childhood care and education'. *Prevention in Human Services*, 6, 109–32.

Sedgwick, P. (1982). *Psychopolitics*. New York: Harper and Row.

Sehl, M. (1987). *The Creation of a Multi-ethnic Housing Cooperative: A Social Intervention*. Unpublished Master's Thesis, Wilfrid Laurier University, Waterloo, ON.

Seidman, E. (ed.). (1983). *Handbook of Social Intervention*. Beverly Hills, CA: Sage.

Seidman, E. and Rappaport, J. (eds). (1986). *Redefining Social Problems*. New York: Plenum.

Seligman, M.E.P. (1995). 'The effectiveness of psychotherapy: The *Consumer Reports* study'. *American Psychologist*, 50, 965–74.

Sen, A. (2001). *Culture and Development*. Paper presented at the World Bank Tokyo Meeting, 13 December. www.worldbank.org/wbi/B-SPAN/sen_tokyo.pdf

Sen, A. (1999a). *Beyond the Crisis: Development Strategies in Asia*. Singapore: Institute of Southeast Asian Studies.

Sen, A. (1999b). *Development as Freedom*. New York, NY: Anchor Books.

Senge, P. (1990). *The Fifth Discipline: The Art and the Practice of the Learning Organization*. New York: Doubleday.

Senge, P., Ross, R., Smith, B., Roberts, C. and Kleiner, A. (1994). *The Fifth Discipline Fieldbook*. New York: Doubleday.

Seskar-Hencic, D. (1996). *Breaking the Silence: New Immigrant Children Affected by War Trauma – Community Needs and Resources Assessment*. Unpublished Master's Thesis, Wilfrid Laurier University, Waterloo, ON.

Seto, M.C. (1995). 'Sex with therapy clients: Its prevalence, potential consequences, and implications for psychology training'. *Canadian Psychology*, 36, 70–86.

Shaw, M., Dorling, D. and Smith, G. (1999). 'Poverty, social exclusion, and minorities'. In M. Marmot and R. Wilkinson (eds). *Social Determinants of Health* (211–39). New York: Oxford.

Shera, W. and Page, J. (1995). 'Creating more effective human service organizations through strategies of empowerment'. *Administration in Social Work*, 19(4), 1–15.

Shonkoff, J. and Phillips, D. (eds). (2000). *From Neurons to Neighbourhoods: The Science of Early Childhood Development*. Washington, D.C.: National Academy Press.

Shure, M.B. and Spivack, G. (1988). 'Interpersonal Cognitive Problem-Solving: Primary prevention of early high-risk behaviors in the preschool and primary years'. In R. Price, E.L. Cowen, R.P. Lorion and J. Ramos-McKay (eds), *Fourteen Ounces of Prevention: A Casebook for Practitioners* (69–82). Washington, D C: American Psychological Association.

Sidanius, J. (1993). 'The psychology of group conflict and the dynamics of oppression: A social dominance perspective'. In S. Iyengar and W. J. McGuire (eds), *Explorations in Political Psychology* (183–219). London: Duke University Press.

Silovsky, J.F. and Hembree-Kigin, T.L. (1994). 'Family and group treatment for sexually abused children: A review'. *Journal of Child Sexual Abuse*, 3(3), 1–20.

Silverstein, L.B. and Auerbach, C.F. (1999). 'Deconstructing the essential father'. *American Psychologist*, **54**, 397–407.

Sleeter, C.E. (ed.). (1991). *Empowerment through Multicultural Education*. Albany, New York: State University of New York Press.

Sloan, T. (ed.). (2000). *Critical Psychology: Voices for Change*. London: Macmillan – now Palgrave Macmillan.

Sloan, T. (1997). 'Theories of personality: Ideology and beyond'. In D. Fox and I. Prilleltensky (eds), *Critical Psychology: An Introduction* (87–103). London: Sage.

Smedley, B. and Syme, L. (eds). (2000). *Promoting Health: Intervention Strategies from Social and Behavioral Research*. Washington, DC: National Academy Press.

Smith, D.E. (1990). *The Conceptual Practices of Power: A Feminist Sociology of Knowledge*. Toronto: University of Toronto Press.

Smith, J.A. (1994). 'Towards reflexive practice: Engaging participants as co-researchers or co-analysts in psychological inquiry'. *Journal of Community and Applied Social Psychology*, **4**, 253–60.

Smith, M.B. (1990). 'Psychology in the public interest: What have we done? What can be done?' *American Psychologist*, **45**, 530–6.

Snyder, C.R., Feldman, D., Taylor, J., Schroeder, L., Adams III, V. (2000). 'The roles of hopeful thinking in preventing problems and enhancing strengths'. *Applied and Preventive Psychology*, **9**, 249–70.

Solomon, P. (1992). The Efficacy of Case Management Services for Severely Mentally Disabled Clients. *Community Mental Health Journal*, **28**, 163–80.

Spector, M. and Kitsuse, J. I. (1987). *Constructing Social Problems*. New York: Aldine de Grutyer.

Sperry, L. (1991). 'Enhancing corporate health, mental health, and productivity'. *Research and Practice*, **47**, 247–54.

Spindel, P. (2000). 'Polar opposites: Empowerment philosophy and Assertive Community Treatment (ACT)'. *Ethical Human Sciences and Services*, **2**, 93–100.

Sprague, J. and Hayes, J. (2000). 'Self-determination and empowerment: A Feminist standpoint analysis of talk about disability'. *American Journal of Community Psychology*, **28**, 649–70.

Stainton-Rogers, W. (1996). 'Critical approaches to health psychology'. *Journal of Health Psychology*, **1**, 65–78.

Stam, H.J. (2000). 'Theorizing health and illness: Functionalism, subjectivity, and reflexivity'. *Journal of Health Psychology*, **5**, 273–83.

Steffy, B.D. and Grimes, A. J. (1992). 'Personnel/Organizational Psychology: A critique of the discipline'. In M. Alvesson and H. Willmott (eds), *Critical Management Studies* (181–201). London: Sage.

Stein, L.I. and Test, M.A. (1980). 'Alternative to mental hospital treatment: I. Conceptual model, treatment program, and clinical evaluation'. *Archives of General Psychiatry*, **37**, 392–7.

Stenmark, D.E. (1977). 'Field training in community psychology'. In I. Iscoe, B.L. Bloom and C.D. Spielberger (eds), *Community psychology in transition: Proceedings of the National Conference on Training in Community Psychology* (159–73). Washington, DC: Hemisphere.

Stoecker, R. (1999). *Are Academics Irrelevant? Roles for Scholars in Participatory Research*. Paper presented at the Annual Meeting of the American Sociological Association.

Stoppard, J.M. (1999). 'Why new perspectives are needed for understanding depression in women'. *Canadian Psychology*, **40**, 79–90.

Stringer, E.T. (1996). *Action Research: A Handbook for Practitioners*. Thousand Oaks, CA: Sage.

Swift, J. (1999). *Civil Society in Question*. Toronto: Between the Lines.

Swift, R. (2001, January/February). 'Health hazard'. *New Internationalist*, **331**, 9–12.

Swindle, R., Heller, K., Pescosolido, B. and Kikuzawa, S. (2000). 'Responses to nervous breakdowns in America over a 40-year period'. *American Psychologist*, **55**, 740–9.

Taylor, D. (1996). (ed.). *Critical Social Policy: A Reader*. Thousand Oaks, CA: Sage.

Taylor, S. (1995). *Health Psychology* (3rd edn). New York: McGraw Hill.

Thesen, J. and Kuzel, A. J. (1999). 'Participatory inquiry'. In B. F. Crabtree and W. L. Miller (eds), *Doing Qualitative Research* (2nd edn). Thousand Oaks, CA: Sage.

Thomas, D.R., Neill, B. and Robertson, N. (1997). 'Developing a graduate program in community psychology: Experiences at the University of Waikato, New Zealand'. *Journal of Prevention and Intervention in the Community*, **15**(1), 83–96.

Thomas, R.E. and Rappaport, J. (1996). 'Art as community narrative: A resource for social change'. In M. B. Lykes, A. Banuazizi, R. Liem and M. Morris (eds), *Myths about the Powerless: Contesting Social Inequalities* (317–36). Philadelphia: Temple University Press.

Thompson, N. (1998). *Promoting Equality: Challenging Discrimination and Oppression in the Human Services*. London: Macmillan–now Palgrave Macmillan.

Titmus, R. (1974). *Commitment to Welfare*. London: George Allen and Unwin.

Tobbell, J. (2000). 'On Freire's *Pedagogy of the Oppressed* and *Pedagogy of Hope*'. *Annual Review of Critical Psychology*, **2**, 204–5.

Tobler, N.S. and Stratton, H.H. (1997). 'Effectiveness of school-based drug prevention programs: A meta-analysis of the research'. *Journal of Primary Prevention*, **18**, 71–128.

Tolman, D.L. and Brydon-Miller, M. (eds).(2000). *From Subjects to Subjectivities: A Handbook of Interpretive and Participatory Methods*. New York: New York University.

Tones, K. (1996). 'The anatomy and ideology of health promotion: Empowerment in context'. In A. Scriven and J. Orme (eds), *Health Promotion* (9–21). London: Macmillan–now Palgrave Macmillan.

Townsend, E. (1999). *Good Intentions Overruled: A Critique of Empowerment in the Routine Organization of Mental Health Services*. Toronto: University of Toronto Press.

Trainor, J., Pomeroy, P. and Pape, B. (eds.). (1999). *Building a Framework for Support: A Community Development Approach to Mental Health Policy*. Toronto: Canadian Mental Health Association/National.

Trainor, J. and Tremblay, J. (1992). 'Consumer/survivor businesses in Ontario: Challenging the rehabilitation model'. *Canadian Journal of Community Mental Health*, **11**(2), 65–71.

Trickett, E. J., McConahy, J., Phillips, D. and Ginter, M. (1985). 'Natural experiments and the educational context: The environment and effects of an alternative inner-city public schools on adolescents'. *American Journal of Community Psychology*, **13**, 617–43.

Truax, C.B. and Carkhuff, R.R. (1967). *Toward Effective Counseling and Psychotherapy: Training and Practice*. Chicago: Aldine.

Turner, S., Norman, E. and Zunz, S. (1995). 'Enhancing resiliency in girls and boys: A case for gender specific adolescent programming'. *Journal of Primary Prevention*, **16**, 25–38.

UNICEF (2001). *The State of the World's Children 2002*. New York, NY: Author.

UNICEF Innocenti Research Centre (June 2000). *A League Table of Child Poverty in Rich Nations: Report Card No. 1*. Florence, Italy: Author.

Ussher, J. (1991). *Women's Madness: Misogyny or Mental Illness?* New York: Harvester/Wheatsheaf.

Ussher, J.M. and Walkerdine, V. (2001). 'Guest editorial: Critical psychology'. *Australian Psychologist*, **36**, 1–3.

Van Uchelen, C.P., Davidson, S. F., Quressette, S.V.A., Brasfield, C.R. and Demerais, L.H. (1997). 'What makes us strong: Urban aboriginal perspectives on wellness and strengths'. *Canadian Journal of Community Mental Health*, **16(2)**, 37–50.

Wadsworth, Y. and Epstein, M. (1998). 'Building in dialogue between consumers and staff in acute mental health services'. *Systemic Practice and Action Research*, **11**, 353–79.

Walker, L.E. (1999). 'Psychology and domestic violence around the world'. *American Psychologist*, **54**, 21–9.

Walkerdine, V. (1997). *Daddy's Girl: Young Girls in Popular Culture*. London: Macmillan – now Palgrave Macmillan.

Walkerdine, V. (1996). 'Working-class women: Psychological and social aspects of survival'. In S. Wilkinson (ed.), *Feminist Social Psychologies* (145–62). Philadelphia: Open University Press.

Walsh, R.T. (1988). 'The dark side of our moon: The iatrogenic aspects of professional psychology'. *Journal of Community Psychology*, **16**, 244–8.

Walsh-Bowers, R., Rossiter, A. and Prilleltensky, I. (1996). 'The personal is the organizational in the ethics of hospital social workers'. *Ethics and Behavior*, **6**, 321–35.

Wandersman, A. and Florin, P. (2000). 'Citizen participation and community organizations'. In J. Rappaport and E. Seidman (eds), *Handbook of Community Psychology* (247–72). New York: Kluwer Academic/Plenum Publishers.

Warwick, D.P. (1978). 'Moral dilemmas in organizational development'. In G. Bermant, H.C.Kelman and D.P. Warwick (eds), *The Ethics of Social Intervention* (147–59). New York: John Wiley & Sons.

Watts, R. (1992). 'Elements of a psychology of human diversity'. *Journal of Community Psychology*, **20**, 116–31.

Watts, R.J., Griffith, D.M. and Abdul-Adil, J. (1999). 'Sociopolitical development as an antidote for oppression – Theory and action'. *American Journal of Community Psychology*, **27**, 255–71.

Webster-Stratton, C. and Herbert, M. (1993). '"What really happens in parent training?"' *Behavior Modification*, **17**, 407–56.

Weick, K. (1984). 'Small wins: Redefining the scale of social issues'. *American Psychologist*, **39**, 40–9.

Weinberg, R. (2001). *Incorporating Mental Health Policy Research and Advocacy in Clinical Training: The Florida Mental Health Institute Predoctoral Psychology Internship*. Tampa, Florida: University of South Florida and Florida Mental Health Institute, Unpublished paper.

Weissberg, R.P. and Elias, M.J. (1993). 'Enhancing young people's social competence and health behavior: An important challenge for educators, scientists, policymakers, and funders'. *Applied and Preventive Psychology*, **2**, 179–90.

Weitz, R. (1996). *The Sociology of Health, Illness, and Health Care: A Critical Approach*. New York: Wadsworth/ITP.

Wells, D.M. (1987). *Empty Promises: Quality of Working Life Programs and the Labor Movement*. New York: Monthly Review Press.

West, C. (1983). 'Ask me no questions...: An analysis of queries and replies in physician-patient dialogues'. In S. Fisher and A. Todd (eds) *The Social Organisation of Doctor-patient Communication* (75–106). Norwood, NJ: Ablex.

Wharf, B. and McKenzie, B. (1998). *Connecting Policy to Practice in the Human Services*. Oxford: Oxford University Press.

White, M. (2000). *Narrative Therapy*. Workshop presented at the University of Melbourne, December.

White, M. (1988/9). 'The externalizing of the problem and the re-authoring of lives and relationships'. *Dulwich Centre Newsletter*, Summer, 3–20.

White, M. and Epston, D. (1990). *Narrative Means to Therapeutic Ends.* New York: Norton.

Wiley, A. and Rappaport, J. (2000). 'Empowerment, wellness, and the politics of development'. In Cicchetti, D., Rappaport, J., Sandler, I. and Weissberg, R. P. (eds). *The Promotion of Wellness in Children and Adolescents* (59–99). Washington, DC: Child Welfare League of America Press.

Wilkinson, R. (1996). *Unhealthy Societies: The Afflictions of Inequality.* London: Routledge.

Wilkinson, S. (2000). 'Feminist research traditions in health psychology: Breast cancer research'. *Journal of Health Psychology*, **5**, 359–72.

Wilkinson, S. (1997). 'Feminist Psychology'. In D. Fox and I. Prilleltensky (eds), *Critical Psychology: An Introduction* (247–64). London: Sage.

Willig, C. (ed.). (1999). *Applied Discourse Analysis: Social and Psychological Interventions.* Philadelphia: Open University Press.

Wineman, S. (1984). *The Politics of Human Services.* Montreal: Black Rose.

Winett, R. (1995). 'A framework for health promotion and disease prevention programs'. *American Psychologist*, **50**, 341–50.

Wolfe, D.A., Wekerle, C. and Scott, K. (1996). *Alternatives to Violence: Empowering Youth to Develop Healthy Relationships.* Thousand Oaks, CA: Sage.

Woodill, G. (1992). *Independent Living and Participation in Research: A Critical Analysis* (Discussion paper). Toronto, Ontario: Centre for Independent Living of Toronto.

Wyman, P.A., Sandler, I., Wolchik, S. and Nelson, K. (2000). 'Resilience as cumulative competence promotion and stress protection: Theory and intervention'. In Cicchetti, D., Rappaport, J., Sandler, I. and Weissberg, R.P. (eds) *The Promotion of Wellness in Children and Adolescents* (133–84). Washington, DC: Child Welfare League of America Press.

Yeich, S. (1996). 'Grassroots organizing with homeless people: A participatory research approach'. *Journal of Social Issues*, **52**, 111–21.

Yeich, S. and Levine, R. (1992). 'Participatory research's contribution to a conceptualization of empowerment'. *Journal of Applied Social Psychology*, **22**, 1894–1908.

Young, I.M. (1990). *Justice and the Politics of Difference.* Princeton, NJ: Princeton University Press.

Index